KEEPING THEM
Wild

Four Decades of Wildlife Rehabilitation with Gila Wildlife Rescue

DENISE *and* DENNIS MILLER

MIMBRES PRESS
of Western New Mexico University

MIMBRES PRESS
of Western New Mexico University

Mimbres Press of Western New Mexico University

www.mimbrespress.wnmu.edu

Media and Publisher Inquiries:

Mimbres Press of WNMU

1000 West College Ave.

Silver City, NE 88062

Cover and interior design GKS Creative

Editing by Shelley Chung and Cindy Doty

Photographs by Jay Hemphill

978-1-958870-21-1 (hardcover)

978-1-958870-22-8 (paperback)

978-1-958870-25-9 (ebook)

FIRST EDITION

First printed in the United States

Library of Congress Case # 1-14532568974

Gila Wildlife Rescue

Visit us on facebook

TABLE OF CONTENTS

This book could not have been possible without the help and support
of my loving, beautiful, intelligent wife who rarely gets the credit she
deserves. I am deeply grateful for Denise coming into my life and will be
forever asking what the hell I did to deserve her.
Thank you, Denise, for everything.
The wildlife and I sincerely and deeply thank you.
This book is and always was dedicated to you . . .
And I do and always will love you with all my heart.

Dennis

Gila Wildlife Rescue

This book documents the true-life accounts of our very close-up and personal experiences with wildlife. These stories take place in Southwestern New Mexico where an incredibly diverse list of wildlife has been rescued by our organization, Gila Wildlife Rescue, for over thirty-seven years, having started in 1979.

Our educational, inspirational, and humorous accounts include heartwarming and heartbreaking experiences. All the photos used to document our encounters have been taken by us and include stunning close-ups of these remarkably beautiful creatures. Not all stories have accompanying photos, but we captured what we could when we could. Most photos are taken when the animals are first examined or when preparing for release to maintain their wildness.

Permitted for the care of all species of wildlife, but specializing in raptors and mammals, we try to convey the importance of keeping these animals wild and keeping their spirits wild. The descriptions and accounts of working with large predatory animals include depictions of these animals' spirits and how important this is for their survival. Personal and deeply moving portrayals of some of our special, more intimate experiences are shared as well.

We are forever grateful and freely share our stories to try to educate readers about the importance of being good stewards of the earth and to not be "ecologically immoral." Since we have a unique view of wildlife, we hope that readers will come away with a changed attitude about their own individual place in the circle of life that we all are a part of, including wildlife.

From Denise:

I was born and raised in Silver City, New Mexico. I left at seventeen and came back at forty-eight—after living in Arizona, Indiana, and Ohio—with a lot of life experiences under my belt.

Dennis and I knew each other in junior high school and were friends, but not close friends. We had a few classes together at Silver High School, but we were more acquaintances than anything. He was always friendly to me. After leaving Silver City as a teenager, I came back as a mother of four grown children and seeking a new path. While living in Ohio, I worked at a doctor's office and was curious because one of the nurses I worked with was talking about a website called Classmates.com. She told me how to connect to it, so I checked it out. As I was perusing the website out of curiosity for people I had gone to school with, I came upon a photograph of Dennis Miller holding a bear cub in the doorway of his office. What?? This really got my curiosity up. He was a biology professor at Western New Mexico University as well as a wildlife rehabilitator. He had been rehabbing animals since 1979, before I came on the scene. To say the least, my interest was sparked! I was communicating with other classmates and decided to write to him too. It was fun finding out what people I grew up with were doing with their lives as adults. We started communicating as friends via AOL Messenger for several months and finally met up in Albuquerque, New Mexico, one weekend. It was great getting reacquainted.

It was our destiny to be together. First friends, then best friends, then partners for life. We married in 2002. The rehabilitation of wildlife came with the territory, and it has been such an amazing experience to watch him and how he handles the animals, birds of prey, and mammals, and him teaching me how to help him care for them. It has definitely made my life fuller and a bit more exciting, to say the least. He told me once that in a life with him there would never be a dull moment. This has been proven to be true!

We've been married almost twenty-two years and have experienced together the care and release of thousands of birds of prey such as hawks, owls, eagles, kestrels, as well as other birds such as pelicans, loons, herons, ducks, geese, etc., and mammals ranging from raccoons, bobcats, foxes, javelina, deer, ringtails, coatimundi, and even a mountain lion! Throw in a tortoise and bat or two to the mix.

It has been a life full of adventure, hard work, some shedding of tears and feelings of frustration—but it has been worth every minute of it. My heart is full of gratitude to have been given the privilege to help care for our Creator's creations. I hope you enjoy this book and that we can convey our experiences in a way that will put a smile on your face, touch your heart with sorrow, and enable you to share the excitement of seeing these wonderful creatures released back into the wild.

From Dennis:

As we started to work on this book, we realized that in many ways this is a love story. A story of two people's individual love of wildlife that is so strong that it encompasses all aspects of their lives even since young children. And especially a love story of two people who were destined to be together and to have all of these amazing experiences together, even though it was a bit later in life.

Denise and I have an amazing relationship that is strong and deep. Having only had two serious disagreements in over twenty years of marriage is proof. Many others have asked what our secret is because they see how much we love and respect and support each other unconditionally. Her coming into my life in 2002 was the beginning of a majority of the experiences we describe in this book and certainly was when my life changed forever. You can just imagine the two of us going through all of the excitement of these experiences pretty much hand in hand and how that has strengthened our love and respect for each other.

Denise, through the years, has not received the credit for the work she does with Gila Wildlife Rescue. Even news articles that interview both of us have not mentioned her at all. Her photos of raptors printed in a publication were incorrectly attributed to me and did not list her as the photographer. I do have more direct contact with the wildlife we care for and am the one holding dangerous animals while she photographs but don't forget the person behind the camera and her thousands of hours of work behind the scenes. There is no doubt in my mind that I could not have accomplished all of this without her being right there as an equal partner in this crazy endeavor.

CHAPTER ONE

The Beginnings

A much younger Dennis and Harris's hawk.

Everyone has probably experienced one of those defining moments that profoundly changes their entire direction and purpose in life. Dennis's came as he was teaching high school biology at the very beginning of his career. One day in early fall, one of his brightest and most attentive students was falling asleep in class. He started teasing her about falling asleep and her reply was, "I have been up all night helping my dad feed baby deer, and I can't stay awake!" That struck a chord deep inside of him and his response was, "Tell your dad that if he ever needs any help to let me know and WAKE UP!" Dennis had no idea how much that offer was about to abruptly direct his life for the next forty-plus years both in how busy he would be and in how it would affect his personal life.

That evening when he arrived home, there was a phone message waiting for him from his student's father, a local game warden for the state of New Mexico. It turns out that he really wasn't supposed to be caring for injured wildlife without a permit, but, with no one in the area for quite a few years permitted to rehabilitate wildlife, they were now desperate to have someone permitted. He explained the process. Dennis mailed the application two days later, with support letters from two of our local veterinarians. A week later, he was trying to figure out how to build cages and get ready to accept animals. After cages were constructed and inspected by the New Mexico Department of Game and Fish, Dennis received permits from both this state agency and the U.S. Fish and Wildlife Service in the name of Gila Wildlife Rescue. More than forty years later, we have built and rebuilt many cages and have proudly cared for nearly ten thousand injured, orphaned, or misplaced wild animals.

Denise and Dennis with a golden eagle.

We run Gila Wildlife Rescue, which sounds like a big organization, but we are it! We, meaning Dennis and who he describes as his partner, soulmate, best friend, and wife, Denise. We do and have done all the work we will be describing in this book, with the occasional help from friends to feed animals when we are away. Some of this story happened before we got together in 2002, but most of the experiences we have had with wildlife that you are going to read in this book occurred after we were married. Denise compliments the program well, as she is totally unafraid, loves wildlife—especially hawks and eagles—has medical knowledge and experience, and a heart of gold.

She is now an incredible partner in all this and can do everything from holding a raptor's legs to control its dangerous feet and talons while being examined, to assisting with surgeries and administering medications. Most of the wildlife experiences in this book occurred once Dennis had this kind of support in his life and was partnered with someone who shared the same passion that he had in caring for wildlife. Denise is a biologist at heart and knows more plants and animals and ecological concepts than many people with degrees in it. She has become an incredible wildlife photographer with some of her photos published in *Raptors of New Mexico* and *Wild Carnivores of New Mexico* both written by Jean-Luc E. Cartron. Ninety-nine percent of the photos in this book are hers as well, so enjoy!

When they were first getting together, Dennis told her it would be a whirlwind at times, and there would probably never be a dull moment. This has proven to be true repeatedly. The stories in this book are proof of that! As you will soon see, Denise is one of a kind and is and always will be an integral part of Gila Wildlife Rescue.

Gila Wildlife Rescue has been in existence since 1979. For the first few years, the organization had twenty-five to fifty wildlife encounters that were dealt with annually. It started out with just one flight cage, a very small deer pen, and very little experience. The New Mexico Department of Game and Fish did not have a training program at the time but did put Dennis in contact with an experienced rehabilitator from northern New Mexico, whom he visited for about a week and received some basic training to get started.

Now, with over forty years of experience and an incredible variety of injuries that have been dealt with, we do quite well, including our own minor surgeries that do not require anesthe-

Red-tailed hawk nestling—first animal Gila Wildlife Rescue cared for.

sia, as well as setting bones and treating a variety of infections. We have gained enough experience and success that at times we get close to 90 percent of the animals we receive released back into the wild. Although we have always been permitted for all wildlife, we have such extensive experience in raptor rehabilitation that we now specialize primarily in this group. As you will see, we also care for some mammals and a few other larger bird species that small bird rehabilitators do not have the facilities for.

Gila Wildlife Rescue's facilities now include three large flight cages, or aviaries, all between sixty and a hundred feet long, a large mammal pen, one medium-sized multiuse cage, and a bank of three mews (smaller holding cages for raptors). We also have a small clinic on the property where initial intake, surgeries, and intensive care is conducted. The appendix at the end of this book gives more details of our facilities.

Our largest one-hundred-foot flight cage necessary for rehabbing eagles.

All the rehab work, cage building, and the encounters described in this book have been experienced by us directly and, in most cases, documented photographically. We do not accept volunteers, which surprises many and is questioned by others. Our paramount mission in everything we do is to return these animals back to the wild and to return them to their vital role in their ecosystem. The worst thing we could do is to expose them to a lot of other humans. Imprinting on humans can be a death sentence once the animal is released. Imprinted animals can view all humans as someone who will feed and help them but that's not reality. We seem to be able to keep up with the workload. The reduction in the chances of imprinting by having less human contact has worked well for us as is evident by our success rate. Our entire facility is located in our backyard as well, so our privacy would be compromised with volunteers. When we are out of town or have a construction project where we need an extra hand, we have a couple of dear friends that we trust, and we appreciate their help.

The other related reason for our success rate is that we do not allow visitors and are not open to the public. Many rehabilitation centers allow visitors to interact with wildlife that cannot be released and are used as teaching animals, but we do not have those. When non-releasable animals are kept in captivity for educational purposes there is some value to educating the public, but the animal itself is suffering. In our opinion, for us to hold a non-releasable animal for use in educational programs we may only do half a dozen times a year or so is unnecessary. Raptors in captivity usually get depressed and die earlier than normal due to not being able to fly free. We have experienced this in birds we have cared for over a long period of time, and it is sad to see.

We are often asked why we do this. Why does Gila Wildlife Rescue exist? How does it operate? Why has Dennis been doing this for over forty years, Denise for over twenty, many times spending a large amount of our own money, spending countless hours of hard work, many hours of heartache, and being tied down all the time not being able to leave town? A quick answer is usually that humans have caused a large percentage of the injuries we treat, either directly or indirectly, so our efforts can counteract or balance the damage that humans cause to wildlife populations and the environment. The longer answer is that our love of wildlife drives us to do what we can to help as our part in volunteerism to contribute to our community. We now feel compelled to continue our efforts because we are the only raptor rehabilitation facility in Southwestern New Mexico and far west Texas. We couldn't imagine what would be happening to all of these animals if we weren't here and hadn't been here for the last forty years.

Golden eagle

With nearly ten thousand animals we have cared for and nearly nine thousand of those released, have our efforts *really* impacted wildlife and the ecology of our area? Some critics of wildlife rehabilitation say that due to the small numbers of animals successfully rehabbed compared to the total populations of those animals in the wild, the impact is so minimal that it is not worth the cost, effort, and permitting. If we rehabbed just passerine or perching birds like hummingbirds, sparrows, jays, and pigeons, this argument may hold some truth, but still does not take away from the good work that these rehabbers do. In quickly perusing the wildlife rehabilitation programs across the country, a large majority (over 80 percent) are these small bird rehabbers, so we can see how critics have this view. But if they were to look at the ones that rehabilitate predators, they will see different results.

Predators of all kinds have a critical role in the ecosystem of any area. They affect others in their food chains more than the rest of the organisms found in their ecosystem. The role of predators in balancing prey populations is crucial and each individual animal has a large impact on the ecosystem they belong to.

For example, if one scrub jay dies or is killed, what kind of impact does that have on the local ecosystem? A mate may not breed that year due to the death, a tiny bit less food would be eaten with this one bird gone, providing a bit more for others. Let's see . . . not much else. If a red-tailed hawk is killed or dies (or is not rehabilitated) what impacts are there? Due to this being an important apex predator (which is at the top of the food chain in this ecosystem without many predators itself), the impacts are widespread and profound. Just think of a balanced ecosystem in some area, say the grasslands southeast of Silver City, and imagine that hawk's role and impact here. They eat at least four mice, or two rats, or a cottontail every day of the year.[1] Using just mice as an example, that makes 1,460 mice in a year that are here because the hawk is dead and not fulfilling its role.

Here is the real lesson: What about the reproductive ability of the mice that are now not eaten? One pair of mice can produce a litter every twenty-two days with a litter having eight babies each on average. That means that each mouse can easily reproduce over 125 mice in a year. If you consider the reproductive abilities of each of these offspring that are mature enough to reproduce themselves in thirty days or so, it is well over one thousand mice each year that are produced by this one pair of mice[2]. That means that if one hawk died or was taken out of this ecosystem, profound effects occur.

Look at it this way: Multiplying the 1,460 mice not killed times the 1,000 mice per year reproductive abilities, the results are 1,460,000 more mice in that ecosystem!

This means that many more mice will be in the ecosystem and eating substantially more food than they would normally. The ecological balance is drastically upset and affects every other organism in that ecosystem. Although there are more factors involved and more predators present, the point is, predators being rehabilitated and returned to the ecosystem to perform this role may have a much greater impact than the rehabilitation of some other wildlife. As a result, we are very proud that our efforts have profound and long-term effects on the environment in our area. We are specialized in caring for raptors, or birds of prey like eagles, hawks, falcons, and owls, and mammals with most of them being predators like mountain lions, bobcats, bears, foxes, etc. We also still take in other larger birds that are not predators, like ravens, ducks, geese, herons, cranes, and the like. Some larger mammals also come to us that are not predators, like deer, pronghorn, and javelina.

There are, of course, other reasons why we rehabilitate wildlife, we will readily admit. Not many people get to work this closely with these incredible animals, although many people would like to. We get to experience their spirited personalities. We see them in a condition

Mississippi kite

where they are almost dead or would die without our care. Then the most rewarding part of all this is being able to release the animal, after working hard, sometimes staying up late, or getting up through the night to care for them, and our efforts are what saved them. Those releases are very special to us. We feel blessed and privileged and are deeply grateful for the opportunity to work so closely with these incredible living things. We have never, nor will we ever, forget that this is all about wildlife, and not about us. To be able to do this has been and *is* one of the greatest and most wonderful things in our lives.

Another reason why Dennis started to rehabilitate wildlife is to use it as a teaching tool. He has been blessed with having a very successful teaching career by, among other things, using innovative teaching methods. One of them was bringing the wildlife program into the classroom. Occasionally, he could bring a raptor in to quickly show classes and use it as a teaching opportunity without stressing the bird. Most of the interaction with the students was through photos and daily updates, and stories of his experiences in wildlife rehabilitation. He used this as an opportunity to teach some basic but extremely important concepts in ecology, including human impact and responsibility, and it has been very effective. Dennis always hoped that by his example he encouraged students to volunteer as adults and make a commitment to something bigger than themselves.

Dennis at age eleven with "Cricket."

He started teaching high school biology at Silver High School in Silver City, New Mexico, in 1979, where he went to high school himself. His parents and their five boys moved here in 1967 after being evacuated out of Nigeria during the beginnings of a civil war. His father was a high school biology teacher and was hired for a USAID (US Agency for International Development) project in that country and it allowed his entire family to live in tropical Africa for three years. During the time there, his father had a few injured or orphaned animals brought to him, as many biology teachers have experienced, and they cared for an owl, a small deer, and some other wild animals.

While in Africa, Dennis had a green vervet monkey and his brother had an African gray parrot as pets. During this exciting experience in the jungles of Africa at the age of eleven to thirteen, at a time when his biology interests were being stimulated beyond compare in this amazing place, these opportunities of caring for wildlife may have helped influence his later passions in wildlife rehabilitation and teaching biology.

After eleven years teaching at the high school level, he was hired at Western New Mexico University to run their Science Education program. Dennis was well-known for how he started out his classes the very first day, walking into the large lecture hall with nearly one hundred students with a hawk, owl, eagle, or large snake. His first words, once the "oohs" and "aahs" quieted down, were always: "Welcome to MY world!" His strategy was to get their attention the very first moment of the very first day and give them that first impression that this was going to be a cool and fun class, so later in the semester, when things were tougher and less exciting, they didn't even notice! It worked so well that the few students that had a hard time being successful in this challenging science class at first had been the students who started late and missed that first class.

The university became a great drop-off point for injured wildlife as well. When something came in from the New Mexico Department of Game and Fish or from the public, or he had to go out between classes and capture an injured animal, the classes that were there that day had some cool experiences. Students were excited to see hawks, owls, and eagles, and even bear cubs because he examined them and did initial treatment right in the classroom with everyone gathered around. Most of these were in lab situations with just twenty to thirty students where everyone could see and interact well.

Dennis has had some great teaching opportunities with students through the wildlife rehabilitation program and has imparted a great deal of encouragement to be good stewards of the land and the living things in it. He liked to teach the term that he invented of not being "ecologically immoral." All of us, as members of this planet, have a responsibility to the other living things around us. Understanding how each person's actions affect other living things around them is one of the most valuable lessons one can learn. This is a clear lesson in morality, in his opinion, and yes, he thinks there is a moral obligation toward wildlife. He discovered a long time ago that using wildlife to teach gave him great power to get this message across in a lasting way.

We have been blessed from the very beginning in that we have always had financial support when we needed it. We have had a variety of fundraisers and have occasionally reached out to groups of local businesses and civic organizations for donations. More recently, Gila Wildlife Rescue has been receiving regular donations from a local mining company and an electric company in our area. They have been very generous with their annual donations, which have allowed us to spend our time working with wildlife and not working at fundraising. We also deeply appreciate our private donors that give anywhere from a dollar to thousands of dollars, some of them who have been regular donors for many years. It would be impossible to do all of this without the outpouring of support that we have had in this community as well as people from all over the United States, and we deeply thank them.

We started out small and needed just a few hundred or thousands of dollars. Now we require between ten and twenty thousand each year depending on if we have more cage building or maintenance to do. Although the funds are used directly for building materials for facilities, transport cages, medications, and gas for vehicles, the primary annual expense is food. Because we specialize in raptors and carnivorous animals, our food bill is outrageous. We spend six to ten thousand dollars for mice and rats alone each year, occasionally reaching twelve thousand. We have not received any grants because we have found very few where we meet their requirements. Almost all grants available require an educational program to be in place for funding. As mentioned earlier, we do not have educational animals. Also, no funds have ever been used for salaries or payment to individuals of any kind. All our work is volunteer.

Our numbers have grown through the years, starting off with twenty-five to fifty wildlife encounters and now between two hundred to four hundred encounters each year—and are still growing.

The required permits are highly regulated. They involve detailed recordkeeping, annual reports, and the immediate contact of both the state and federal agencies when an injured eagle or endangered species is received. We have been permitted by the New Mexico Department of Game and Fish and the

U.S. Fish and Wildlife Service since Gila Wildlife Rescue's inception, so for over forty years. A permit is required to conduct wildlife rehabilitation for two reasons: for the protection of the animal and for the protection of the rescuer/rehabilitator. Without proper knowledge, you could extend an animal's suffering and cause more harm than good, and it can be hazardous to the rescuer. Without proper training and experience, serious injury could occur, or diseases could be spread.

So now that a bit of Gila Wildlife Rescue's background has been introduced, let's start relating the amazing experiences we have had that we would like to share. We look back in awe at many of the stories you are going to read and even writing all this brings back strong emotions where we need to wipe away tears to be able to continue. Some of the animals we have cared for have deeply affected us and we find it almost impossible to control our feelings.

A good example of that was when we first started working with the amazing veterinarians at the El Paso Zoo. We brought an immature bald eagle to them that we had rescued near the Gila Cliff Dwellings National Monument north of Silver City. We drove it to El Paso to give it immediate care and arrived with high hopes of a successful rehabilitation. Once the bird was examined and diagnosed, we received depressing news that it would have to be put down due to its injuries. We shocked the veterinarians when both of us got teary-eyed, very visibly upset. Even after caring for thousands of animals, they still get to us every time they don't make it. We often worried that after a while this stress would make us quit doing this, but we finally realized that these failures are learning situations that allow us to save more in the future, even though a few tears are lost in the process.

CHAPTER TWO

Thor's Saga

We had already had a busy spring at Gila Wildlife Rescue, this typically busy time having come a bit early. We were dealing with some of the spring's young hatchling raptors and a few long-term recovery birds from the previous fall. After a few weeks of respite, we got a phone call about another wildlife injury. This call was from an obviously frantic woman who was yelling into the phone, "We have an injured eagle! Where can we meet you?"

Dennis asked, "Where are you? Where did this happen?"

She replied, "Highway 180 between Deming and Silver City. We saw it get hit and stopped and picked it up. My husband is driving, and he had you as a teacher years ago and knew you could help him."

It's not unusual to receive wildlife calls from former students. They are familiar with the routine of calls since they would frequently come in during class. He gave her instructions to meet him at the Walmart parking lot and headed there himself.

Eagles are always exciting for us to get in, although we cringe when eagles or any of these creatures get injured. They are so strong and powerful. The spirit that is incredibly strong in all raptors is especially powerful in eagles, as Native Americans have always known. You can feel their spirit being broadcast out from them like the strength you see in the bearing of a powerful leader. They view the world as their domain, one in which they are on the top of, both literally and figuratively: they happen to be the top predator in any food chain they are a part of, and they frequently fly very high and often hunt from lofty heights where most other birds are never seen. An eagle can easily spot the movement of a small mouse from two miles away![3] We see this power and spirit in every eagle we have cared for, which is nearly a hundred now, and are always in awe and feel blessed to care for them.

Dennis drove up to the meeting point at the same time the rescuers did. Arriving in a minivan, they slid the side door open, revealing an excited man sitting on the floor of the van hugging this incredibly large golden eagle wrapped in a sleeping bag. Even though his arms were wrapped around it holding it tight, Dennis could still see this was a very large bird. Probably a quarter of the eagle calls we get are red-tailed hawks or something that is misidentified as an eagle. *This* was definitely an eagle! With a triumphant look on the man's face he said, "We rescued him!"

Dennis smiled at him and thanked them profusely. He wanted to get the bird into a large pet carrier as quickly as he could in case the bird, who seemed dazed at the time, became more alert and aggressive. Eagles have massive feet with not only a wide span and large talons, but the muscles to squeeze those talons are some of the most powerful muscles in nature, having a grip strength of over 700 pounds .[4] This is true of all birds of prey, so as one would expect, the largest raptors have the strongest feet. Eagles are very aware of the fact that this is their only weapon, and they use it to their advantage. (Contrary to what most people think, their beaks are not very dangerous at all and just a bite by itself would doubtfully cause even a break in the skin. On the other hand, if the eagle is gripping its prey, using its powerful leg muscles to help tear, then a big chunk can be torn out.) He quickly positioned the pet carrier near the van, reached in and grabbed the bag and the eagle together, and took him from his rescuer. As he was repositioning his grip and got the eagle clear from the sleeping bag, the rescuer and former student started to tell his story.

They were driving along the highway coming home from Deming, New Mexico, which is a long, flat stretch of highway with desert scrub vegetation. They were following a woman who was going the speed limit, but kind of holding up the usually faster and impatient Friday-afternoon traffic. We were having one of those typical windy, late-winter days where you must maintain a tight grip on the steering wheel. For birds, these are days that only the strongest of fliers are out. As this couple was driving behind this car, they saw a large eagle on the side of the road that was eating a roadkill jackrabbit. Just before the car whizzed by it, the eagle unfortunately jumped up and tried to fly off before the cars reached him. The second the bird did this, a stronger gust of wind tossed it directly into the car in front of them. The eagle kind of tumbled over the top of the car after making solid contact with the windshield, fell to the side of the car, and rolled onto the shoulder of the road barely in time for them to avoid hitting it with their minivan. He pulled over to the side of the road and noticed the car that hit the bird had pulled off the road farther up. He grabbed a sleeping bag and used it to collect the eagle without getting hurt (he said he remembered how Mr. Miller had taught them in class the proper way to do this) and wrapped it up. His wife started driving and called Dennis while he was holding the eagle, and they drove to Silver City as fast as they could. They noticed that the car that hit the bird had pulled out and was continuing on the highway but was going very slow. As they passed the car, they thought they noticed the windshield was cracked but weren't sure.

Dennis thanked them again and quickly drove to our clinic, all the while being very concerned about its condition and probable results of the impact at sixty-five miles per hour. Was there a concussion? Internal organ damage? Were there broken bones? What was the extent of the damage done? Surely, it had

Dennis holding Thor minutes after arrival.

to be extensive. Taking the bird out of the carrier to examine it once arriving home, we were again amazed at how large this eagle was.

He laid the eagle on its back on the examining table in our clinic. The eagle fought him for a second, and it surprised us at the amount of strength it was exhibiting, knowing what it had just gone through. It calmed down, sensing we were helping, which is very common in birds we care for. Denise grabbed its legs just above the bird's powerful feet. These were massive, far larger than her entire hand. She gripped the eagle firmly and got ready for a possible struggle as he got ready to examine it. Dennis felt for wounds, breaks, or loose joints. He examined its eyes, including pupillary response, and observed its demeanor and spirit. After everything was closely examined, we stopped and looked at each other in awe. We were totally and completely blown away. This bird had *no* major injuries. It was certainly bruised, in shock, stressed, and very scared, but it still had a lot of spunk. Having no broken bones, no concussion, no lacerations, no major injury of any kind after this massive collision was downright miraculous. We hadn't yet seen the damage done to the vehicle. That was to come.

Since it seemed strong enough to stand and perch, we placed the eagle in our large flight cage, leaving it just inside the door to calm down from its ordeal, including its examination by us. Later, as we were just finishing dinner, the phone rang. We receive between ten and twenty calls each week dealing with wildlife issues and rehabilitation, sometimes more. Most of the time, it is another injured animal coming in. We are frequently just sitting down to dinner when calls invariably come in and interrupt things. It is also our experience that animals come in groups, usually of three, and since we just got this eagle, we were not surprised to get another call.

Dennis answered the phone, and it was a friend of ours who was very distraught. "Dennis, are there any vultures around here this time of the year?" was her somewhat bizarre question out of the blue.

He replied, "No, vultures don't return until the spring equinox the third week of March, and this is just March second."

She started freaking out and went crazy over the phone. "Oh my God! Oh my God! I am going to prison!" she hysterically yelled. "He was right. It couldn't be a vulture, and so it had to be an eagle!"

Dennis said, "Slow down. Take a big breath and tell me what the heck you are talking about."

She was so upset that it took a few minutes for her to calm down and start talking coherently to tell her story. She was driving home from Deming and the wind was blowing very strong. The traffic was heavy when she drove up on a large dark bird on the side of the road. It jumped up to fly away and a gust of wind blew it directly into her car. She said she tried her best to miss it, but she hit it squarely. She described it being so large it totally covered her windshield. She was so shaken up that she pulled over. It was then she realized that the impact had totally shattered her windshield, having collapsed it in on the passenger side about six inches. She had a hard time seeing through it, but eventually limped her way to a friend's house in the village of Hurley just up the road. When the two of them looked closely at the damage to the windshield and saw a place on the metal of the top of the car that was dented, they thought that this bird could never have survived. There was even blood and guts all over the windshield. They were amazed she could drive that far with all the damage and viscera blocking her vision.

Still thinking she has hit and killed a vulture, with the adrenaline impairing her thoughts, she had her friend take her home. Even after arriving home, she was still highly excited and she shared her incident with another close friend. He then explained to her that the only large bird that could be on the highway at this time of the year would be a golden eagle. Her friend said that it is too early for vultures to be back, which was correct. Then he teasingly told her that killing an eagle like this is a crime and that she was going to go to prison. Unsure of what she just heard from him, she decided to call us and find out, because now she was a bit worried.

Things started clicking in his mind as they talked, and Dennis then realized the connection. When he finally calmed her down so she would listen to him, he told her that we had received an eagle from the same place at about the same time as the one she had hit, and that it had to be the same bird. She went from being

Damage to car that hit Thor—you can see what looks like blood on the top photo; bottom photo shows the dent in top of car.

distraught because she thought she killed an eagle and was surely going to jail, to being elated that the bird was already rescued! The next day, we went to her house to look at the car and were shocked at how much damage the windshield sustained. It was completely shattered, and a basketball-sized area on the passenger side was pushed in about half a foot. Just as she described, there was even a small dent in the metal close to the top of the windshield.

How could an eagle, a ten-pound bird, have had this serious of a collision with thousands of pounds of steel going that fast, and basically walk away from it? This was one tough bird. On closer examination, the windshield had what looked like blood and guts all over it, but the eagle didn't have injuries that could have caused this, and we were confused. We recalled the driver's story where she described the gore on the glass. The only way this could have happened is that the eagle must have been hit squarely in the chest, and her description of the moment of impact confirms this. Remember, the bird had just been feeding on a jackrabbit, so its crop was probably very full. The crop is the first chamber of a bird's stomach that stores food for later, and then it is ground up in their gizzard to go into the stomach. The impact was most likely cushioned by the crop absorbing much of the force and caused the crop contents to be sprayed all over the windshield. This wasn't the eagle's blood or viscera—it was the jackrabbit's blood. More than likely, this is what saved this bird's life. After realizing the enormity of the collision this bird experienced and to be in this relatively good condition, we felt it was a miracle.

The local newspaper published a small article about this incident. This was seen by a reporter from an Albuquerque, New Mexico, television station. He called us and we told him the details. He asked if he could interview us via a Zoom call, and we agreed. He called later that afternoon, and we once again told the story of this bird's survival for the article. The story aired on the television news that night.

The next day, we received a call from an eagle researcher with Eagle Environmental Inc. located in Santa Fe, New Mexico, who is affiliated with the U.S. Fish and Wildlife Service. Their research consists of attaching tracking devices on golden eagles to learn more about their life histories and to eventually protect them. He was wondering if they could put a tracking device on this eagle. We hesitated at first because a few months earlier we had an experience with tracking devices dealing with an Aplomado falcon. A hiker found a dead bird in a barbed wire fence with the strap of the telemetry device hooked in one of the barbs. He called us and we identified it as an Aplomado falcon and contacted the researchers through the information on the device. Aplomado falcons are an endangered species in New Mexico, and several of them were released in far southern New Mexico as part of a reintroduction program. When we saw what happened to the falcon, we were frustrated that this happened at all and contacted the researchers in charge of the program to report it. They admitted that this was the third falcon they had released that ended up caught in barbed wire out of a dozen originally released. Because of this, we struggled with the decision and weighed the pros and cons, then with some reservations, we decided that the ability to determine if our methods were successful was worth it.

A few days before the researcher arrived to install the tracking device, he called and asked if we had named the eagle yet. We kind of laughed and said that we don't name our charges and if we did, we would have run out of names a long time ago. He explained that they name all the eagles they track to keep them straight. He told us that they usually name them after where they were found, so we could name him Deming or Silver City or something. He didn't want to name this eagle the normal way. He thought it would be cool to give him a name that showed his strength and power, since it survived this crash. The researcher was asking us for ideas but had one himself that he wanted to run by us.

"How about Thor? He smashed things, right?" remembering the windshield.

With laughter, we immediately agreed, seeing that this name—the Norse God of thunder and strength—was indeed fitting. The eagle had been called Thor ever since, including in his research data.

We timed the tracker installation for when Thor was ready to release. By the end of March, just four weeks after the collision, this very tenacious eagle was fully and completely recovered. Just hours after the incident, he was perched on a low branch, moving around, but not flying. A few days later, he was attempting to fly from one low perch to another. After a week, he flew to the high perches and eventually all over the cage. This bird's recovery was remarkable and now it was time to return him to his rightful place in the web of life.

Video Links: ThorNotFlying   ThorStartingToFly

The last step before freedom was to install the telemetry device. Although we were not totally comfortable with the process, it had great promise of giving us some valuable feedback. We have always wondered about how well the animals survived after release and this was finally an opportunity to find out. Little did we know the surprises that lay ahead!

The Eagle Environmental researcher and his assistant, a graduate student from New Mexico State University, arrived the day before release. It was an amazing process to watch this transmitter being installed, and we had front row seats. Denise was documenting the whole thing with her camera, and Dennis was holding Thor the entire time.

After he caught the bird, it was weighed, had a dozen or so measurements taken including head, beak, foot, and talon lengths. A sample of blood was then drawn for a genetic profile, and feather clippings were taken to determine the age and sex of the bird. We were pretty sure it was a female by its size but were curious to find out the definitive results.

Video Link: ThorTransmitter

Preparing to install transmitter as Dennis holds her legs.

In birds of prey, females are considerably larger than males. We eventually found out that Thor was a female and was five years old. Although named after the wrong gender, he was she. From here on out in our story, Thor will be referred to as "she." She was hooded to calm her down and he then held her belly down on a table so they could access her back and she was carefully fitted with a harness and the tracker. We were very impressed at how gentle and patient the researchers were, making sure the device was installed correctly. The eagle didn't seem to mind too much until she had been held for about an hour and decided she had had enough of all this. Struggling and trying to get out of his grasp, he repositioned his grip and she calmed down again. It was another hour before Dennis could relax his grip on her legs, though. The process took that long.

Once completed, Thor had a small box on her back about the size of two AA batteries, with a short antenna sticking up about three inches. It was held by nylon straps that had pads carefully placed in strategic places so the straps would not chafe her. The unit had a solar panel for power that was designed to last for around five years or so, with some units still transmitting after ten. Thor was finally ready for her release.

Installing
transmitter as
Dennis holds
her legs.

Trimming
straps—bird
is hooded for
the two-hour
process
to keep it calm.

One evening, about a week before the event, we had a thought. The chapter on releases will explain this more, but releasing an animal can be a very strong healing experience that has lasting results. We have seen and experienced it many times. The thought was that we should use this very powerful eagle's release to help a friend of ours, and his family. He had lost his teenage son recently to suicide, an event that rocked the community as his very large family is well-known in the area. The damage to the family was sad to see, and we wondered if they would be interested in releasing this eagle as part of a private ceremony to symbolically send their son on his way and to send with it their grief, and maybe reduce their burden. Our friend was ecstatic and immediately agreed. We told him that this would be private and that only immediate family could attend, say five or six people.

On a bright, warm Saturday morning, the last of March, we met his family to drive to the release site. There were five vehicles full of over a dozen people! His "immediate" family was still quite large, but we said, "Come on." We drove to our eagle release site in the Burro Mountains, south of Silver City, in the southern section of the Gila National Forest. We have used this site periodically for releases, especially when we are releasing a bird that needs to migrate right away. This eagle, for example, was getting dangerously close to it being too late to migrate back north and would have had to be kept until fall to release. She must have been spending the winter either in our general area or somewhere south. This release site is located in a very remote area and is situated directly on top of the Continental Divide, a landmark commonly used by migrating raptors. It is located on a ridge that looks out in all directions. Mountains in Mexico can be seen in the far distance to the south, and Arizona is spread out majestically to the west. On a clear day, you can see almost all the way to the Rio Grande Valley to the east.

We unloaded the pet carrier, and Dennis gathered the bird in his arms. We assembled the family around us, and said a few words about this bird, and how she may be significant to their loss. We suggested that they could let the eagle symbolically help take some of their grief away. We encouraged them to imagine their son, grandson, nephew, and brother, with his spirit symbolically now inside this powerful creature, flying to the heavens. The family then took turns in saying prayers and encouraging each other to use this for healing. We all said a prayer for Thor after that, like we always do when we release an animal, praying for her strength and protection, and giving thanks for the opportunity to help her.

Dennis then asked our friend who he wanted to release Thor. Did he want to? He suggested that his grandfather, Pete, the patriarch of the family, be the one. He was eighty-some years old and a bit reluctant at this suggestion. When Dennis asked him if he wanted to, he looked at us with a hesitant and confused look, but his wife nudged him with her elbow, urging him, "Say yes! Say yes!" and we all got a chuckle.

With Grandpa Pete standing next to him we prepared for the release. He transferred Thor to his aged but strong arms and explained what he needed to do to release this eagle. We usually try to toss birds up in the air enough to get some height as they fly away so they don't collide with bushes or trees. He said he understood and was ready, although a bit nervous.

As we were waiting for cameras to be set up, and the family to clear out of the way, this very proud, stoic man asked Dennis something that eventually he realized was extremely profound. "Do you understand how important this bird is to my people?" the patriarch asked.

Not quite understanding what he was referring to, and a bit surprised by the question, Dennis replied, "No, tell me."

Pete said very proudly, "I am Apache, the great-great-grandson of Geronimo. Eagles are very important and powerful to my people," was all he said.

Dennis was amazed at what he shared and was a bit in shock. He had not known of Pete's heritage and for this patriarch to share that was very emotional for Dennis. This was a very powerful moment indeed for both of them. Dennis was deeply honored and touched.

Grandpa Pete and Thor

When everyone was ready, we all counted out loud, "One, two, and three." Grandpa threw him up in the air the best he could, and Thor was off. She flew south for a few hundred yards and landed on the top of a tree, possibly to get her bearings, and then took off again, curving around the massive rock bluffs behind us, heading north.

Denise, Dennis, Pete, and Cookie who accidentally hit Thor.

The family was deeply moved and grateful. We were glad that Thor could help them deal with this tragedy. We were also glad that Thor was successfully rehabilitated and released after her ordeal. Once again, we were touched by how releasing an animal like this can be so healing and at least help to make it through difficult experiences.

Excitement was building for us now to be able to finally track an animal we rehabbed and see how successful our efforts were. Was all the effort worth it? Did we make the right decision that she was completely healed and ready to be released at this time? Did we make the right choice in choosing a release site? How successful are animals after we release them? Do they return to where we found them? These are questions we have always had but never received any answers to. We were anxious to see what Thor could teach us.

We did not have long to wait. The next morning, we heard from the researcher that Thor traveled an incredible distance on the first afternoon of being released. She flew from the southern Burro Mountains of New Mexico to the Chuska Mountains near the Four Corners in northeast Arizona, in just six or eight hours and nearly five hundred miles. She seemed to be in a hurry to migrate north. Is it possible she had a breeding ground and mate waiting?

Throughout the next few weeks and months, we received periodic updates from Eagle Environmental. Thor continued to amaze everyone. The researchers assumed she was like most of our wintering eagles in New Mexico, migrating to Colorado or Montana areas for the summer. This bird kept flying through western Colorado, Wyoming, western Montana, and into Canada close to Glacier National Park. She had now traveled for five weeks and continued flying north. A few New Mexico eagles had been known to summer up in Canada, but very few.

Interestingly, Thor followed the Continental Divide almost perfectly on her travels thus far. After another two weeks, she settled for a short time, maybe to mate or to attempt to establish a territory, in the Cassiar Mountains of Yukon, Canada, near Haines Junction. We thought this was her summering grounds and that she was at the end of her journey, but no, she eventually started heading north again.

Thor's release.

Where Thor ended up for the summer was on the north banks of Alaska, shocking everyone! This is at the east end of the Brooks Range, close to where Alaska and Canada join. It is located only twenty miles from the Beaufort Sea, part of the Arctic Ocean, and is in the Arctic National Wildlife Refuge. Thor basically ran out of continent! Her three-thousand-plus-mile journey followed this divide almost exactly from the southern end of it near the border of Mexico, to the north end of it in far northeast Alaska. What an amazing journey, and what a powerful animal!

After researching the longest migrations recorded in golden eagles, we discovered that Thor was close to tying the record. One piece of information that was missing is where her wintering grounds are. We would need the location of the end of the migration to calculate the total length. Thor could have been wintering farther south and was migrating north when she experienced the collision. Calculating from where she was hit, she was close to the record.

We waited patiently throughout the summer to see if Thor would begin her migration south to our area, but it was difficult. We had been ecstatic that the first leg of her journey was so epic and could not wait to find out what the return journey would reveal. On August 23, 2013, we received another report. Thor had moved 2 degrees south, or about 140 miles, and it looked like she was on her way back south. We thought, "Here we go!" and our excitement grew.

During this entire process, we had been posting on our Facebook page about Thor. We try to keep fans of our program informed on new intakes and post release videos. From the first day we did the intake on her to this point and through her entire journey we posted regularly to update our readers. When we first told the story, a few hundred people were reached. Once the migration started, we gained hundreds more. Once the migration became so heroic due to the incredible distance and the strength and tenacity of this magnificent eagle, we gained hundreds more and the "shares" began adding even more. Thor's saga was becoming popular, and people were telling us they couldn't wait for the next update.

Throughout the next few months, we received updates on her progress. She followed a very similar path, many times the exact duplicate of her northern journey. On October 26th, she was in western Wyoming, then

Thor's journey. Red is the north bound route, green the south. bound

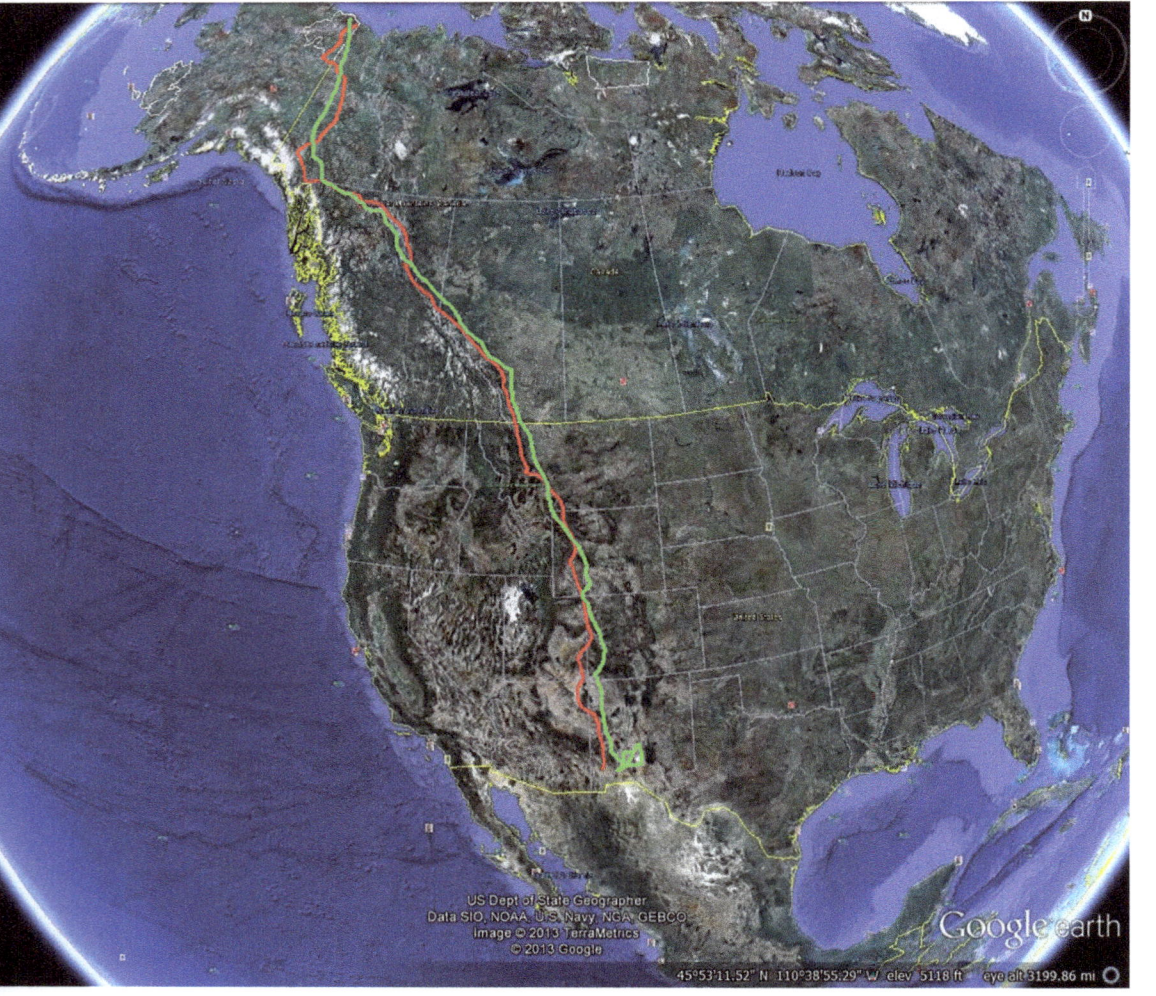

continued north, spending time again in the Cassiar Mountains of Canada. She arrived in New Mexico on November 24th, flying directly down the Continental Divide to the same area along the highway where she had been hit. She stayed in the same general area, switching between one power pole and another between Silver City and Deming, using them as a hunting platform all winter long. This proved that this was her wintering grounds.

We drive this highway often, since it is our only major access east when we need to go to Las Cruces, New Mexico, to shop, or to El Paso, Texas, to catch a plane. The most frequent reason, though, is that we are on this road to pick up another injured animal. As soon as we were told that the telemetry data showed she was perched on a power pole on the Deming highway, we didn't have to wait for an excuse. We immediately set out to see if we could actually spot her. We were disappointed when we did not see her, but the chances of seeing Thor were slim anyway. Recognizing her from the other handful of eagles that winter in that area each year may also be tough. So we were patient, and we kept checking the next few times we traveled in that direction. Denise even snuck off to see if she could spot her when Dennis was busy.

In mid-December, returning from a short getaway, we saw a big eagle on a power pole as we drove up from Deming to Silver City. We pulled off the highway and got out our binoculars. Denise grabbed her camera, quickly putting on her long telephoto lens. Dennis focused on the bird and immediately yelled, "It's her! It's Thor!"

Denise said, "Are you sure? How can you tell?"

"I see the antenna sticking out of her back. It HAS to be Thor!" was his very excited reply.

It might help to understand our excitement. This is the ultimate thrill that any wildlife rehabilitator could have. Having an animal that we rehabbed and released to be so successful was an incredibly rewarding thing to

Thor returns home.

experience. To have her return "home" after such a legendary journey was so amazing that words could never do justice to the feelings we had right then. You may have to be a rehabilitator to fully comprehend our emotions at this time, but needless to say, we were elated. We both had tears in our eyes, then we quickly exchanged the binoculars for the camera, and he started taking photos. We wanted to document this, to be able to prove that it was not our imagination. Holding the powerful zoomed-in lens as still as he could, which was a challenge as excited as he was, he just started clicking. We watched her for ten minutes or so and she eventually flew off, probably a bit disturbed at the attention. We're sure she didn't recognize us, but we would not want that anyway because that would mean she was imprinted on us.

When we got home, we downloaded the photos, and he had taken 211 pictures! After all that, due to his excitement, we ended up with only one decent photo of Thor that clearly showed the transmitter box and the antenna on her back. It was all we needed for positive proof! Thor had returned home and had been successful for one year after this horrible collision. Our prayers were that this would continue for many years to come.

Thor on her favorite power pole along Highway 180.

The next spring, Thor was tracked again, documenting her northward journey to her summer home, starting on March 23, 2014, close to the date we released her the previous year. More and more Facebook fans were following this impressive bird. She followed the same path again, varying slightly, but not much. She again spent a bit of time in the Cassiar Mountains of Yukon, possibly to attempt to establish a territory and to mate. She then continued her journey to the north banks and the Brooks Range, just like the previous summer. It is interesting to note that how we could tell if she was actually breeding is that making a nest, incubating eggs, and rearing her young would show in the data. She would be at one location for much of the day and for a long period of time. She never exhibited this behavior.

Her return journey that summer was documented as well. She returned to the exact same power pole as the previous winter on November 6, interestingly three weeks earlier than before. We were privileged to see her again on many occasions and looked for her every time we drove by each winter.

It was an incredibly exciting eight years to have witnessed the journeys of the mighty Thor. We were elated every November when we would see her perched on her power pole near Deming. In early November 2020, we received our usual email from the researchers that Thor had completed her eighth full migration successfully.

As usual, we jumped in our truck and headed toward mile post 150 on U.S. Highway 180 to greet our former charge and congratulate her on her long journey home. We didn't see her and figured she might be out hunting for a meal to rejuvenate her, so we came back home.

After a few days, we got a phone call giving us the horrible news that Thor had been found dead in a stock tank. We asked the rancher if she was sure that it was our bird. She sent us a picture of a golden eagle lying face down in a moss-filled metal stock tank. The next picture she sent confirmed that it was indeed Thor. She had removed the tracking device and sent the photo with the identifying tag. Needless to say, we were crushed. Our hearts sank in our chests. There was a moment where we were in disbelief, but kept going back to the photos, knowing this was real.

Thor's body in tank and tracking device tag.

Although we had great trepidation in our hearts, we knew we had to retrieve Thor's body, so made arrangements to meet at the rest area. With dread, we walked to the back of the truck and saw her stiff, lifeless body that was still damp from the bottom of the stock tank. The rancher described to us in detail how she and some of her kids were out checking their cattle. The kids were riding in the back of the truck and as they drove by a large metal stock tank, one of the kids told her to stop because he had seen something in the bottom of the tank. They saw the eagle lying face down and quickly retrieved it, noticing the strange box on her back. That's when they called, informing us of the news.

We transferred her to our truck and made the drive home in silence, which seemed to take forever. After a while, we started asking questions. Had she been shot? Had she eaten something that had been poisoned? Unfortunately, we were assuming the worst. Dennis called Eagle Environmental and informed them about the sad news of Thor. They asked if we had retrieved the transmitter and gave us instructions to put her in the freezer while he started working on the arrangements for a necropsy (an autopsy in animals). We all wanted to know what happened to her. We eventually heard from the University of Georgia College of Veterinary Medicine in Athens, Georgia. They gave us instructions on how to mail her and sent a mailing label. We found a large box, and with great sadness, we carefully packed her with dry ice and prepared her for shipment. So many memories of her journey from the time we rescued her, rehabilitated her, released her, and watched her for those eight years came flooding in as we said our final goodbyes. It was truly a sad day for us.

On February 12, 2021, we received the results of the necropsy via the eagle researchers. The results the researcher relayed to us were: "She died of a heart attack caused by an underlying intestinal disease. Is there any more to be said? Old age? She had a good life. She died doing what she loved to do. Migrate!" He then said, "Why did it happen at the end of the journey and not on the way?" He didn't know.

Thanks for the experience, Thor!

Dennis's answer to this was: From the very beginning, Denise knew that we would be the ones to be present at the end of her life. To our relief, this meant she died of natural causes and not at the hand of humans, which had been our fear.

In the eight years that she was tracked, she traveled fifty-thousand-plus miles from one end of the North American continent to the other for eight full migrations. It was truly a blessing to have been a part of this incredibly wonderful story. Fly free in the heavens, Thor!

Thor's research data not only added to the growing information that is used to determine more about the life histories of eagles to help protect them, but also added to the amazing range of these birds with Thor's near-record migration. Golden eagles are ecologically imperative to the ecosystems that they are a part of, and the need to protect them is paramount. We were honored that we were able to be contributors in this effort. Without Thor, this would not have been possible. Thank you, Thor. We are forever grateful for the experience you provided us and all of your fans who followed you for so many years.

CHAPTER THREE

Injuries and Treatments

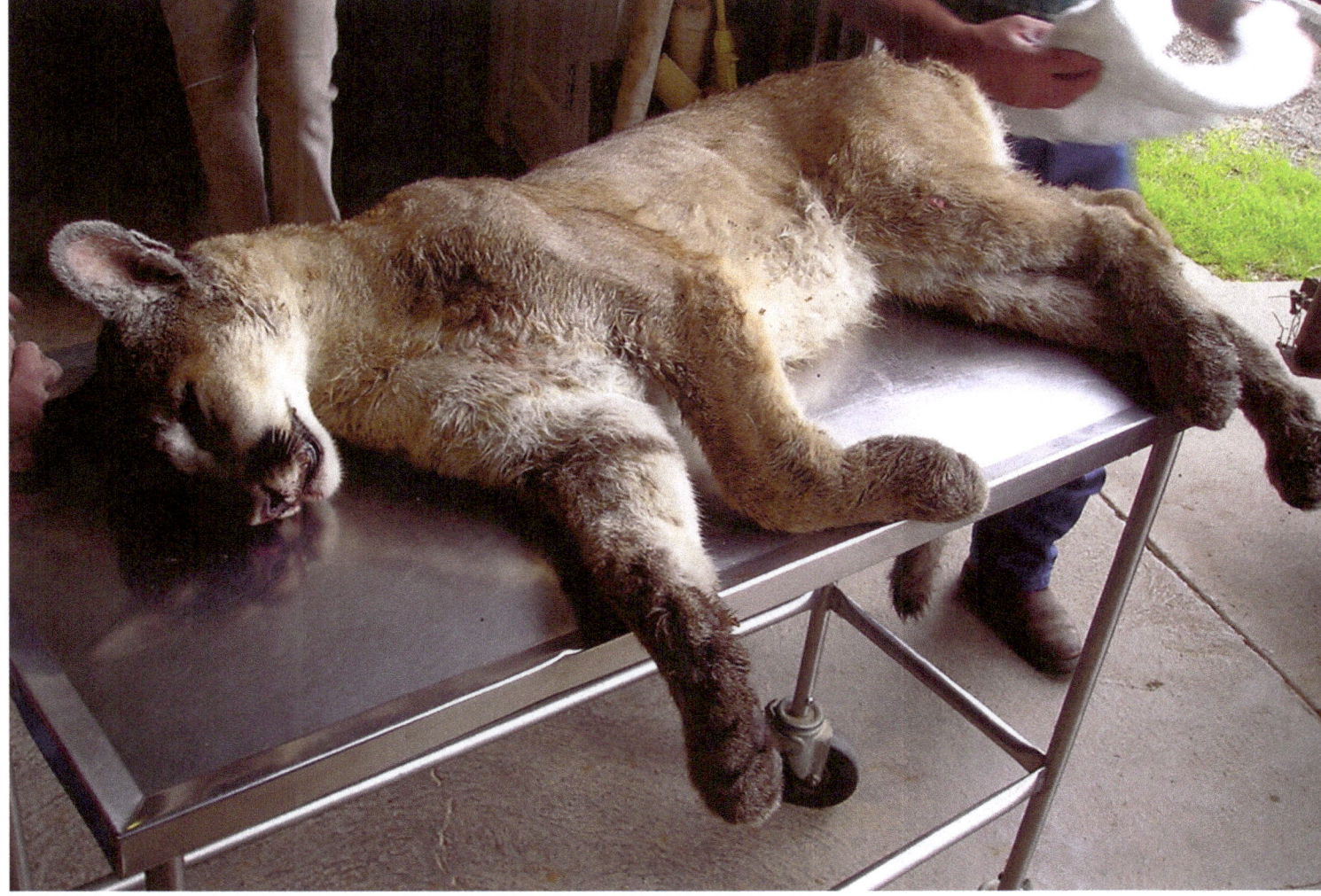

Tranquilized mountain lion hit by car.

Gila Wildlife Rescue has experienced a wide variety of injuries and conditions throughout its existence, varying from small lacerations and abrasions to head injuries, broken bones, and infections. Some of these infections have been unusual but an important part of our education to help future animals in our care. Most of the animals we receive are treated by us in our clinic unless the animal needs anesthesia, which can only be administered by a veterinarian. We have been blessed with vets in our area that have never hesitated to help and do so free of charge. They also perform complicated surgeries for wildlife and provide medications that again can only be prescribed by veterinarians.

Around 2010, we started a relationship with veterinarians at the El Paso Zoo in El Paso, Texas. They had been running a rescue program for raptors and were working with a rehabilitator in El Paso to complete their rehabilitation and release. They contacted us when the rehabber fell ill and had to quit. This partnership immediately doubled the number of birds we cared for, but we gained access to the incredible experience and knowledge that the veterinarians provide. The zoo conducts the initial evaluations and treatments and when they are sufficiently healed and ready for rehabilitation, they are transferred to us. We then continue the animal's care to the point they can be released.

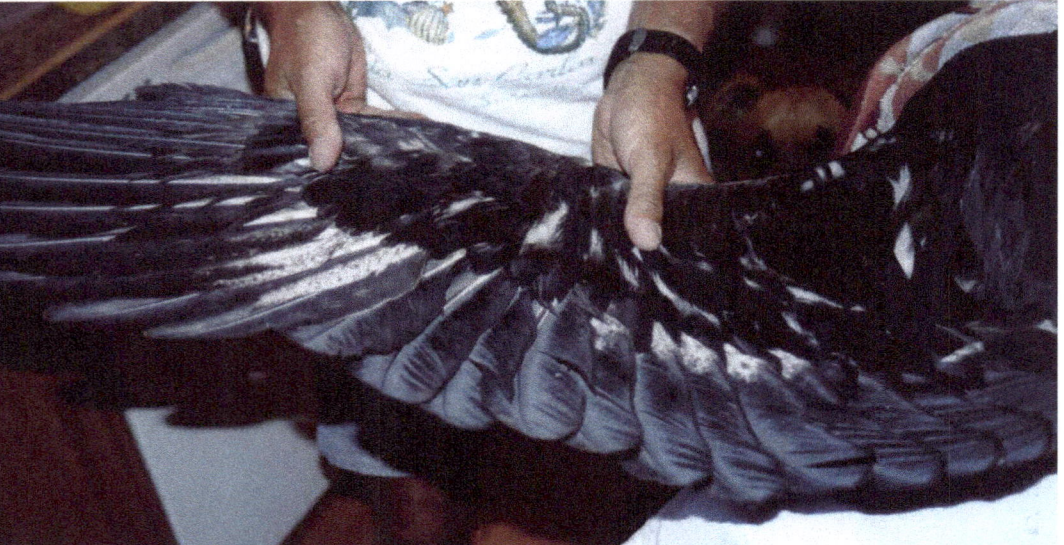

Golden eagle wing being palpated.

When we take in a new animal, the first thing on the agenda is a thorough examination. The general demeanor and the level of spirit it displays are two of the most important signs to observe. Birds of prey that are injured hang their heads just slightly, and both birds' and mammals' pain is revealed in their eyes. Examining the eyes for head injury comes next by shining a light to determine if pupils are constricting and reacting the same in both eyes, then a slow and methodical process of palpating the body to feel for broken bones, or lacerations, or punctures.

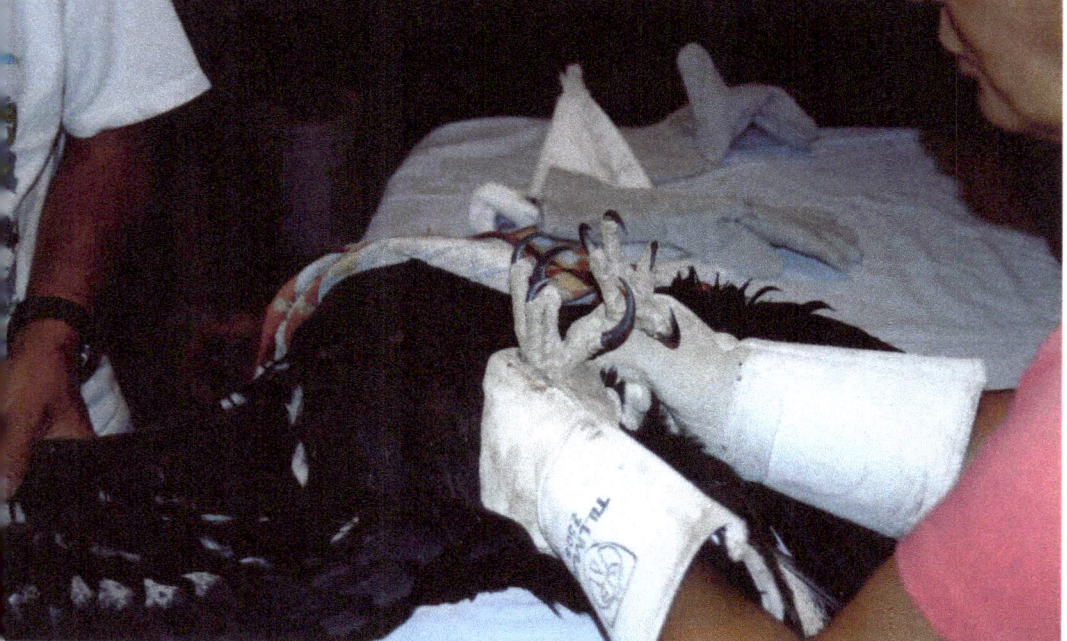

Denise holding golden eagle down and protecting us from talons.

We work as a team at this point because in order to feel the body and bones, Dennis must take his gloves off. This leaves him vulnerable to the lethal talons of raptors or the bite of a mammal, so it is Denise that he puts his complete and total trust in to protect him. She holds the legs and keeps the animal from struggling as the animal is examined.

She has never once failed in controlling these dangerous animals, and neither of us has ever been seriously injured, but each of us has been grabbed by talons a few times. Denise's hand was grabbed by a barn owl as it was being released, which was Dennis's fault for not bring-ing gloves. A great horned owl grabbed Dennis on the forearm above his gloves once while examining the bird after being delivered to him during one of his biol-ogy lab classes. That one was difficult to get off, to say the least! When the owl grabbed Dennis's arm, he was frozen in place because if he strug-gled, the talons would just sink in deeper. He yelled for

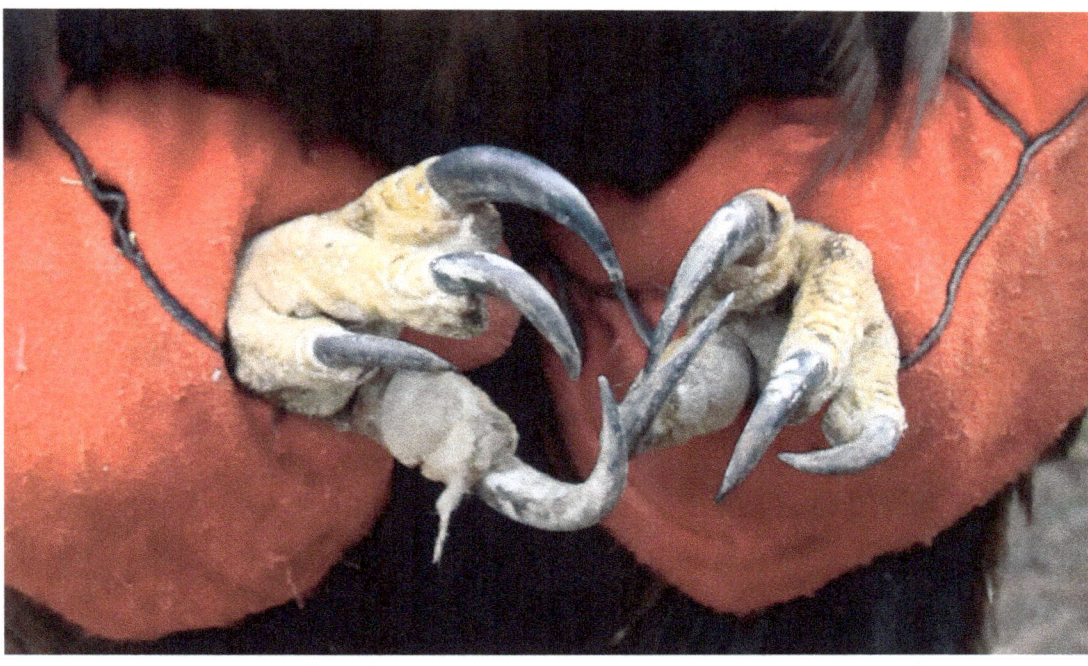

Golden eagle talons, each claw the size of a finger.

help and three professors came running down the hall to his aid. It took the four of them, each pulling on one of its toes and talon, until the bird weakened enough to let go. It took about ten minutes and during that time, Dennis had one of the talons stabbing his arm bone causing intense pain.

The only other time this happened was an even more frightening experience because it was with a large golden eagle. One of the vet technicians at the zoo had a difficult time catching an eagle to transfer it to a transport cage. We had just arrived to pick this bird up, and Dennis offered to catch it for them since he had quite a bit more experience. He handed Dennis a pair of well-worn leather gloves and he started to capture the eagle. As he reached down, the bird grabbed his arm, which happens frequently, but that is why we use gloves that protect the forearm. Little did he know that the gloves were so old they were brittle, and the eagle's hallux—the largest back talon on raptors—pierced the glove like it wasn't there and sunk deep into his forearm. Intense pain caused him to yell for more help and everyone came running. Dennis was lucky that when he let go of the legs, the bird thought he could escape and released his vicelike grip to run to the back of the cage.

The next attempt captured him without any more injury to Dennis, and he was placed in the transport cage. The pain was so excruciating that we were starting to worry that this was a more serious injury. On the drive home, it became so bad that Dennis almost asked Denise to stop at the emergency room, but with some painkillers it eventually abated. He was very lucky that it did not cause any serious damage and that he had all necessary immunizations.

We have found that once we start examining them, birds tend to calm down some, their breathing slows, and struggling stops. It may be a fright factor that makes them so afraid that a human is touching them, but we have observed a calmness that comes over them with gentle examination. We try to do this quickly, quietly, and with a calmness but assertiveness that lets the animal know we are in charge, but we do not intend to hurt them. The wildlife we care for, nine times out of ten, seem to accept this invasion of their space as helping them and they coop-

Peregrine falcon in scale.

erate well. There are times though that they do not accept that we are helping them and are fighting us throughout the entire examination.

Depending on what is found in the hands-on examination, the animal is commonly weighed as the next step. Their weight tells us if the animal is emaciated. Close to one-quarter of the adult raptors we receive are simply starving, having become so weak that they cannot fly and would have died unless a kindhearted human picked them up and brought them to us. We see this often in the winter where birds hatched the previous spring, who are full adult size, end up lacking the hunting skills to catch enough prey to survive. For some strange reason, when we put birds on the scale to weigh them, laying them on their backs, they calm down and they will just lay there for a while, looking silly.

Normally, injuries we experience will show themselves by this time in the examination, but if we still find no cause for the animal to be down, then we look at feces that may have been left in the transport carrier or the animal's cage. If it is bright green, then it is an indication of a possible poisoning. If the droppings of mammals are white, or dark sticky black, then infection is likely. We are always on the lookout for a severe type of diarrhea in mammals called scours that needs immediate treatment. If this provides no answer, we take a blood sample to the veterinarians to send off for testing because lead poisoning and West Nile virus is common in large raptors like eagles. If all this fails to provide an answer, then we look at the possibility of an aged animal that is at the end of its life.

One of the most common conditions we see are head injuries and eye injuries. Concussions are difficult to treat and are one of the most life-threatening we encounter. We most frequently see concussions in great horned owls due to collisions with cars when they are feeding on a roadkill at night. This diagnosis is easy to make because symptoms are so clear. A lack of proper pupillary response, which is a classic sign of concussion, is easy to see in these large owls because their eyes are so huge. On the other hand, in barn owls and some hawks, it is more difficult to test pupillary response because their eyes are so dark their pupils are almost invisible. Additionally, the pupils can be blown wide open, or one eye will react differently than the other. Occasionally, the bird will also exhibit a characteristic head turn, most frequently seen in owls, where they slowly turn their head in one direction to about 90 degrees and then quickly snap it back to the straight position, and they repeat this constantly, all day and night.

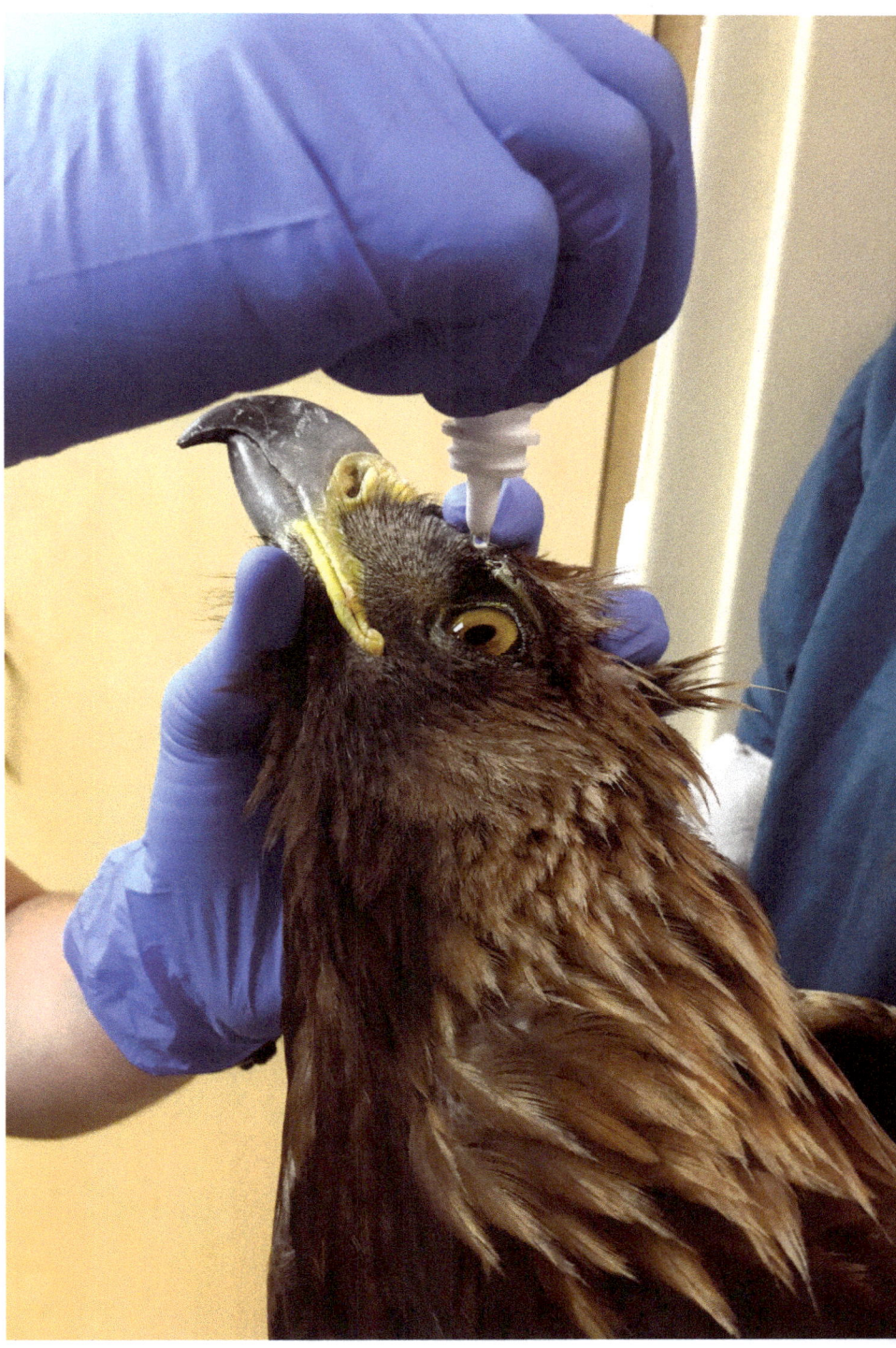

Golden eagle being treated for eye injury.

To treat concussions, we inject a drug used to reduce swelling in the brain. Hydration may be needed but may contribute to brain swelling, so it must be regulated. This is one of the most acute injuries we deal with. We save more animals than we lose, but concussions cause more deaths than other injuries.

Another common injury is caused by barbed wire fences. Again, common in large owls more than others, we also have had many hawks, eagles, falcons, deer, and javelina that have been torn up in this manner.

Burrowing owl with "blown" pupil.

Golden eagle—lacerations caused by barbed wire.

With birds, the harm is worse than with mammals. Not only is a bird's skin very thin and tears easily, but when they hit the fence, they struggle to escape and always seem to spin their bodies around and around, tearing more tissue. Our task is to get the wire untangled from them without causing more damage, and that is a challenge. When these birds are found, we cut the wire on each side and take the bird with the wire to the clinic for surgery. Note: We always repair the fence where the wire had been cut to free the bird.

Often what we see is a mass of twisted, tangled skin and feathers with no clear sign of where to start or which direction the bird had spun. Eventually, with a great deal of patience and stamina (Denise has held the legs of raptors for as much as three hours straight during this kind of surgery), we remove the wire with its offending barb and now have another large task, closing all the skin that the barb damaged.

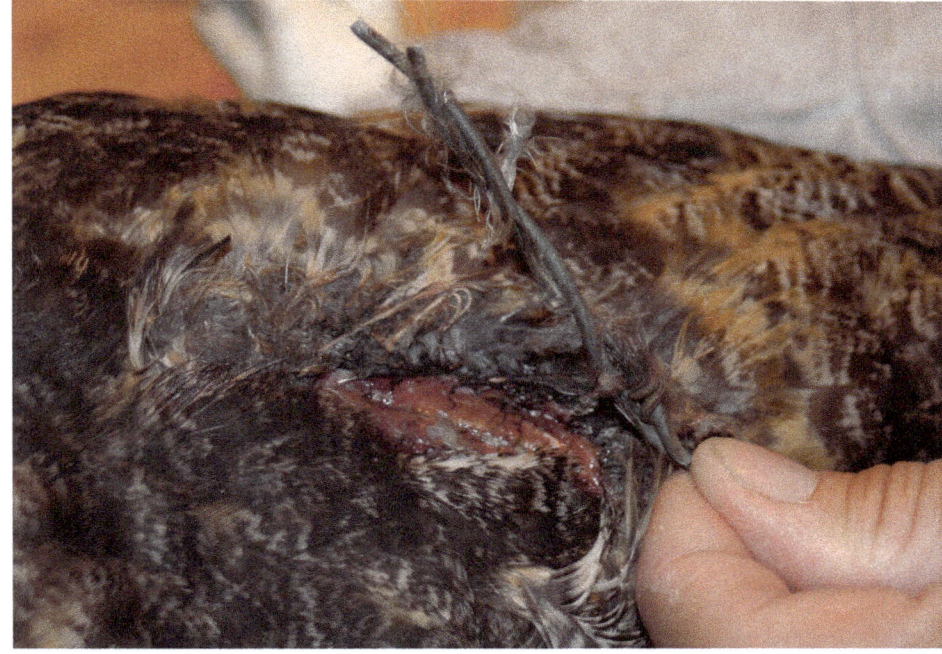

Barbed wire removed from great horned owl.

Small sutures, gentle tugs here and there, occasionally using artificial skin products and medical-grade honey to stimulate skin growth, we get the task completed. It is one of the most difficult things we do, and it seems to leave us dazed and our energy spent for a while after the surgery is completed.

In the past few years, we have observed an increase in these entanglements, and they often come in batches where we will have several animals with barbed wire injuries that come in during a short period of time.

Barbed wire removed from birds of prey.

Speaking of things happening in a series, we have observed this time and time again where we receive several animals with the same injuries, or the same cause of injury. For example, having four or five barbed wire incidents in a few days, or a series of auto collisions, or head injuries, or broken bones.

Surgery to repair skin tears in peregrine falcon.

Broken bones are always challenging. When a mammal breaks a bone, it usually requires casting and even pins. Animals like deer and pronghorn don't do well with casts on their legs, but it is necessary at times.

Pronghorn fawn with leg cast.

Birds, on the other hand, have hollow bones to reduce weight for flight and seem to be easier to set. They also can have a pin put in them that extends from one end of the bone to the other without damage because of this hollow trait. Birds' bones heal amazingly fast. This allows for quick recoveries and quick returns to the wild. We tape the wing, once set, to prevent it from extending.

After the bone has healed, in about six weeks the wrap can be removed, and the bird is placed into a small cage for some intermediate care. The restricted movement in the smaller cage does not put stress and pressure on the wing bones but continues to keep muscles loose and moving. After a few weeks in the smaller cage the bird will be transferred to a large flight cage to strengthen the flight muscles in its breast.

This takes between one and three weeks. Once a bird starts flapping its wings for flight, an incredible amount of stress—or "wing loading"—occurs that places extreme forces on a wing. Perfectly designed in nature, wings are a marvel of engineering to be so light and delicate, yet to be able to withstand amazing forces of pressure during flight. Birds like great horned owls and eagles have the highest wing loading of any bird,[5] being quite large and placing more stress and pressures on these wings as they fly fast and dive for prey. A total period of seven to ten weeks and the animal is back in the wild hunting!

On rare occasions, raptors are brought to us with a broken leg. Often, this is such a massive injury that they must be euthanized. When surgery is successful, they are difficult to treat because they cannot put any weight on the leg for at least three weeks. To achieve this, we have to suspend the bird in a hammock-like device and hand-feed it until ready.

Peregrine falcon with broken humerus showing figure eight wrap.

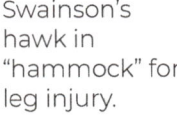

Swainson's hawk in "hammock" for leg injury.

One of the most fascinating processes we use to help birds is a process called "imping," developed by falconers centuries ago. This is a procedure where we take feathers from a deceased bird and transplant them to a bird that has lost or broken feathers. They can then be released almost immediately instead of having to wait for feathers to grow back. When we receive a bird that has been injured, but the damage is just broken or lost feathers, we normally would have to wait for them to grow back naturally, which could take up to a year. Many of these cases are birds that have no other injury, but the feather loss has either left them unable to fly or not able to fly well enough to catch food efficiently. A bird can be grounded even with just a few feathers lost. If the loss is on one wing and not the other, their balance is thrown off and they cannot fly, at least well enough to catch food regularly. Waiting for the long period needed for natural feather growth to occur increases the chances of other injury and imprinting and stresses birds, so imping when needed is an important tool to use. A fascinating fact of nature is the way the molting process is perfectly designed to have the same feathers on the left and right

Juvenile red-tailed hawk with feather loss.

wings molt at the same time, and another pair starts to get ready to drop once the other feathers grow in.

Here is the process: Wings from deceased birds are kept for imping purposes along with molted feathers that are in perfect condition (which is rare). When a feather needs to be replaced, it must be the exact same feather as the one that was lost. For example, if a hawk has lost the third and fourth feathers on his right wing, we must use the exact same feathers from the same wing of the donor.

Dremel tool to make smooth cut on frayed shaft.

Blade used to cleanly split the shaft.

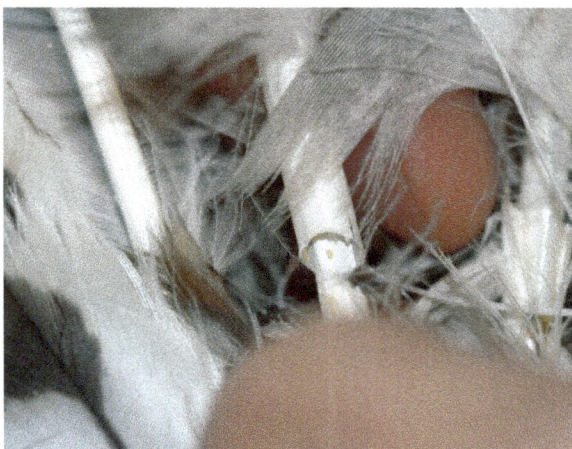

Carefully inserting and aligning the shaft.

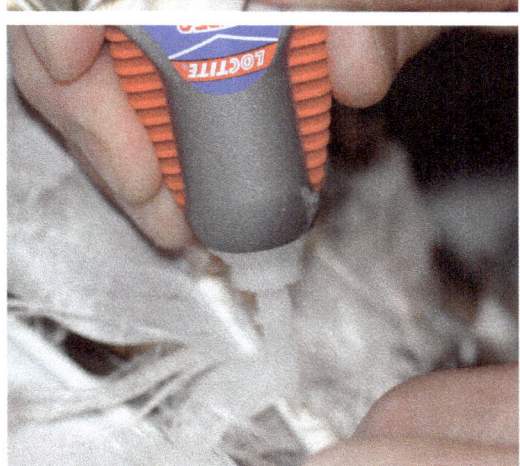

Superglue new feather.

Imping complete and bird ready to release.

Once the correct feather has been obtained, a high-speed Dremel tool is used to cut the broken shaft of the feather cleanly behind the frayed edges of the broken shaft. This tool works best because the feather shaft is hollow and using other tools just shatters and splits the shaft. The donor feather is then placed inside the hollow shaft of the broken feather, at the appropriate length, and is glued together with superglue. Like it does on human skin, this glue can cement tissues together and works great for feathers.

This process is repeated on all lost flight feathers until the plumage is again complete. In almost all cases, we use the same species of bird for the donated feathers but every once in a while, we have to mix and match. We have probably confused a few local birders by releasing red-tailed hawks with Swainson's hawk feathers or put adult red-tailed feathers on a juvenile bird, giving him a crazy-looking combination of brown and red feathers on its tail. But as long as it gets the animal released as soon as possible, then it is worth it. They will molt the broken feather shaft along with its donated feather on their next molting process and have a new fresh feather replacing our "imps."

Deer fawns with scours, a severe form of diarrhea common in livestock, requires a completely different skill set that involves learning how to read the animal. If scours can be treated early, the prognosis for survival is good. The problem is that the primary cause of scours is simply stress. The animal becomes very stressed by being captured, much less the stress it may have experienced from the injury. Fawns may change their behavior, start drinking more water, or their eyes become glossy and sad looking. Catching these wily critters to administer injections without stressing them is impossible without some direct interactions that encourage them to think you are helping them. This causes another problem by getting them at least acclimated to humans, if not imprinted a bit. These are the tough, intensive-care types of cases and not the norm, but we have good luck using our no contact method after this period of close contact treatment to get them back to being "wild." We have medications now that we can inject into fawns as soon as we get them that help to prevent scours and reduces a condition called capture myopathy, both of which can be fatal. It doesn't work all the time but has reduced the problem somewhat.

As you can see and will eventually learn more about, we have gone to great lengths at times to rehabilitate an animal to the point of releasing it. Some wonder why all that effort and, at times, expense? Ecologically, these animals have one of the most important niches, or places in nature, of any animal. Raptors are at the top of any food chain they are in, which makes them extremely important for the survival of the entire ecosystem. It is always important to return an animal that has been injured back to the food chain it was participating in. In the case of raptor nestlings that fall out of the nest, there is another significant benefit of saving them. When nestlings fall out, they often naturally die either from the fall itself or from predation.

Some would question why we interrupt this natural process where not all the nestlings make it to maturity. Humans kill thousands of animals each year with cars, poisons, shooting, and on and on. If we have opportunities to return most—if not all—the nestlings to the wild, we are making up a bit for the other deaths that humans cause. The counterbalance we provide to the ecosystem in this manner has had to have had a profound effect, especially if you realize that we have been doing this for over forty years and close to ten thousand animals.

As raptor rehabilitators, we have had to be inventive at times to bring a bird to successful release. It is usually the tough cases that require us to develop our own methods of care. For example, one year we had an eagle that after his wing was healed, would not fly. After working with the bird for months, he eventually would fly across the flight cage but from one low perch to another, never trying to reach higher perches. For release, we needed him to fly strong and powerful, but he was not. After using every method that we knew and researching new methods that also failed, we struggled for a solution. We put our heads together and constructed a twenty-foot-long narrow ramp, covered in fake grass carpeting to give it traction, and placed it in the cage with one end up on the high perch. After coaxing the eagle up the ramp a few times with food, he eventually walked up the ramp to the upper perch, then flew off the perch to the opposite end, one hundred feet away. Success! This eventually was used for a few more eagles as well.

The injuries and treatments Gila Wildlife Rescue has experienced have been varied and complicated at times, but thankfully we have always had our local veterinarians help us with X-rays and medications. Since we started our work with the El Paso Zoo, we have also expanded our knowledge and our ability to save birds that we were not able to in the past. Their knowledge of healing abrasions and growing skin back is amazing. They can almost always surgically repair a broken bone, utilizing the latest technology and methods successfully. Here is a video of Dr. Vicki releasing a golden eagle that was initially treated by the zoo.

Video Link: GoldenEagleDr.Vicki

We received a golden eagle from our colleagues at the El Paso Zoo early one spring. The zoo has an awesome raptor rehabilitation program and conducts excellent

Golden eagle "El Paso" with West Nile virus.

initial treatment and care along with surgeries for us. When long-term care and flight cages are needed, they transfer their patients to Gila Wildlife Rescue where we complete their rehabilitation and release them. We have a one-hundred-foot-long flight cage which is mandatory for receiving a rehab permit that includes the care of eagles.

Sticking to the system our eagle research friends normally use, this large juvenile male eagle that was between one and two years old was named El Paso because he was found in El Paso on the Fort Bliss Army base. The veterinarian at the zoo had already completed blood work, x-rays, and other tests and determined that this bird, although down on the ground and not able to fly, had no discernible injury or infection.

The only thing she could find that could possibly cause this huge bird to be grounded was that he tested slightly positive for West Nile virus. When we received him, this information did not seem to be important because he improved quickly, and we thought he was on his way to recovery and release. After a few days running around in the big flight cage, he started to jump to higher perches and make some short flights across parts of the cage. In a couple of weeks, he was flying across the length of the cage and doing great. Surprisingly, the next week he started flying less, started using lower perches, and slowly became less active. We entered his cage one day to check on him and noticed a few large flight feathers on the ground. At first, we discounted this as the normal molting process. It wasn't significant until a few days later when there was a pile of eight or ten large feathers under one of the perches. Now we had a problem and needed more information because we had no idea what was going on. It was possible that the West Nile virus infection was progressing and the cause of this.

We conducted an extensive search for information on this relatively new virus that we were more familiar with infecting domestic horses and had never encountered before in wildlife. It turned out, to our great surprise, golden eagles are very susceptible to West Nile virus[6] and it was decimating populations in some areas. The fact that they migrate and can infect summer and winter range populations exacerbates the problem. Birds that summer in northern reaches had higher incidents of the infection due to more exposure to large swarms of mosquitoes, the vector that transmits this disease. When an eagle contracts this disease, it will slowly become so weak that it is on the ground and cannot fly. This also can be caused by feather loss. Once down, it will survive for a while running after prey on the ground. This action further damages their tail feathers and the primary flight feathers (longest feathers most important for flight on the ends of their wings) as they use their wings to propel themselves after prey. Soon the bird is too weak to catch prey, and this suffering, possibly taking many weeks, continues until it dies.

Those lucky birds that get discovered by caring people who report them can survive only with "coordinated care" until they are strong enough to return to the wild. Coordinated care is simply providing everything the bird needs for as long as it takes until they either survive, or they get worse and pass away. When El Paso started losing feathers in this very uncharacteristic molt, we contacted other rehabilitators and fish and wildlife officials. Most had never heard of this kind of feather loss. Two of the contacts gave us the exact same information: "West Nile virus does very strange things to eagles," because it does different things in different birds. Therefore, they were not surprised that the molting process was affected.

El Paso— beautiful but very sick.

El Paso eventually lost all of his flight feathers. That sounds awful, like we are describing a totally featherless, naked bird. No, what happened was that the infection from the virus triggered its molting process but in a very unusual way. The virus caused it to change from the normal, slow molting process to a process that made him lose feathers at an unnatural rate and left him unable to fly due to feather loss. The normal process of molting in birds, during the season when they normally do this, is to lose a few feathers at a time, then these grow back and they lose a few more. Feather growth is phenomenally rapid, so this switching out of old feathers for new, with equal feather loss on the left and right wing so flight is balanced, occurs without ever leaving them flightless.[7] The exception to this is in a few birds like some species of geese. They lose all their primary flight feathers at once, and it leaves them flightless for a short time.[8] These types of birds migrate to islands or similar areas with no predators to safely get through this molting period. The normal molting process also includes losing and replacing every feather on their body, but the small ones are not as noticeable, unless the bird is in a cage with West Nile virus and its molting process has gone completely haywire. Then it is very noticeable! El Paso eventually had piles of smaller feathers as well. New feathers were growing back quickly to replace them.

What was happening with El Paso was that he was losing feathers far too rapidly, and because it was caused by a hormonal imbalance triggered by the virus, it was not symmetrical (equal on each side) like it should be. He was weakened, flightless, and starting to become depressed. At least we had an explanation for his bizarre symptoms. We also learned that the only treatment we could give him to get well was to keep him fed and safe until the virus ran its course and his feathers grew back. It took many, many months. We are required to contact the New Mexico Department of Game and Fish and the U.S. Fish and Wildlife Service if we have any animal that we keep longer than ninety days. They review the situation and approve another ninety days. We had to do this three times with El Paso because he was with us that long.

Feather regrowth in El Paso's wing.

After a period of repeatedly molting through three cycles, he stopped losing feathers and just continued growing them back. Once fully feathered, he started flying again.

Here is a short video of the capture of an eagle in order to examine how well feather growth was progressing:

El Paso "pounding the perches"— notice all feathers have grown back.

Video Link: GoldenEagleFlightCageCatch

El Paso's muscles had atrophied to the point that he could barely fly at first, but soon, due to his spirit returning because he was starting to fly, he was "pounding the perches." This is a term we use for describing the way most raptors start flying when they are ready to be set free. They fly back and forth across the cage most of the day and fly very aggressively, hitting perches quite hard as they land. You can hear a clear, audible *thunk* as they pound the perches. We listened to this message he was expressing to us by the forcefulness of his flying across the cage and knew it was time to set him free. El Paso flew off into the sunset on a warm autumn day, exuding the confidence and power that these eagles show so brilliantly. This was one lucky bird to have survived this ordeal.

Another unusual case was also one of the few bald eagles that Gila Wildlife Rescue has ever cared for, the majestic birds being quite rare in our area. The call came at about 11:00 p.m. one evening from a New Mexico State Police officer. "Are you still takin' care of birds and stuff?" he asked, "I have an eagle for you!"

Luna with lead poisoning.

Sure enough, he was another one of Dennis's former students who remembered he rehabilitated wildlife from being in his class. It turns out the eagle was reported to their dispatch as sitting in the middle of the road, directly on the line between Arizona and New Mexico on U.S. Highway 180, west of Luna, New Mexico, watching cars zip by him. The officer had wrapped it in his jacket and had it in the trunk of his patrol car. He was around two hours away and was checking with me before he headed in our direction.

"The bird is shaking his head, like tremors or something," he told me.

Dennis replied, "Get him here ASAP!"

An hour and fifteen minutes later the cruiser pulled up in the driveway and the officer got out and opened his trunk. We were assuming this was going to be another golden eagle, having cared for dozens of these more common eagles in this area. Imagine our amazement, surprise, and horror when we saw lying down in a box in his trunk the unmistakable white head and yellow beak of an adult *bald* eagle!

This was our first bald eagle, but how horrific. This rare bird had been injured or was sick and was suffering.

It also hit Dennis that this was probably one of the breeding eagles that were on Luna Lake, which is located less than a mile from the location where he was picked up. A pair of bald eagles had recently started successfully breeding there, which was a rare thing in our part of the world. The loss of one of a breeding pair would compound this catastrophe. Our hope was that it was one of the offspring coming back to visit, and not the mature breeding pair.

Dennis examined the bird, shaking the whole time with excitement. Upon examination, there were no broken bones, no lacerations, no sign of head injury, and no tremors. He could find no cause for her to be down on the ground, but the bird was obviously in trouble. She was alert and had an intense stare that seemed to look right through you. She could stand and perch but did not move at all past that. Her pupillary response was very quick like it should be but the pupil of one eye constricted a bit slower than the other. Dennis checked it multiple times and got worried. Pupils not responding to bright light are a sign of head trauma and possibly a concussion. Pupils responding to light but the response not being equal in the left and right eyes can be signs of neurologic problems of some sort and may not necessarily be caused by head injury.

We quickly drove her to the veterinarian's office early the next morning with a blood sample that needed to be sent to the state vet's lab for a rush job and to get this bird some x-rays to make sure there were no other injuries. At 10:00 a.m. the next morning, with the eagle getting weaker, the vet called with test results. The bird had lead poisoning. We normally think of lead poisoning as something humans may get from contaminated drinking water or lead paint in the environment. The uninformed may think that for a bird like this to get lead poisoning they had to have been shot by some immoral human. How eagles really get this is a different, unfortunate story.

If a bird like this bald eagle were to get shot with lead shot, say from a rifle (where it is less likely to survive to develop lead poisoning) or more likely from a shotgun pellet, it would not likely develop lead poisoning. Again, assuming he survives the shooting. When a bird is hit with a few pellets, but not enough to bring it down or kill it, the bird's body grows tissue around it. This seals it off and protects the body from this foreign object. If enough pellets, or larger bullets, are lodged in the body, there sometimes can be enough leakage and dissolving of the lead to where it can enter the bloodstream, and the bird can develop lead poisoning, but this is rare. Upon examining x-rays, many eagles have pellets present and have survived, which demonstrates how they could survive being shot and not develop this serious poisoning. Remember though, an x-ray had been taken of this eagle. Bullets and pellets show up on these scans like bright light bulbs in the film. Anything metal does, and this bald eagle, Luna, had none.

Luna—still lots of spunk even though very sick.

How would a bird get lead poisoning without getting shot? Ingesting a lead pellet would accomplish this, and, in fact, it may only take one pellet to be eaten and enough lead could be released into the bloodstream to cause death.[9] The sad part about this whole scenario is that the only way the eagle could have eaten lead shot is if his prey, in this case probably a duck on Luna Lake, had been shot with lead shot, which is very illegal, and to us, ecologically immoral. The hunting industry themselves cleaned up the entire sport once it was discovered that lead pellets from shotguns, used to hunt waterfowl like ducks and geese, can contribute to lead poisoning in humans and other animals. States nationwide banned the use of lead shot for waterfowl and eventually a national law was enacted. The alternative, endorsed by Ducks Unlimited and many other hunting organizations promoting conservation for future duck hunting, was to use steel shot, which does not cause toxicity like lead does.

This means that someone was hunting ducks with lead shot, which is something used only for quail and dove away from waterways where it does not cause harm. Bald eagles have frequently been observed predating on ducks on Luna Lake. This eagle likely ate a duck that had not died from being shot but had formed a cyst around a pellet it was shot with, probably in muscle tissue. The digestive enzymes of these primarily, but not exclusively, fish-eating eagles are so strong that they can dissolve the entire body of a fish in a few hours, skeleton and all.[10] Sadly, the digestive enzymes are also strong enough to dissolve that lead pellet the eagle ate. There is a toxic level of lead in just one pellet dissolved in the stomach of a bird, and this bird may have eaten multiple pellets.

A quick side note of importance here is that golden eagles also have a serious problem with lead poisoning and may be one of the leading causes of death.[11] They ingest lead from the carcasses of hunted animals that are left in the field instead of taken off and eaten or disposed of. Both coyotes and jackrabbits are commonly left in the field after being shot. The larger bullets from the type of guns used to hunt these animals have a great deal more lead than shotgun pellets, so are even more lethal.

This diagnosis was outside Dennis's knowledge base, having never dealt with a case of lead poisoning. He contacted the veterinarian in northern New Mexico that we use as a resource, and she instructed us to immediately rush the bird up to her for treatment. Gila Wildlife Rescue did not have the proper medications or equipment to do what was needed to give Luna a chance at survival. We placed her in a transport box and drove her to our regional airport. She was flown to Albuquerque where someone was waiting to transport her to the clinic in Española and the awaiting procedure.

The procedure she needed is called chelation and is used in some cases (for both humans and other animals) to pull toxins out of the bloodstream. The specific treatment for this eagle involved intravenous application of a drug that the dissolved lead in the bloodstream can bind to, and then as blood is filtered through the kidneys, the drug and the lead it carries can be eliminated out the patient's urine.[12] In a speedy relay to give the

Luna

bird the best chance possible at survival, Luna was hooked up to the equipment for this procedure within one hour of leaving the Grant County Airport. If we drove, it would have been six hours before treatment.

The procedure did not produce any improvement, however, and after the lead levels were tested more accurately, the vet realized that this bird had twice the level considered necessary to cause this kind of damage and death. They quickly scrambled to contact other rehabilitators that may have tried another chelation drug with better success. Just as they found out about a drug used by some rehabilitators in Minnesota that pulled the lead out more efficiently, Luna surrendered the fight.

We were kind of glad we weren't there for that transition. We had a hard enough time with the news once hearing it. What we saw in this instance was that Luna's death was appalling because a human who did not care enough about the other living creatures around them, who could have easily followed the law of man and the code of hunting, chose to be malicious and caused deep damage to this eagle by using lead shot. But we also saw that because we found a new drug for this procedure, Luna helped the rehabilitators of the region obtain a new tool for the arsenal of helping these poor creatures when humans are so ecologically immoral.

Since this case, there have been several advancements in the treatment of lead poisoning.[13] One of the newest drugs being used now can easily remove all the lead at levels even higher than Luna had. If caught early, this horrible infection is a treatable condition where in the past it was usually fatal.

The other silver lining was that Luna helped in the continued protection of eagles by making the public aware of this problem and taking some action. We contacted the local newspaper, and they quickly did a story for us. They have never turned us down in the past when we have made requests like this and have been very supportive. Issues with photos on the front page, like a close-up of a bald eagle's head looking straight at the camera, doesn't hurt sales and circulation either. This time they wrote a great article about this eagle's death and connected it directly to the unknown hunter that used lead shot. It detailed the law, history of it, and the reason for it, something some hunters may not have known completely. We helped to educate them. This article was reprinted in an Albuquerque newspaper and reached a statewide audience of sportsmen. Dennis wrote letters to the New Mexico State Game Commission, the governing body of the New Mexico Department of Game and Fish, and expressed his concern along with telling them the story of Luna and including copies of the press articles. They produced a press release that was part of an insert in the Sunday papers statewide a few months later that again helped educate everyone about the importance of using steel shot for waterfowl hunting. See, Luna, you did some good after all!

In the spring of 2021, we received a call from Desert Willow Wildlife Rehabilitation Center in Carlsbad, New Mexico, asking us for help in caring for an adult bald eagle. Always ready to accept and help any wild animal, we readily agreed, but this was also only our third bald eagle, having normally cared for golden eagles. The center had completed the initial treatment of this bird for severe lead poisoning and needed a rehabilitation clinic that had an eagle flight (must be at least one hundred feet long) to continue his rehabilitation. We worked out a transport and held him in our eagle flight for six weeks or so until he was strong enough to release. When he was ready, we contacted the Mescalero Apache

Tribe in Mescalero, New Mexico, to make arrangements to release the bird. The bird was initially discovered next to a small pond with trout in it on the Mescalero Reservation. This pond, popular with fishermen, ended up with fish that had either ingested lead fishing weights or had swallowed the line and sinker attached to a fish they captured. Three bald eagles were catching and eating fish there as they passed through during their spring migration. Two of them died before someone noticed, and the third was captured and taken to Desert Willow Rehab.

Mescalero, as we now started calling him, was successfully rehabilitated and when the eagle was ready,

Mescalero

we contacted the tribe to get permission to release on tribal grounds. Their head wildlife officer met us at the site where the bird was found originally. After a few photos, the bird was released successfully. The officer then gave us a private tour, taking us back to his offices via a private route that was through incredibly beautiful backcountry. He then made us feel even more welcome by giving us a tour of their fish hatchery facilities. The entire process was very heartwarming and encouraging. The Mescalero Tribe takes great pride in the wildlife on their lands and work tirelessly at protecting and managing it.

Video Link: MescaleroRelease

Early one summer, we received a call from the New Mexico Department of Game and Fish in Las Cruces, New Mexico, saying they had a litter of newborn gray fox puppies they needed us to rehabilitate. We were shocked at first. Around five years ago we were barred from rehabilitating a specific group of carnivores that were susceptible to rabies and distemper, which they had a long history of, and an increase in exposure to humans had been recorded along with some population crashes due to the diseases.[14,15] This group included foxes, skunks, coyotes, and raccoons. Having

Gray fox pup.

raised all four of these species in the past, we were concerned about the ban and tried to work with the department on why there was a ban and how we could possibly work around it. Almost all stories of our experiences with these amazing creatures occurred before this ban took place.

The disease expert for the department basically ruled that the animals cannot be rehabilitated due to the danger of exposure to rabies. Rehabilitators could be exposed to the disease and the possible spread of the disease when the animal is released were the major factors in the decision. The argument we used—that all animals raised by Gila Wildlife Rescue are free from disease when released and have received vaccinations for rabies—did not persuade him. Even the fact that we and most rehabilitators that handle wild animals have pre-exposure rabies vaccinations did not budge the decision.

So you can imagine our surprise and frustration when we received four very cute fox pups just old enough to start opening their eyes. The reason for the change of heart by the department was due to the fact these animals had been rescued by a local rancher in an irrigation ditch, mother dead nearby, and several people knew about the rescue including a reporter wanting to write an article. Their initial reaction to the revelation that the animals would be euthanized due to this ruling was so negative that they realized backtracking was prudent here. Although they were not infected, they could not be raised and released by rehabilitators. We were contacted and allowed in this one last exception to complete the rehabilitation process.

As is common in trying to feed milk to wild animals, these cuddly babies were brought to us already suffering from an infection causing a bit of diarrhea. We were experienced with this and were not concerned at first. This frequently happens with wild babies due to the stress of being picked up and taken away by a human, normally their mortal enemy. Our normal protocol is to switch to electrolytes and then slowly start introducing milk replacer. One puppy died the first night, and we knew we had to change tactics due to an infection and not simply stress.

Our local veterinarian who volunteers his time and resources to the program provided us with an injectable antibiotic that we quickly administered, hoping for the best. The little black balls of fur with tiny eyes poking out were so adorable but were starting to become weaker. Dennis sat up with the remaining three the next night, giving them milk every fifteen minutes. One died early in the morning, another later that afternoon. After consulting our veterinarian, we switched antibiotics. The last baby was hanging in there and starting to get stronger but early the next morning, after sitting up with it again to feed it regularly, it succumbed as well.

The following day, Dennis started to feel bad and eventually started having diarrhea. Initially, he did not make the connection, but after two straight days with no relief, Denise realized the connection to the foxes. Two days later he was in the emergency room, and after conducting numerous blood tests they could not identify the cause of the infection. He was sent home with no treatment except a broad-spectrum antibiotic.

As Denise was picking up the prescription a few hours later, she received an urgent phone call from the emergency room. It seems that one of the tests, which takes a bit longer to get results, finally showed that he had a *Campylobacter jejuni* bacterial infection, most likely from the foxes he was trying to save. Dennis even received a call from the New Mexico Department of Health, interviewing him as to how he contracted the infection just in case it was from a restaurant or some other source that could spread it to others. They were a bit surprised when they heard about the source of the infection in this case! With a more specific antibiotic to fight it, Dennis recovered quickly. The more serious infection explained a bit more why they were so difficult to save and possibly why the mother died in the first place.

CHAPTER FOUR

Orphaned Wildlife

Bobcat kitten.

Another large group of animals we care for are orphaned wildlife, usually making spring and summer our busiest time. Not usually needing treatment for an injury, these animals still need very specific and complicated care to get them to the point where they can be released and succeed in the wild. Often the event that orphaned them and the subsequent rescue by a human causes a great deal of trauma that must be dealt with immediately. Whether it is falling out of a nest that is high up in a tree, or their parents being killed due to collisions, being shot, or poisoned, the addition of humans handling them can put them in shock.

Each spring Gila Wildlife Rescue is inundated with baby raptors. In early spring we receive great horned owls, later in April we get red-tailed hawks, followed by smaller raptors like kestrels and Cooper's hawks in May. Also, later in the spring young mammals like bobcats, foxes, and raccoons come in. In July and August, we used to get busy with baby deer. (As you will read in a later chapter, we no longer care for baby deer.) In later summer we start to get Swainson's hawk orphans, who nest a bit later than other raptors. The numbers of orphans can vary a bit from year to year, but each year it varies depending on what the most common species is. In 2015 we had one of the largest nurseries ever, raising more than thirty barn owl nestlings, twenty great horned owl nestlings, fifty American kestrel nestlings, and twenty-five Swainson's hawks, along with a few red-tailed hawks, peregrine falcons, burrowing owls, and Cooper's hawks—all nestlings. On top of all that, we cared for four gray fox pups, all within a four-month period!

Gray fox pups.

In the past, we would raise ten to twenty baby raptors each year, but in recent years the count is often well over a hundred. With the adults and mammals we cared for, we had nearly three hundred encounters that year. We also had even more hawks transferred to us from a rehabber in Carlsbad, New Mexico, along with more owls, hawks, and falcons from the El Paso Zoo. We received many transfers that year, often with multiple birds being shipped and as many as twelve raptors coming to us all the same day! Each year since then we have had similar numbers, and they are not decreasing. It is interesting that during the deepest part of the COVID shutdown there was a large increase in the number of people that were out camping. We expected a larger number of animals needing rescued simply due to more people out recreating and encountering them. Surprisingly, this did not happen, and, in fact, that was the only year that we had any significant decrease in the numbers of animals we cared for.

Our rule with raising orphans of any species is that we do not raise them unless we are sure they are orphaned, or it is impossible to return them to their parents. There are a few caring but uninformed people who assume that if the baby is alone and they cannot see the mother around that it is abandoned and now orphaned. This is especially true with baby deer. Much of the time, the babies are not really orphaned and by picking the animal up and bringing it to us they are not helping and are possibly writing a jail sentence or death sentence for them. Most wild animals do not abandon their young unless the animal has severe birth defects or injuries. Occasionally, the orphan does not have a chance to make it and parents can sense the problem and leave their doomed offspring to predators and scavengers. As a result, we normally raise babies that are truly orphans, which means the parents are dead. It is always far better to have babies raised by their parents, and every effort is made to return them to their parents. The exception to this is the raptor nestlings that get pushed out of their nest by a sibling and would not survive without our help.

We would like to point out that our decades of experience have shown us that many humans have a blind spot when it comes to deciding if a wild baby should be picked up. The strong urge to help any baby is part of it, but the stronger subconscious urge to be "the" one to rescue and "save" it is more of a driving force. The need to pick it up and hold it and pet it is a strong urge but is never ever the best thing for the wild orphaned animal. It only fulfills urges in the rescuing human! This drive to be the savior is due to both the person's own personal fulfillment and the desire to brag to other people about the event. In the past, this was a common occurrence, where someone picks up a baby deer or other animal without thinking first or contacting someone about what to do before touching it. Recently, we have been receiving more calls asking what to do before they touch, so people are becoming more aware of the possibility that their interaction could cause more harm than good.

Baby Birds

The most common reasons we end up raising orphaned birds are nestlings that have either fallen out, been blown out of the nest, or the nest has fallen out of the tree. It is also very likely that one of the other babies has pushed out its sibling. Whichever way, we sometimes must raise the baby at this point. Putting the baby back into the nest is one solution, but it is not always possible due to the height of the tree. The nestling also may come right back out anyway and risk sustaining an injury once more due to the fall.

Nestling red-tailed hawks.

With many types of birds, and in particular raptors or birds of prey, more chicks are hatched than can normally be fed each year. The largest and oldest chicks will push out the younger, weaker chicks as they compete for food. It is a natural process that seems cruel to humans, but it ensures that if the first laid eggs and hatchlings don't survive, there are backups to make certain reproduction will be successful that year. In some years, all of the young make it because there is plentiful food, other years only one survives. The hatchlings that get pushed out or fall from the nest will perish by starvation or predation unless a well-meaning human picks them up and brings them to a rehabilitation center like ours. With raptors, the bird should not be returned to the nest because it will likely just get pushed out again. With some other birds, like small perching birds, they can be successfully returned to the nest and their parents.

There is an interesting false belief that if you put a bird back into the nest the mother will just kick it out again. First, there is really no circumstance where a mother bird would kick her baby out, but it is very common that the siblings in the nest would have done the pushing as they compete for food.

Another false belief is that the mother would kick it back out of the nest because she smells the human that touched it. The best way to correct this is to simply point out that birds can't smell very well. They have a somewhat poorly developed olfactory sense compared to other vertebrate animals.[16] At one point, it was thought that they did not utilize their sense of smell much at all, but recent research has shown that birds, including raptors, use it more than once thought.[17] Either way, they do not smell well enough to be bothered by possible human smells and then have a negative reaction. The only birds that rely on smell are a few species with a specialized diet of something like carrion or specialized smell for fish in marine birds. The easiest way to find rotting meat is by the smell, so vultures are one of the few birds that have adapted to utilize a well-developed olfactory sense.

So how can you tell if the chick should be put back into the nest? First, determine if it really is a helpless chick. Most often it is a fledgling that is trying to learn how to fly so should be left alone. The young bird may be at the fledgling stage all birds go through where they are down on the ground learning to fly, but seemingly injured or too young to fly. This stage lasts for a few hours or a few days and is often when the animal is susceptible to predators or to being picked up by well-meaning humans. These animals should not be captured and should be left alone. If it is obviously too young to fly, then the general rule is if it is a small sparrow to robin-sized bird, an attempt should be made to put it back into the nest. If this can't be done, put it in a small basket or small box and nail it to the nesting tree as high as can be reached. Parents will normally come down and care for birds in both "nests."

Great horned owl nestling.

If it is a larger bird, especially a bird of prey, it is more likely that the largest sibling has pushed the smaller, younger chick out of the nest due to competition. If it is placed back in, it will most likely get kicked right back out. In this case, the best thing to do is to get the nestling to a licensed rehabilitator.

Here are a few baby owl videos we saved:

FeedingSwainsonsChick

GHOInCage

GHOFledglingShowingOff

GHOLearningToFly

GHOReleaseBest

Orphaned Mammals

Having raised baby deer, javelina, raccoons, foxes, bobcats, bears, beaver, and even jackrabbits over the years, we have had our share of this difficult work. In the past ten years or so this has changed. We have had a handful of bear cubs since Gila Wildlife Rescue started, but none in the past twenty years. In previous years, we raised many deer fawns, but since educating the public and ourselves, we do not even need or have facilities for them anymore. Just a few years ago for public safety due to rabies, the New Mexico Department of Game and Fish has not allowed us to care for adult bobcats, or any age of fox, coyote, raccoon, or skunk. We are hoping this ban is temporary but still have recently only raised bobcat kittens and javelina babies. Much of our mammal experience was between 1998 and 2018. Remember, we have been doing this since 1979!

Baby javelina.

Once babies are in our care, be it bird or mammal, we have a series of challenges that we deal with. When we first receive orphans, they are very delicate, and getting them past this tenuous stage before they succumb to complications is a daunting task at times. If they make it past the first few days or weeks, they usually will survive and can eventually be successfully released, depending on the severity of stress they have experienced.

The dietary needs of orphaned wildlife are the most difficult challenges to deal with, particularly if they come to us before being weaned. Fed the wrong food, they are susceptible to serious digestive system ailments. Once the animal's gut is inflamed and infected, the animal is in critical condition and may not survive. The goal is to not stress the animal's system too much, and complications like diarrhea or scours can be prevented in most cases. Unfortunately, just the act of catching the animal and putting it into our cages and pens can be enough stress to cause scours without any other dietary complications.

Another difficult task is that these babies do not have their mothers to teach them things, and they cannot watch and mimic their parent's behavior. A great deal of this behavior is instinctual, but our job is to provide opportunities that provide these important lessons on getting food and protecting themselves from other animals including humans. We utilize a variety of methods to help teach the young animals how to find and capture and kill their food. We also give them a long period of time to get well experienced before they are released.

One more challenge, and to be honest the most difficult, is to keep these very cute and cuddly looking babies wild. It is so tempting to talk to them and touch them, but this would imprint them on you or any humans, which may prevent their successful release. It is paramount in their care to take great lengths to keep them wild in order to have them succeed once released.

We have found that the use of donated fur coats is effective in giving them something to cuddle with and get comfort from. We also use a plush toy with an artificial heartbeat for added comfort. Here is a baby javelina enjoying those furs while being fed.

Video Links: JavelinaInBox   Javelinamovie

One of the more bizarre orphan experiences we have had in caring for wildlife was early in Gila Wildlife Rescue's existence, when Dennis was still teaching high school biology. A wildlife officer walked into his classroom one day with two baby beavers, which was a huge surprise, never having even seen such an animal up close, much less a baby. They were incredibly cute, curled up and all fuzzy, about the size of a baseball. Beavers are found along rivers and streams in our area and these two were found along Duck Creek, a tributary of the Gila River, near Cliff, New Mexico. The officer who delivered them was not the officer who took the call originally, so he could not give Dennis any details. It was great that he was able to show them to his classes throughout the afternoon before he took them home at the end of the day. They were adorable balls of dense brown fur with tiny eyes that they constantly kept hidden.

After getting the pups home, he fed them and set them up in a cage with a warmer. Then Dennis called the officer in Cliff to find out the details of what happened. The story related to him was hard to believe at first. It was so bizarre that we doubted if there was much truth to it at first. The story was related to him by the woman who called about the young beavers, so Dennis was curious and got her number and called to hear about the experience firsthand. The story she told was so detailed

Baby beaver after remarkable rescue

and was so passionately expressed with so much enthusiasm that he couldn't doubt it once he heard all of it. She also seemed like a very nice and honest eighty-something-year-old woman.

Here is her story:

She was walking her dog along Duck Creek that morning, like she did every morning, and her dog ran up ahead of her and out of her sight. She heard some commotion up ahead with her dog yelping in pain. She ran up to a bend in the river and saw her dog in the clutches of a very large adult beaver. The beaver had the dog by the chest, and it was acting crazed and would not let the dog go. She yelled and screamed, and the beaver still held on. She was fearful for her dog and so used the walking stick she always carried and hit the beaver a few times until the animal let go. The next thing she knew was the dog was hightailing it back home and the mother beaver was laying there dead. She had no idea why she died but thought she must have hit her too hard. She still didn't think the couple of blows she gave her would have done anything but made the beaver loosen her bite.

Things were a bit quiet at this point and she thought about what to do next, wondering why this beaver was acting so crazed. She had never heard of a beaver attacking like this. She looked at the beaver and turned it over. She noticed that it was way fatter than normal and decided that it might be pregnant. No wonder the beaver was acting that way, she thought. She was reasoning that the beaver was probably about to give birth and the dog was a big threat.

You must understand that this is a mature, elderly ranch lady who has seen and experienced a great deal while living on remote ranches. She was curious to see if the beaver was pregnant, curious if this is why it behaved so strangely, so she took out her pocketknife and slit open the body to see. She had assisted with births of horses, cows, dogs, and cats, so she said she found it easy. When she did this, the first thing she found was a dead baby beaver, half rotting and blocking the birth canal. No wonder the mother was so crazed. The mother beaver was also near death due to this, so she understood why just a few whacks with her walking stick was all it took to kill it. When she continued, she found two more babies inside, still attached with umbilical cords and fully formed. They seemed like they were dead and were not moving. She felt a bit sad but realized now what had happened and why.

She wondered if the fetuses could go to some use, remembering that the high school biology teacher at Cliff High School had a bunch of specimens in jars of formaldehyde. She picked up one of the pups and noticed now it had blood and dirt and gravel all over it from where she laid it, so she quickly rinsed it off in the water of Duck Creek. But as soon as the little beaver hit the cold water it moved, it twitched! She realized it was still alive, but it wasn't breathing. She did what she had done many times when animals she has helped deliver are not breathing at first, she gently blew into its mouth and nostrils. She described placing her lips over them and gently blowing. With only a few tries, she got the little one to start breathing on its own. She then took the second pup and repeated this procedure, and he started breathing as well. But the second one would not keep breathing, so after two tries of mouth-to-mouth resuscitation, she decided his heart was not beating, so she used her finger, gently pressed over and over again on the beaver's tiny chest. Another breath in the mouth and this time the beaver started breathing and joined his brother. She took them home and called the New Mexico Department of Game and Fish.

You can probably see why Dennis didn't believe the story the first time as told to him by the officer. An elderly woman slits the body of a dead beaver open and saves the fetuses by giving them CPR! Hard to believe, but you had to have heard it yourself. If you listened to the details this woman related and excitement about what had happened, you also would have no doubt.

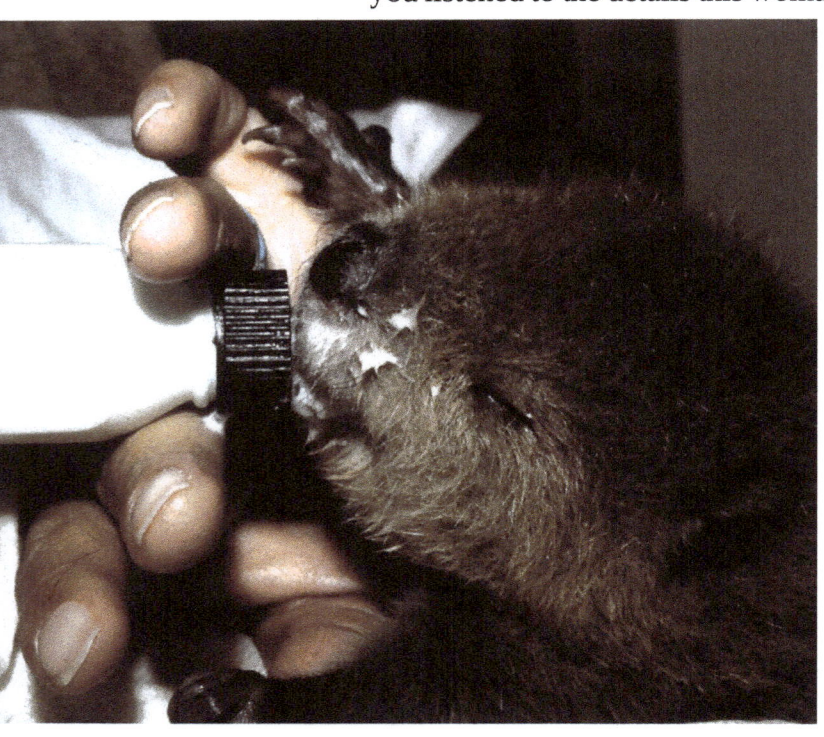

Baby beaver prior to weaning—eyes still closed.

The beavers were raised by Gila Wildlife Rescue until they were weaned. As we were starting to figure out how to prepare them for release, looking into the best ways to do this and determining at what age they should be released, we got a call from the Santa Fe offices of the New Mexico Department of Game and Fish. They were calling because they had heard the report about the beavers being found and had a request for us.

The Abiquiu Ghost Ranch is an educational retreat in northern New Mexico that has a small display of native wildlife. They have had a pair of beavers for many years, and they never had a litter. Surprising everyone, the female gave birth to two pups that year. Sadly, the day before the call from Santa Fe came to us, the babies were found dead of unknown causes. The game department was asking if it would be possible to have these adults who just lost their babies adopt these young pups. We were floored! We were trying to figure out how to raise them without adults around and how they would learn the necessary skills they need to survive. We didn't know what behaviors are instinctual and how much is learned from their parents such as building their beaver dams. Our experience with carnivores, including raptors, was that much of it was instinct, and experience gained was sometimes all they needed. To have a mother beaver that is still lactating to lose a litter and at the same time receive another litter that is orphaned is not only good timing, but a blessed event.

We took the pups to Abiquiu and as soon as the pups were put in the cage, the mother beaver waddled up to them and started squealing quietly. She got very excited as if she had just found her lost babies. She had them eagerly suckling her from her nipples in minutes. We had reports for the next few years that they were doing great and had become a mature, healthy beaver family.

This was early in the rehab program, and we had not developed opinions about the wildlife we save being transferred to zoos. In this case though, the successful raising of two unique animals with very unique lifestyles and behaviors would have been jeopardized by being raised by humans. Once raised, their success in the wild may have been in question without parental training and following parental example. Although not ideal, this gave them a chance at least. We were not sure if we would ever do it again, but in this case, it was for the best.

A lone raccoon came in from Las Cruces, New Mexico, east of us, in late summer. A farmer in the Rio Grande Valley near there was setting up to water his fields. When he turned the water on, a tiny young animal shot out of an irrigation pipe. This little guy was wet and bedraggled looking when we received him. Once warmed and calmed, he eventually fed and came through the ordeal without too much damage. There was damage done though because now he was an orphan and he had to be raised alone, since we didn't have any other raccoons at the time. The farmer looked around diligently for the mother or more babies but could not find any. So this guy was a lone orphan.

We placed him in our mammal pen and started his care. He stayed in his shelter for a few days before coming out. We could tell he had not moved by looking for his tracks in the sand lining the bottom of the cage. Once he decided to come out, he roamed over the entire cage, as his footprints showed. Little star-shaped tracks covered every square inch of the sand.

He did not eat well at first, barely getting anything down. We weren't sure if he was weaned or not, so we tried a variety of things including milk for carnivorous mammals and some mixtures of milk and foods. He ate a little bit at first, but over the next couple of days he slowly stopped eating. We were very concerned and confused since he had shown no signs of infection or disease. We were worried we had a capture myopathy case and were bracing ourselves for the worst. Then we found bright white diarrhea in the cage, and we knew he had an intestinal infection that needed antibiotic treatment as soon as possible. Luckily, he responded quickly and started eating better.

Everything was progressing satisfactorily over the next few weeks but then we started noticing odd behaviors. He would come out of the shelter when we went into the cage and would shyly walk toward us and then run back into the shelter, the whole time making a soft, guttural purring sound that is unique to raccoon pups. This started with just one short vocalization and developed into a noise he constantly made whenever we were in the cage. It was coupled with a coy behavior of looking at us and then hiding

A lone raccoon baby washed out of water pipe.

his eyes bashfully, but still working his way timidly toward us. Again, we were not talking to him or petting him but had to enter the cage daily because he constantly defecated in his water, and it had to be cleaned.

We were worried about him being a lone orphan, and the deficiencies that raising him alone may cause that could prevent him from surviving once released. There are wide variations in living things in the amount of parental care offspring are required to have, and how much teaching by parents is necessary for their survival. Some mammals can survive on instinctual behaviors developing and may be successful without much parental teaching. We have found that bobcats are successfully raised without parenting and seem to naturally have hunting skills from birth. Skills taught by mom will give them a better chance at survival, but the skills they were born with may be enough. On the other hand, other mammals absolutely depend on parental care for longer periods of time, as in mountain lions.

All this information was going through our brains as we started to worry about this young lone raccoon. We had to be careful again not to anthropomorphize and attribute a human behavior like "feeling lonely" to him. There is validity to the fact that some mammals, especially those that are gregarious (living in groups like herd and pack animals), need parental bonding and contact and fostering to eventually survive on their own in the wild. We weren't experienced enough with raccoon orphans to know how much parental training was necessary.

Denise quickly researched the subject and discovered that raccoons are one of the most sensitive mammal orphans to raise, particularly when it comes to the need to be raised in a group. All efforts should be made to raise them with at least one other cub. Interaction and touching are necessary for their brain development. She found some great advice on how to deal with raising a raccoon without a parent or sibling for it to interact with.

Baby racoon.

Dennis was elected to be the surrogate parent because he has the pre-exposure rabies vaccination that protects him from this disease. We rarely care for adult raccoons due to rabies. They have very high rates similar to what skunks have, which at times can be 20 percent of the population.[18] He walked into the cage and got down on one knee. The pocket-sized ball of fur came out slowly and then darted back. Being patient, Dennis waited for the baby to return, and he did, this time a bit closer. The little guy eventually worked himself up to where he could smell Dennis, who reached up and touched the baby's back. The baby immediately pulled away, but not all the way back into the shelter like before, and at the same time made that purring noise very loud. He liked the contact but was afraid.

Throughout the next few days and weeks, Dennis worked with him and eventually could get to the point that he would nervously walk up to Dennis and accept his soft scratches. The raccoon obviously liked and needed it and nuzzled back and purred. He started eating better and gained weight quickly. He needed this contact. Once he received it, he thrived.

Raccoon youngsters close to release time.

As he matured, he slowly started to become more and more wary of Dennis and did not seem to like the contact as much. He eventually got to the point that he was hissing and would not come near. Now he was back on track. The touching and nurturing did its job, but now he was back to being a wild animal. From then on, we had no further contact except when absolutely necessary.

We got lucky with what happened next. One of our friends had a serious raccoon problem at his house. He started trapping the animals and relocating them, trying to protect his poultry. He eventually trapped something like eighteen of them. We knew about his problem because he called us for advice and borrowed some live traps. As soon as we got this baby raccoon in, we contacted him and asked him if he ever caught any babies to let us know. We could then introduce them to our raccoon and let them bond and touch and nurture each other. It was a long shot, but it was worth letting him know in case he could help us out.

Sure enough, just about the time we were thinking about releasing our raccoon, he caught two youngsters the exact same age as ours. He brought them over and we introduced them. The original loner started hissing and spitting at them and he slept outside the shelter that the new raccoons had taken over. The next night they spent together, all three curled up in a ball. We raised them for another month, until they were about "teenage" size and released them. Immediately upon reaching freedom, they climbed to the very top of a tall cottonwood tree along the banks of the Gila River and started their lives in the wild.

We had another successful introduction like this a few years back, this time in the wild. Another friend had rescued a tiny raccoon from imminent death on a bridge near downtown Silver City. He was walking his dog and heard the faint cries of a baby raccoon. Recognizing this sound from childhood experiences with raccoons, he located the scared orphan before it fell from the bridge.

We were raising this very lucky guy by himself, so we were on the lookout for another raccoon or a wild group with babies that this one could join. We were out on Sapillo Creek in the mountains north of Silver City one day with the baby raccoon in tow because he had to be fed every few hours and miraculously found a group of raccoons, a mother and three babies, foraging for food along the stream. Placing it close to the mother and the babies, but around the corner of the stream where we were hidden, we backed off and waited. We had observed that the family was working their way in the direction of our raccoon, so were hoping for an encounter with another baby before the adult saw it. A young raccoon came up to ours, sniffing and making mewing noises. Then they both got excited, acting like they were long-lost brothers. The mother came up and simply smelled him and licked him a bit, then continued foraging with now all four babies in tow. A successful reintroduction!

Recently, we had another interesting reintroduction as well as learning a valuable lesson ourselves. We work very closely with individual officers from the New Mexico Department of Game and Fish. We received a call from one of the more mature and experienced wildlife officers whom we have worked with many times throughout the years and trust explicitly. He was on his way to check out a large golden eagle that had been reported in a housing development on the east side of Las Cruces and was confirming our availability and whether the bird should be picked up. We told him we were ready to receive it, not knowing anything about the bird's injury or disposition, but he said it was reportedly walking along one of the paved streets in a new, busy housing development on the east side of town near the base of the Organ Mountains. We met in Deming, New Mexico, which was only a one-hour drive for both of us, and he transferred the eagle to us in a large box.

Fledgling golden eagle "Ladera" found near Ladera Canyon near Las Cruces, New Mexico.

When we arrived home and examined Ladera—named after the location he was found, near Ladera Canyon close to Las Cruces—we were immediately struck at how beautiful the bird was. His body was dark brown with golden tips to wing feathers, and his head was covered with long, golden-brown feathers that were perfect and undamaged. In fact, every feather on the body was perfect with no wear or damage, and the colors were vibrant and amazingly magnificent. As we were performing a thorough examination, he was eventually turned over on his back and wings stretched out to check for injuries, we noticed a great deal of white in the feathers on the underside of the wing that did not show when the wings were folded closed. We quickly realized at this point that this was a very young bird, possibly a first-year hatchling, and had probably just left the nest, attempting to fly for the first time. His feathers were so pristine and fresh-looking because they were brand new. In the forty-plus years we have been caring for eagles, we have been privileged to take care of close to one hundred of these magnificent creatures, but this was the first newborn eagle we have ever had.

At this point, despite being excited and somewhat in awe of what we had taken in, we also started to worry a bit. The little we knew about eagle hatchlings and fledglings spurred us to seek advice. We knew that parental education was paramount in eagles, and they tend to stay with parents for many months or even years, unlike many of the smaller raptors we care for. If we were to attempt to raise this ourselves, it would involve a training program using falconry techniques that we did not have the necessary training or certification for.[19] We would have to transport it to a rehabilitator in California to conduct this training.

Ladera ate well and tried to fly across the cage but never really got airborne. Dennis exercised him a bit and tried to get that first real flight that he needed but with no results. He ate well and was otherwise very healthy and feisty.

Video Link: LaderaTryingToFly

We then consulted with our researchers from Eagle Environmental. It turns out *we* needed an education. Although Ladera was found in a housing development on a busy street, he normally should have been left alone. He was in danger and needed help, but we should have taken him up the canyon and left him there, even though he could not fly. Instead, he was captured, transported to the El Paso Zoo, and a week later transferred to us. It turns out that eagles are just like baby deer: They should never be picked up unless the parents are dead. They need to get through a period where they are on the ground, parents feeding and protecting them, and then they start flying better and are on their way. Coupled with the fact that their survival depends on the training and care from parents during their first year.

Ladera starting to fly.

We asked the game officer to investigate the canyon for us near where he was found and discovered that the parents were still in the area, just east of the site up a remote canyon. Following advice from our experts, we quickly transported him there the next morning. After getting him out of the large pet taxi, Dennis carried him, wrapped in his arms, up the trail a mile or so to a flat area so that he could be visible to his parents. We did not see any eagles during this transport, but we released this somewhat scared bird with a great deal of apprehension. We were betting on the parents being able to spot him and come to care for him but had our doubts.

We walked away and found a place to hide a quarter of a mile away and observed through binoculars. We waited all afternoon with no sign of the parents. She jumped up on a yucca and tried to fly a bit, but never got airborne. So we left her with trepidation. The next morning, we went out and looked for her and could not find her anywhere. She was not in the release area anymore. We spent the entire day searching for her to no avail. We worried and wondered if she had flown and was doing good or if she was in trouble.

The following morning, we went back out and saw two adult eagles flying and observed them landing on the ground and greeting a third eagle. She was a long distance away and we could not see for sure if it was the young bird we released with lots of white on it. It was our hope and prayer that this is the eagle we released, and she had been successfully returned to her parents. Thank you, eagle researchers, for your help and advice as well from the New Mexico Game and Fish officer for his assistance.

We learned a lesson with this bird. Although this one was found in a housing development with traffic and was correctly picked up, it turns out these young fledgling eagles normally should be left alone. Much of the public is aware of the importance of not picking up baby deer . . . this is the same situation with baby eagles. Our best advice if any wildlife is found is to contact a wildlife rehabber or local game department and get the expert advice on what should be done.

Many more experiences Gila Wildlife Rescue has had with orphans appear in later chapters of this book.

CHAPTER FIVE

Bear Stories

Dennis with
starving yearling
black bear.

Despite the variations of brown colors that also appear in bear populations, the only species of bear in New Mexico are black bears. Grizzlies, a type of brown bear, have been extirpated by overhunting from our area for well over a century. We have many black bears that are dark brown, light brown, a reddish cinnamon, and even almost blond colors, but they are all still "black bears." In fact, only 50 percent of black bears in the

Rocky Mountains are black.[20] As a biology educator, Dennis has often been frustrated with these inaccurate common names and clearly sees why biologists use scientific names like *Ursus americanus*. These animals should have the common name "American bear," which is its Latin meaning.

We have cared for a few young bear cubs. Some with eyes barely open and others that were an eighty-pound ball of fur, teeth, and claws. Early on in our rehabilitation program we did not have steel cages to house larger adults like we have now. As a result, most of the bears we have helped have been cubs. Once they were weaned and ready for the next stage, we transferred them to rehabilitators in northern New Mexico who had more experience in raising them and had steel cages for when they are larger.

Our toughest bear case was the yearling that was found by hunters near Reserve, New Mexico. They heard some noise inside a steel water tank and, sure enough, a bear cub was discovered in the mostly empty tank and had not been able to get out. They wondered how he got in there in the first place, but then noticed a small sapling next to the tank, just large enough for the cub to climb up and get trapped. There was a bit of water in the bottom, and during this drought year, the little guy had been looking for a drink. The hunters turned the cub over to the New Mexico Department of Game and Fish who then transported it to us. This is a typical way for an animal like this to come to Gila Wildlife Rescue.

The very reddish-brown-colored black bear was alert and awake but was acting strangely. He hung his head down and had a strange, faraway look in his eyes, like he wasn't quite aware of what was happening. We placed him in a cage, prepared some food for him, and tried to get some nutrition into the cub. We used a mixture of our wildlife milk formula, then added oatmeal, honey, and raisins. At first, he lapped it up with gusto, but quickly slowed and only ate about a quarter of it. This worried us because he had to be very hungry and knew from previous bear cubs that he should have had a better appetite. We captured him in the cage and made a much more thorough examination, looking for puncture wounds, lacerations, or some sign he may have been injured by a bullet or an arrow. There were none.

His blood test showed no infection and no toxicity. He still had that strange look in his eyes, and the next day he was hanging his head even more and acting more lethargic. We tried every trick in the book to get him to eat and did everything we could think of to figure out what was wrong with him, all to no avail. We then contacted the veterinarian and wildlife rehabilitator in Española that we work with. She listened to all the symptoms, the examination and testing results, and was confused too. We decided to get him up to her immediately.

We contacted the New Mexico Department of Game and Fish, and they had an officer who was headed to Santa Fe the next morning and could take the bear to Española. We loaded him into a bear tube, a transport trailer and trap used to capture bears and other large mammals, and he headed north.

The next morning, we had an early call. The vet gave us very bad news, but it explained everything and taught us all a new lesson. When she received the very lethargic and sick bear, she was also confused. She went through the same examination and testing that we did and could find no infections or injuries. She did find something in the blood work that indicated a concussion though, so started examining a bit further with x-rays. Sure enough, the x-ray revealed that the starving and dehydrated cub had eaten some prickly pear cactus pads. One cactus spine had punctured his mouth and had worked its way between the bones of the palate on the roof of the mouth into the brain cavity. The symptoms of concussion now made sense. She carefully did surgery to remove the spine, but as soon as she did, the cub died. The pressure changes in the swelling around the brain once the spine was removed had killed him. It was such a sad story, but like many incidents that seem like tragedies, they end up being blessings in disguise because we learned something new. We know now how to look for this in young animals that show no injury but are showing signs of a concussion. Too bad he didn't make it, though. He was a beautiful little bear.

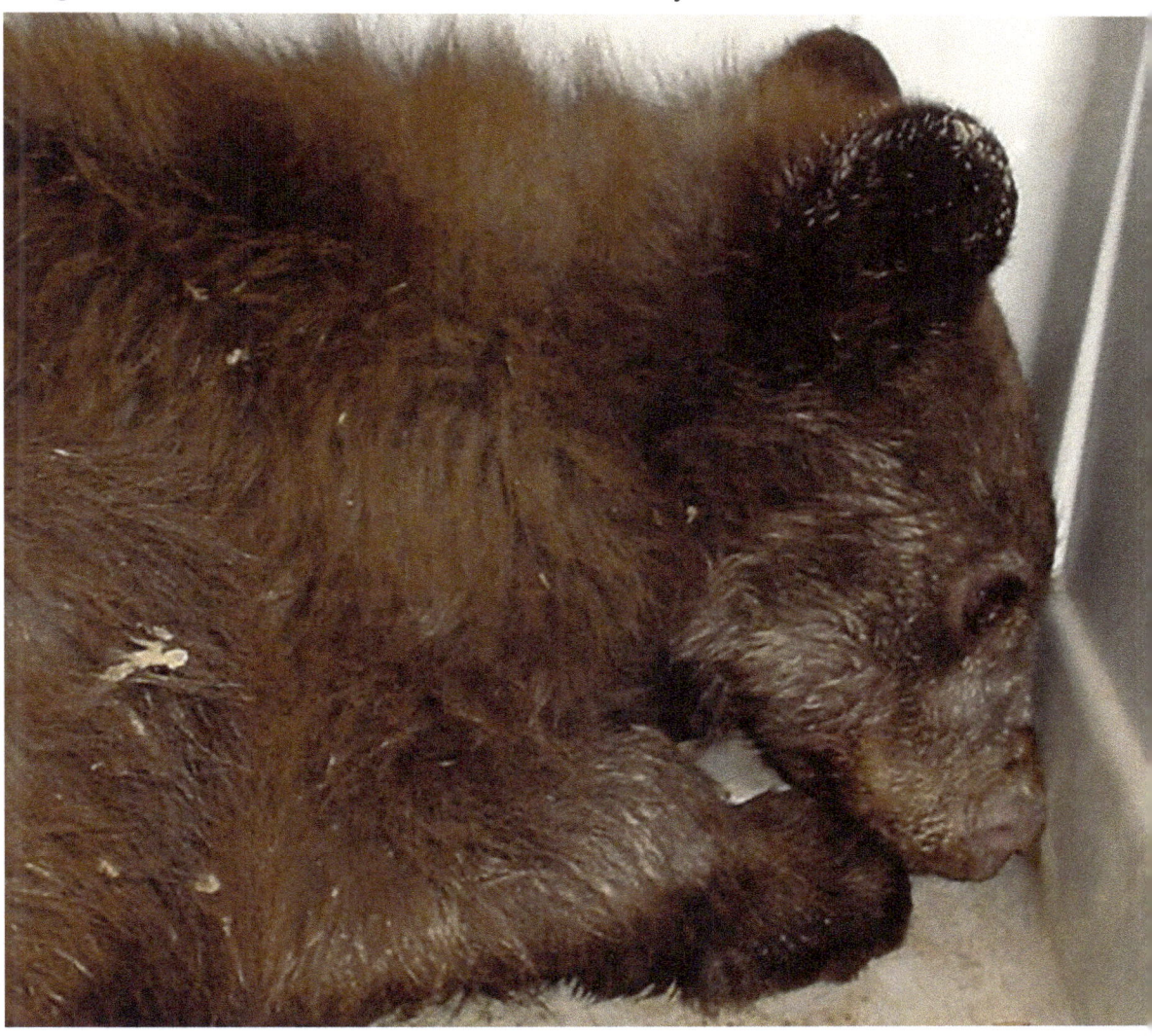

Black bear yearling with cactus spine in brain.

The most interesting bear cub story is one of our most bizarre stories of all. In the mid-1980s we had been suffering from a bad drought in our area. It was typical for bears to come out of the mountains and into at least the outskirts of communities looking for water and food. It was also normal for cubs to be seen with mothers during these summer drought periods. Pinos Altos, a small community just north of Silver City, was no different and a good number of calls to us and the Department of Game and Fish came in about bears coming out of the mountains and foraging for food and getting into trash. There were reports of mothers with babies and even some with twins.

Baby black bear girl tries to take home for pet.

A little eight-year-old girl who loved animals was getting off her school bus to go home when she spotted a little bear cub. She described being able to walk up to it and just pick it up. The cub let her hold it, but the girl had other ideas in mind. She wanted to take this fuzzy ball home with her and keep it as a pet. When she started to walk home holding the little guy, the cub tried to struggle and get out of her grasp. It was when she held on to it a bit tighter that the event occurred. The cub bit her. It really was just a superficial scratch on her arm, but it was technically a bite. She was extremely lucky the mother was not around, or the situation could have been much worse.

As many of you may know, when an animal—wild or domestic—bites a human and the skin is broken and saliva from the animal has a chance of getting into this break, contraction of rabies is a possibility. Rabies is a disease that many people have become complacent about, and they shouldn't. Since most people regularly vaccinate their pets and rarely hear of a human that has contracted rabies, we tend to let down our guard and not be as aware as we should about this deadly disease. Here is the bottom line. Rabies has a 100 percent death rate in humans and other animals.[21] No one has survived the terminal disease. A few years ago, a woman from the Midwest was bitten by a rabid bat and a cocktail of drugs were used to treat her. At first it looked like she would be the first to survive, but she eventually died due to the damage to the brain by the virus.

Once a human has contracted rabies and the disease is fully progressed, there is no cure or treatment.[22] There really are not many diseases out there that once in full infectious stages have no treatment. If the treatment for rabies exposure is applied *before* the disease takes hold, humans can and almost always do survive. The treatment, a series of injections, has a small risk of complications, so is not given indiscriminately to everyone who is bitten by an animal. Animals that have bitten someone must be tested and then treatment given if the results are positive for rabies. To protect himself, Dennis has received the "pre-exposure" vaccine for rabies. This vaccine, which is a series of quite expensive injections, is a vaccination that is exactly like a vaccine given to a dog or cat, in that it protects him at all times from exposure to the disease. It is not practical for the general population because the level of exposure for most people is quite low, and the cost of the medication is high.

For wildlife professionals and animal control officers it is a lifesaver. For Dennis, it saves the lives of many animals we care for. If he were to be bitten without this protection, that animal would have to undergo testing. As we will soon explain, the animal must be killed to test for rabies, which is counterproductive to what we are trying to do. This way everything is safe for both of us. Even AIDS, that we thought had no cure, has some drugs that can now treat it. Not rabies. You don't fool around with it. Every state in the US has laws, usually in their health department statutes, which are connected to controlling rabies outbreaks.[23] All of them require any human who has been bitten by a wild or domestic animal to be tested, treated, and reported to the state health department. Most states, but not all, also include laws about not keeping certain animals as pets (such as skunks and raccoons) due to the danger of contracting rabies.

So with this knowledge of rabies, you can see why Dennis reacted the way he did when unexpectedly one day he received a phone call about this bear cub.

"Mr. Miller!" the distraught mother said. "My daughter just got bitten by a bear! What do I do?"

He could not believe his ears! The call came from the child's mother, who was in his college biology class the year before. "Take her to the emergency room immediately!" was his reply. "Why are you calling me? Get her to the hospital!"

He knew no details about the age of the bear, how severe it was, or anything, but even if she told him at the time that it was just a scratch, he still would have told her to go to the hospital and get it checked and reported. It would have been his duty also to follow up on it too, to make sure the girl did get examined and the incident was reported.

The next strange turn in this bizarre experience is that an hour later we received a call from a law enforcement officer for the Gila National Forest who had captured a baby bear in Pinos Altos. At first, Dennis was relieved but had a nagging feeling in his gut that something was off. He just couldn't place what it was yet. The young man delivered the cub to us, and we started its care, getting a cage ready and preparing a gruel mixture similar to what we described in the previous bear story. The cub was starving! Her voracious appetite had to be slowed down a bit—she was eating so fast. She also spread the gruel all over herself and the cage, so when she was through, she was a mess. This was standard bear cub behavior, and we were encouraged that this girl seemed healthy and was doing so well this quickly.

Often when we receive young orphans it is very difficult to get them to feed, and all sorts of tricks must be utilized to coax them into eating. Once they get a taste for it and realize what it is and that you are trying to help them, they do fine. This girl did not need coaxing. It was one of the first bears Gila Wildlife Rescue had ever dealt with, this incident coming in the first ten years of rehabbing wildlife, and it was so exciting and amazing to observe this cute little cub. She was just a ball of thick but very soft fur, about the size of a volleyball. Her tiny little bear feet were strangely similar to our own. Her small dark eyes looked right at you with very little fear and a bit of fiery defiance. She was incredibly cute. Once again, we tried to keep our contact with her to a minimum to prevent stress and imprinting problems in the future. The photos shown were taken quickly as the cub was being transferred to secluded cages.

Baby black bear on intake—decision to euthanize to test for rabies still in question.

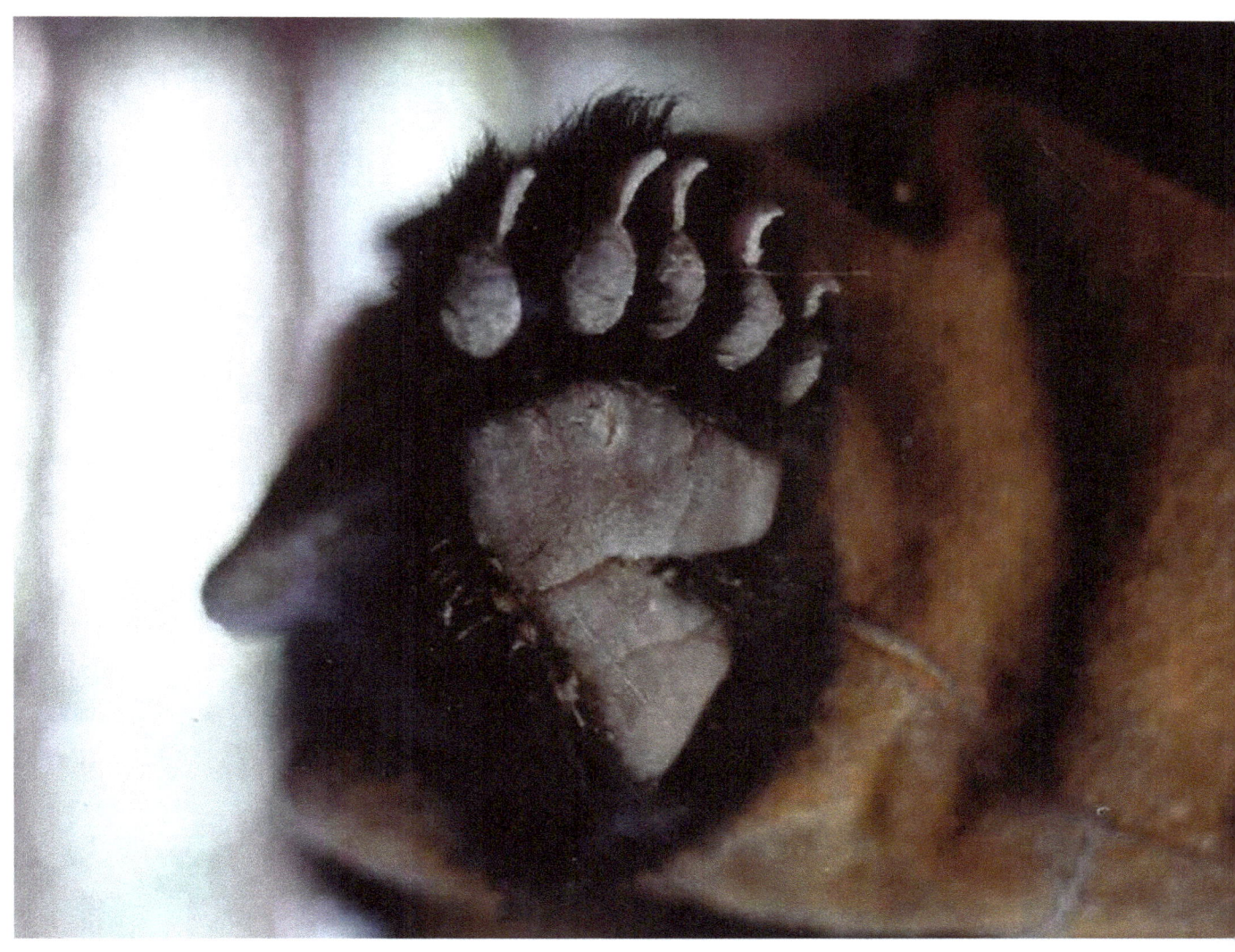

Baby black bear's tiny foot.

Remember Dennis said that states have laws that include reporting rabies cases? He received a call from the doctor in charge of the New Mexico Department of Health. He had been notified of the incident by the Gila Regional Medical Center in Silver City and was contacting us about the bear cub. His message was simple. "We have a case of possible rabies. I understand that the offending animal has been captured, and so I am requiring you to euthanize this cub. I need you to cut off its head, and immediately send it to this office for testing," he said. Notice he used the term "requiring." It was not "requesting." It was and is a requirement by law.

Dennis felt like someone had hit him upside the head with a sledgehammer. He was flush and his heart was racing. He was devastated. For some reason, Dennis will never know why, he did not think of the possibility that the bear would have to be put down. He also would never have thought that he was going to have to be the one to kill her and then cut off her head! Being fairly new to wildlife rehabilitation, this was our first rabies case. He was excited at first to have this young orphaned but otherwise healthy bear cub to care for, and the thought of having to kill her never entered his mind. So you can imagine his reaction to this official's statement on the phone about the situation. He was going to have to kill an otherwise extremely healthy and unbelievably cute animal to have it tested. When it comes to the life of a human, though, in this case this young wildlife lover, there is no question. To ensure this girl's survival it must be done.

The only definitive way to test for rabies is to examine brain tissue upon necropsy (autopsy on nonhuman animals).[24] When a person's life is at stake with this completely fatal disease, you cannot take any chances. That is why the law is there. These euthanasia cases to test for rabies occur by the hundreds every day in the US, and a large majority of the time they are negative; the animal is free from rabies and thus harmless. It is sad that they had to die, but the answer to the testing for the human is always the more important factor. It would be great if someone would develop a new method to evaluate for this deadly disease that would not entail the need to kill the possible culprit every time.

At this point, things started to get complicated. The mother of the girl that was bitten found out that we were going to have to put the cub down to be tested for rabies. She called me on the phone terribly upset. "Is it true? Because if it is, we will just volunteer to take the shots to save the cub." It was a noble thing to do, so Dennis told her he would talk to the Department of Health about it.

He called the official back and told him about the girl and her mother volunteering to take the shots. The official said it did not matter and by law the animal had to be tested. He seemed genuinely nice and caring and had even heard of our rehab program and the work we do. He was sympathetic to what Dennis was going to have to do, but he was very firm in his demand. Dennis eventually pleaded with him: "Please! Isn't there anything we can do here? You and I both know that although it is possible in any carnivorous mammal, there has never been even one case of rabies in black bears in the United States."

He was silent for just a bit, then asked, "Tell me the details of what happened, one more time."

Dennis explained again. "This little girl was walking home from school, encountered a young bear, picked it up and a very minor bite occurred. The cub ran off, and an hour later the bear was captured by a Forest Service law enforcement officer and brought to us."

He was silent for a long while this time and eventually said, "I am going to ask you one simple question that I am documenting as we speak. I need you to be very careful about your answer and just give me a yes or no without adding anything."

Dennis was very confused and somewhat apprehensive of the way the official was wording things, but replied, "Okay."

He said, "Are you absolutely, 100 percent sure that this is THE very bear that bit this little girl?"

In a millisecond, Dennis's mind saw what he was trying to do and why he was wording things so carefully. He obviously had obligations to protect this young girl's health, but also had enough compassion to figure a way out for the bear and still do the best thing to protect the little girl. Dennis's instant reply was simply, "No." He documented it.

Dennis was then able to explain to him how the area had recently had numerous bear reports including cubs and even twins. He further told the official the details of when the girl was bitten, she dropped the bear and it ran off while she ran home crying to her mom. An hour or so later, the officer came out and caught "a" baby bear in Pinos Altos, but it could have been another cub, not the one that bit her. If the captured animal were tested and found to be negative, we could have made the wrong decision to not have the girl undergo rabies treatments.

Baby black bear about to become a celebrity.

That decision could have been tragic. She could have developed the disease and it might not have been caught in time to save her. It easily could have been another bear that bit her, and we were not 100 percent sure that a different bear wasn't captured. To protect this child, the Department of Health's decision was that she must undergo rabies treatments *and* that Gila Wildlife Rescue could now rehabilitate this bear.

The girl's mother was relieved that the bear was going to be okay and clearly knew that this "volunteering" to undergo the treatment did *not* save this bear's life. We made sure this was explained clearly and we understood that the Department of Health reinforced this. He thanked her for the gesture, but also wondered what the little girl thought about all this. She was worried about the injections coming but was excited about the attention and her mother was encouraging it.

By now, the public had heard about this incident, and Dennis was approached by a reporter from our local newspaper. He wanted to write an article and use one of his photos for the front page. Dennis knew we were sitting on a tinder box, so he warned him up front that we do not want to give the public the impression that this girl's mom's volunteering to take the rabies shots saved this bear cub's life, because it did not. He explained that if the article did this, it would give people the impression that this is an option, and by law it was *not* an option.

He did an amazing job. He wrote a clear and balanced article that explained things accurately. That was the last time a reporter did this with this story. Everything since then has been twisted and sensationalized just to sell papers and make a buck. It was not this poor reporter's fault, but the excellent article got some attention quickly. The morning after it appeared in our evening paper, Dennis received a call from an Albuquerque newspaper. They wanted to reprint the article and use his photo. He agreed but on one very specific condition. He told them very clearly, "Do not write anything that would even give the *impression* that someone can volunteer to take rabies treatments and save an animal's life. It is state law in New Mexico and in other states that the animals must be tested." That seemed very clear to me.

Baby black bear photo seen around the world.

Imagine our surprise and concern when we looked at the Albuquerque newspaper the next day and the headlines read in big bold letters, "GIRL VOLUNTEERS TO TAKE RABIES SHOTS AND SAVES BABY BEAR'S LIFE." It was a new article that had taken some of the original text and twisted it around and downright fabricated some additional facts. It turned out that an inexperienced new reporter, who had been assigned to our part of the state, really wanted to get that *big* article and be famous. The results were astounding and occurred within minutes of reading the article myself. Phone calls started coming in asking for permission to reprint the photo of the cub from newspapers and news agencies around the nation and the world. Over the next two days, Dennis probably received fifty calls, everyone from CNN, Reuters, the Associated Press, United Press International (UPI), *The New York Times*, the *Chicago Tribune*, and even newspapers and news agencies from Japan, Sweden, England, and Spain. The attention was flattering and exciting, but through it all he kept his head and kept insisting on the same thing over and over again: "If you reprint this photo, you MUST not use the same headline and you MUST be clear that the girl volunteering to take the shots is not what saved the cub's life. We were not positive this was the same bear that bit her."

Every one of those newspapers and agencies promised that they would do this, and that they understood they should not give a false impression. But *none* of them did. The newspaper article appeared worldwide that day, and the following day pieces appeared on all the morning television shows like *Good Morning America* and *The Today Show*. They *all* just reprinted the original article from the Albuquerque paper with its inaccuracies. Dennis was incredibly angry and frustrated. At this point, there was nothing he could do about it, but he really did try to get them to report the facts accurately.

The next day he received two more calls. One from the head of the Illinois Department of Public Health in Chicago who was irate and blaming us for the article that was giving people the false impression they can volunteer to take rabies shots and save animals. Once Dennis told him the whole story, he understood and chuckled a bit. He decided to contact the *Tribune* and get an article printed with the correct information to inform at least the people in Illinois about the truth. We really hope that this did not cause any serious problems with other state health officials in dealing with rabies incidents. If we did, we would be deeply sorry.

So then, the second call. By this time, Dennis was deeply burned by the press. Late in the afternoon when he had just finished teaching a long and grueling biology lab class, and he was tired and frustrated by the audacity of the press, Dennis got a call from Jay Leno's "people." They asked nicely at first if he could come on the show and bring the bear cub to show everyone. Dennis politely explained that this was not going to happen, that it would not be good for the cub to travel and be around so many people when we were trying to keep it wild for eventual release. He also explained to them that the reason they wanted him on the show was false anyway and told them the true story.

At this, they started pressuring him to still go on the show to explain the truth to the public and how it all got twisted around. That kind of lit a spark of interest, but again, realizing something, he asked a quick question: "If I come to tell the true story, do you still want me to come if I don't bring the bear?"

There was a brief pause, then, "Well . . . no."

Dennis just hung up. They tried reaching him for two more days, but he ignored them. Now, thinking back on all this, he realized, "Darn it! I missed my chance to be on *The Tonight Show*!"

But he would have had to compromise the recovery of this young bear, and he's glad it was not even an option to us, and the way Gila Wildlife Rescue has always operated. We must do what is in the animal's best interest, not our own or a reporter or whoever. Our overall objective must *always* be focused on keeping these animals wild so they can be successful when released.

The mother and the little girl, on the other hand, had other ideas in mind once they were tempted by the lights of notoriety. They were picked up by a limousine from their house in Pinos Altos and flown to Los Angeles for *The Arsenio Hall Show*. And you *know* what the sensationalized subject was all about. Oh, well, the little girl got to go on an adventure and see the big city. Needless to say, we did not watch the show.

We raised the bear past weaning stage to about thirty pounds in weight and then transferred her to the facilities in northern New Mexico. She was eventually released with a tracking collar on her as part of a study by the New Mexico Department of Game and Fish. She ended up becoming somewhat famous in the biology world because she was recorded migrating from the Jemez Mountains west of Santa Fe to mountains west of Denver, shattering a record for the longest distance a female black bear had ever been recorded migrating.

We hope she lived long and prospered in Colorado due to our decisions. This bear has likely had many litters of young and is still reproducing, contributing to maintaining healthy populations of these powerful yet gentle creatures that have such a significant role in ecosystems of the Rockies.

Black bear cub ready for transfer.

Although we miss interacting with bear cubs, we are not upset in any way that we have not had any bears for many years. During the first twenty years of working with wildlife, we cared for around ten bears. Since then, we have not had any brought to us for care. Based on the patterns we have observed in other animals we care for, this usually means that conditions have changed to allow cubs to be successfully raised by their mothers and not become orphaned.

CHAPTER SIX

Dangerous Encounters

Mountain lion release.

Caring for wildlife is certainly dangerous at times with even the smallest of raptors possessing very sharp beaks and talons, much less the bite and scratching danger posed by larger carnivorous mammals and eagles. These are wild animals, and we are their mortal enemies. Unless habituated to humans, any contact with wild animals can elicit a protective response that can get us bitten, clawed, gouged, scratched, slashed, or in some other manner injured. In more than forty-plus years of doing this, we have rarely been injured due to our constant vigilance and respect for these animals and the dangers they present when we are handling them.

We wear protective gloves, use capture sticks or nets, eye protection, and thick clothing when necessary. We also have learned to subdue and hold the animal's weapons. For example, great blue herons are a long-legged, long-necked bird with a long, sharp

Mountain lion
with thorn in
paw.

beak. Unlike the beak of a raptor that is used primarily for feeding and not defense, these birds use their beaks for protection. They can reach out and stab quite a distance, but usually aim for the predator's (or human's) eyes. We handle them by grabbing that beak first, eliminating the threat, and never letting go until we are through examining or transporting. We hold the legs of raptors when handling them to remove the threat of their talons. They are amazingly strong and must be held very tightly without letting go or the person examining is going to get grabbed by those talons and be seriously hurt. When the bird needs treatment that could last a long period of time, we let them grab a few cotton balls then wrap the feet in tape so talons cannot open, removing the threat.

This danger is constantly on our minds when working with wildlife. It helps us to handle them without getting hurt, but it also helps keep the animal safe. The care and patience needed to handle an animal without getting yourself injured is the same care and patience needed to handle the animal without injuring the rescued animal. With carelessness, capturing or transporting an animal can injure or stress it even more than it already is.

Early on in rehabilitating wildlife we received a young mountain lion that weighed about fifty pounds. This size is deceptive because although they don't have the strength and agility of an adult, they are still formidable, being very strong and dangerous. When they are younger and smaller than this, they are easier to handle because their size and their demeanor is that of a kitten. This guy was not a kitten and not docile. A cactus spine in his paw had become infected, leaving him lame. He had become weak and was luckily found by hikers before he died. We placed him in a very stout (3' x 4' x 4') wooden cage covered with welded wire. An adult lion could escape from this, but it held the youngster just fine for the short duration of his stay.

His paw was infected and swollen. He could not put weight on it and was constantly licking it. The obvious treatment was to remove the spine, treat the wound, and start him on antibiotics. He also had other treatments needed because he was emaciated and dehydrated. Regular feeding and providing lots of water took care of that problem, with him eating two adult jackrabbits a day for the first five days. But the paw was another story. The spine needed to be removed, each day he needed injections, and every other day the wound needed to be cleaned and treated. How were we to do this and not get severely mauled?

For some reason, Dennis had little fear, but once again, this was early on in rehabilitating wildlife, so he was still inexperienced, and this was his first lion. That lack of fear protected Dennis, but he still had to figure out ways to treat this teenager without injuring himself, which is what the age of this lion was in equivalent human years. Dennis put on his "armor," which was a very thick leather coat that reached to his thighs, thick gloves, insulated pants over denims, and even a hockey mask to protect his face. He probably looked silly but was ready.

The first job was the removal of the spine. Two problems arose. One was how to get the thorn out without him injuring Dennis and without using tranquilizers. Tranquilizer darts are difficult to get permission to use, and in this area the only people allowed to have them are wildlife officers. The primary reason for this is that the most common drug used is ketamine and it is often misused as a recreational drug. Rigorous training is needed to apply this drug without increasing the chance of mortality of captured animals, which is common.

The second problem was the difficulty of getting a cactus spine out. When looking at a spine under the microscope, millions of tiny backward-pointing barbs can be seen, totally covering its surface. This design allows the spine to slide in easily but makes it very difficult to pull out. It grips so tenaciously that if you pull the spine straight out it will often break off, leaving some of the spine in, or a large amount of tissue will be torn with it, causing a nasty wound. The spine needs to be cut out, or at least a blade slid down the length of it on one side where it can be lifted out rather than pulled straight out. The other choice is to push the spine all the way through, if possible, as it slides forward easier and does not grab tissue. Dennis remembered a veterinarian doing that

Very angry and aggressive mountain lion.

to a dachshund they had when he was growing up. The dog had gotten a cholla cactus spine in his paw, then used his mouth to get it off himself, and ended up with spines in his lips, cheeks, and tongue. Most of them were removed by simply pushing them all the way through, the way they came in.

Dennis ended up getting very lucky. The cat came in about 9:00 a.m. one morning, brought to his house by a wildlife officer. When he went into the garage later in the afternoon where the cage was, the cat was sound asleep with his paw against the side of the cage. Dennis peeked in at it and saw that the cactus spine was sticking out within reach. He quietly snuck up on the lion with a pair of pliers and a tiny scalpel. If you can imagine this, he was in his bulky clothes, sneaking up on this very wild animal. He got down on his knees next to the cage and leaned down almost to the floor while trying

This mountain lion's weapon of choice.

to be as quiet as possible. Dennis knew that when the lion awoke it would be startled and he may lash out. Moving as quickly as he could, Dennis grabbed the spine with a pair of pliers, sliced down the side of the spine, and pulled it out in one swift motion. The cage erupted and almost knocked over as Dennis fell back onto his side, scrambling to stay out of the way of the slashing claws of a very pissed off lion. He looked at the pliers in his hand and there was the spine! Like we say, luck!

From then on it was much more difficult to treat him. We couldn't sneak up to him and treat the foot, nor would he hold still for injections. He was never caught sleeping again. Dennis had to catch him each day with a catch stick, quickly injecting him in the shoulder, then getting a rope on his injured paw and holding it away from his biting mouth and slashing claws—but it got the job done. It was not easy to accomplish without any injury. Dennis was getting good at handling animals solo by this time, the way he did most of the work with wildlife in the beginning of the program. It was difficult to find someone who was not afraid, and like we mentioned with handling eagles, you *must* be unafraid and aggressive with them, or they will get you.

(Now that Denise helps, Dennis always has that dependable assistance.) This mountain lion's treatment progressed well, and he was released a week later.

At times, the animals themselves may not be dangerous, but the act of saving wildlife becomes the danger. Dennis has been hoisted up on lifts and cranes to get up to nests and dangled from slopes and cliffsides with entire fall safety teams at our local mines. But most of the time it is work that is accomplished alone and with little safety equipment, except his own common sense. We are always wary and careful not to injure the animal or ourselves when capturing wildlife.

One of the craziest raven cases we ever experienced was a good example of this. A little note here: Many people call the large black birds in our area crows. Although crows are common in northern states, they are rare here. These birds are ravens, either common ravens or Chihuahuan ravens. They are much larger than crows and are much more of a scavenger, taking the place of the vultures that migrate from here during the winter. Common year-round, these phenomenally successful and intelligent birds unfortunately are often misnamed. Ravens and the Corvidae family that they belong to are considered the most intelligent of all birds.[25]

The call came in that a nestling was hanging upside down out of a nest, having been caught in a string of some sort. The neighbors in a trailer park north of town were alerted to the problem when the bird's parents started constantly cawing very loudly. As Dennis drove up, he saw a large raven nest with a young raven hanging from it, almost at the top of a seventy-foot ponderosa pine tree. The parents were still vocalizing their concern and flying around nervously. The three nest mates had fledged (taken flight out of the nest) and were perched in a nearby tree, crying softly.

The tree was easy to climb up into, but as Dennis scrambled higher and closer to the dangling baby, the parents decided this was a threat and started cawing much louder and tried to attack him. Obviously being terribly upset, they started dive-bombing him and slapping him with their wings, even nipping with their beaks. Dennis fended them off and reached the baby. Along with things like sticks, electrical cord, and trash bags, the parents had incorporated the bright-colored cord used to tie hay bales to make their nest. Unfortunately, living around humans who don't care or don't know any better, and who leave these dangerous materials around, these were readily available for nest building.

The young raven's foot was not only tangled in the bright yellow cord, but it had been tangled for so long that his skin had grown around it. He probably was tethered to the nest for quite some time without even noticing much, but when he tried to take his maiden flight, the poor guy made just a flap or two before the cord pulled him back and left him like a dangling, wiggling, very noisy ornament on a Christmas tree. It might have been a humorous and almost cartoonish thing to witness though, the moment of his first flight. You can just imagine him extremely excited, finally getting the courage to jump and take the first big risk of his life, and how disappointing that must have been. Or is that anthropomorphizing? Maybe it was how "scared" that he must have been.

Dennis worked as fast as he could. The parents had already nipped him pretty good on the forearm once and were starting to dive-bomb again, trying to hit with more force. He didn't think they could knock him out of the tree, but wasn't about to test it, now being sixty or so feet in the air. He said he kind of felt like that dangling raven for a minute there! He quickly cut the cord, grabbed the fledgling, and dropped out of the tree like a squirrel to keep away from the parents. The parents followed the entire way as Dennis walked back to his truck, and even driving partway down the road, they were flying just above and expressing their anger. He hated to steal their nestling, but the bird needed surgery immediately. The raven was rushed to the clinic where we removed the cord, but small incisions had to be made to get it free. To be honest, the foot was so damaged that we were concerned he would not be able to be released.

Raven with foot damage from nest materials from humans.

Raven foot showing how tangled the cord was.

Raven's foot after surgery to remove cord.

We have learned through the years to be patient with tough cases and give them a chance, especially if they stay spirited and show a promise of healing like this bird did. Sure enough, the next morning he was standing on the damaged foot. His toes were still clutched together instead of being in a perching spread, so he was not out of the woods yet, this being an impediment to his success after release. Over the next few days, by allowing him a bit more movement in a larger cage, but not letting him fly yet, he slowly improved to the point where he was putting all of his weight on that foot and spreading his toes normally. He was released a week later at the location where he was found. This guy surprised us all. Hopefully, the rest of his life will be a bit less traumatic.

In another section of this book, we describe an episode about a mountain lion that was hit by a car. During the release of this animal, we were definitely in a dangerous predicament. The release of an animal like this is always precarious because the large, powerful predator can always turn on his rescuers, not knowing they are trying to set him free. As this lion was being released, we were prepared to protect ourselves but were praying we would not have to. The Game and Fish officer who accompanied us stood ready in the back of his pickup with a shotgun. Luckily, he did not have to use it and the lion ran off directly away from us and was not threatened. The horrible consequences of having an animal turn on us and have to be shot after all the effort to save it was too much to even think about. We were very thankful that all went well on the actual release.

One reason that those who work with wildlife must be permitted is due to this imminent danger that is always present with the large predators we rehabilitate. We have seen people capture hawks and owls and end up going to the emergency room due to their inexperience and ignorance. Others have had to go through rabies treatment, a series of uncomfortable and painful injections. To have an inexperienced person handle a sick baby animal and have that infection spread to them and their family is a scary prospect. We strongly encourage everyone to never try to handle injured or orphaned wild animals ever. Please wait for an experienced rehabilitator to protect both the animal and you. The fines for caring and possessing wildlife without both state and federal permits are not something that anyone would want to pay, often leading to thousands of dollars being assessed and possible jail time.

CHAPTER SEVEN

Unusual Animals

White pelican

Through the many years of wildlife rehabilitation, Gila Wildlife Rescue has had a variety of strange and unusual experiences, but they also include some strange and unusual animals, at least for this area. There are so many examples of this that it is difficult to pick just a few, but the list of species we have cared for in the appendix of this book can give you a better idea. The most unbelievable example was a zebra that Dennis advised with a local veterinarian about! A circus was in town and their zebra had given birth on the way here. They stopped at a local veterinarian's office for help when the newborn started to become ill, and Dennis was called in for advice, the vet being uncertain about this somewhat "wild" animal. The animal was very weak and had scours. With IVs to hydrate and medications, he survived and continued with the circus. Here are a few more notable stories.

Pelicans, of All Things!

Yes, pelicans, right here in Silver City, New Mexico. One of them was found in a woman's fishpond in a tiny backyard in the middle of town. It sure surprised us when we got the first call. The first two were white pelicans, and since then we have cared for a couple of brown pelicans. Whites have a wingspan of over ten feet, the second longest of any North American bird, with only the California condor being longer.[26] They have a large, turkey-sized body and huge bill, so this woman was shocked when she found one in her pond with all her fish gone. It tried to get off the ground and fly but was too weak and kind of stuck in the tight area of her backyard.

The only problem this bird had was that it was emaciated and hungry. It saw a bit of water and dropped down during migration to feed its starving stomach. We had a few trout in our freezer, so placing her in a pen, we gave her some fish. She would not eat at all. She refused anything else including cut up fish, fish from the store, and fresh shrimp. We tried everything. She didn't look right, like she was uncomfortable, but we discounted it at first, thinking it was just fright from being captured. Worried, Dennis finally listened to that message in her demeanor and thought about it for a while.

The only place we have ever seen this species of bird is at the Bosque del Apache National Wildlife Refuge in central New Mexico. It is along the Rio Grande River, where we always observed them in the water. We didn't remember seeing any on land. Maybe we just needed to change our approach. Sure enough, when we borrowed our kid's plastic wading pool and put it in the cage with water, she jumped right in it, splashing and bathing, obviously much happier.

The fish were placed on a block next to the pool and we expected her to eat now that she was more content. The next morning, she still had not eaten. We were very worried now because her condition was deteriorating and the only treatment was to get food into her, so an attempt was made to force-feed the bird. Has anyone ever tried to force-feed a thirty-pound bird with a ten-foot wingspan? Of course you haven't, you aren't that crazy—but he had to get this bird some nutrition. You can imagine him standing in the pool with her, trying to get her mouth open, her huge wings like mammoth fans beating him on the sides. Dennis was getting frustrated because every time he put a fish in her pouch, she just spit it right up. In frustration, he stepped out of the pool and threw the fish he had in his hand back into the water with the pelican. To his amazement, she immediately attacked the fish, dexterously flipping it up in the air and catching it with her built-in fishnet and swallowed it in a matter of seconds.

"What just happened?" he thought, and then it dawned on him. She is accustomed to finding and catching her food *in* the water, not off a block on the ground. She didn't recognize it as food and probably had an instinct to not pick dead fish up off the ground. She wanted the fish *her* way, not his.

Pelican fishing

She rapidly ate all the fish from the freezer, and we quickly saw that purchasing enough to fill her up was going to cost over a hundred dollars a day, so we tried to figure out a way to get this monstrous pelican fed. Dennis would have loved to go fishing every day to keep her fed, but at the time, he had a heavy teaching load that did not allow for even thinking about that possibility. He had contact with a local fly-fishing club, so he called them to see if they could help. It was heartwarming to see these guys come to the rescue. They organized the club members to go out and catch bluegill on Bill Evans Lake, close to town. We had a small ice chest of fish waiting for us when we got home every day. The bird fattened up quickly and after a few weeks, was ready to release. Knowing they needed a long runway to run across and get airborne, we took it out to Bill Evans Lake for release.

White pelican release—notice the ten-foot wingspan.

The large pelican was placed in the lake, and she started flying without delay, running across the surface of the water. She started flapping and pushing with her feet, pumping faster and faster, then surprisingly she put on the brakes and stopped in the water. Our thought was, "Was she not ready to release? Should we have waited?"

Getting a better view of her with binoculars, we watched the pelican for a while as she was clearly turning and paddling around in the water. Confused at first, it all became clear when she suddenly plunged her beak into the water and came up with a bluegill, the same type of fish she had been fed this entire time. She was trying to fly away, but when she saw more fish, she just couldn't resist. We waited for almost an hour and were about to give up and leave her there, hoping she was strong enough to migrate, when she started another charge down the runway of the lake. This time, she ran for a longer distance. By the time she was ready to be airborne, her legs were pumping in a blur, and she lifted off, heading north, never to be seen again.

A brown pelican that we cared for was strange as well. Unlike white pelicans that regularly migrate through New Mexico, usually along the Rio Grande Valley, brown pelicans are quite rare here. The twist that made this case so unusual was that he mysteriously showed up at the fairgrounds in Cliff, New Mexico, during the annual Grant County Fair. We examined him thoroughly and found no injuries. His problem was that he was starving. Having learned that they like bluegill, we immediately released the bird at nearby Bill Evans Lake. He hung out there for a few weeks, and then continued his migration.

Another brown pelican we dealt with had, from all we could tell, confused a local highway with a river. It was reported by half a dozen drivers along New Mexico State Highway 90, the main road south out of Silver City. When Dennis drove up to him, he was just sitting on a post for the guard rail like it was a dock. He flew away when approached, so was not injured, but just glided right back to the highway, lining up with

White pelican running across lake to get airborne.

Immature
brown pelican.

it and landing slowly, even placing his feet in a position like it was landing on water. As soon as he hit the pavement he crashed and rolled a bit, confused and dazed. The late afternoon sun was just at the right angle so that the pavement was shiny and did almost look like water. It was a kind of "pavement mirage" that confused this poor bird. After repeated unsuccessful attempts to capture him, Dennis ended up just hazing him away from the highway and the area. We did not receive any more reports of him, so we hope he got "unconfused."

Badgers

Badgers are found primarily in the grasslands of our area and the savannas that are composed of grasslands with scattered trees. They are secretive animals, primarily

Badger with injured foot

nocturnal, so are seldom seen, and many residents don't even know they live around here. They are brawny animals with short legs, an abundance of strong muscles, and a perpetual mean disposition. Badgers live singly, at least in this area, interacting only to breed, and pretty much live the life of an old grouchy recluse that goes about his business each day not caring about anybody but himself.

Badgers are well described as "a wolverine with short legs" because they are very similar mammals both physically and genetically. Badgers are quite a bit shorter but just as stout. Though shorter, there is no reduction in its aggressive disposition. They all are in the weasel family of mammals (Mustelidae), so both are just large, very fat weasels.[27] The only species in North America is the American badger.

Badger—just a big fat weasel— in the same family.

Most of our experience is in capturing nuisance badgers and relocating them, although we did have a baby one year. These animals are so muscular and violent once cornered or trapped that it is an adventure to catch one. These are the second most aggressive animals we deal with. The most dangerous encounter was with an adult javelina that Dennis caught with a catch stick (a stick with a loop in the end like a dog catcher uses) that flailed around so much trying to get away from him that when the animal ran into a small shelter, the catch stick hit the side of the shelter and bent it in a 90-degree angle in a blink of an eye! That stick was also keeping the animal from attacking Dennis, and now the stick wasn't very solid anymore and was bending even more in the middle as he struggled. This was a catch stick made from tubular aluminum with a steel core that the javelina bent like it was a cardboard tube. He quickly grabbed another catch stick and got the javelina into a transport cage before he hurt him or someone else.

Amazingly, about a year later, a similar incident happened with a badger we were relocating. This is the event that taught Dennis a valuable lesson in always listening to his wife Denise. We were at our favorite breakfast restaurant in town one Sunday morning and as we were finishing our meal, he received a wildlife call. It was a gentleman who had a badger trapped inside his fenced yard, and despite numerous attempts to get him to go out a gate, the animal was still trapped and getting more and more crazed by the minute.

Dennis turned to Denise and said, "Good timing! We finished breakfast just in time to go on a wildlife call. You get to help me catch a badger!" We excitedly paid the bill and got in our SUV. We keep catch sticks and pet carriers in the vehicle, so we are always prepared. As they were leaving, Denise said to him, "Hey, should we go get your truck? Could that badger get out of the pet carrier inside this SUV and then be loose inside here and attack us?"

Dennis's reply was quickly given: "Nah, we will be okay," and we started down the road. But this little voice inside him said to listen to her and he is very glad he did. Dennis

Adult badger captured for relocation.

decided to take her advice and turned around.

"Why are you turning around?" she asked.

"I decided to not be stupid and, instead, listen to my wife" was his reply.

We went home, got the truck and an even stronger pet carrier, then headed out to catch this grouchy old badger.

It was hard to get the loop of the catch stick around the badger but that was accomplished, and Dennis held on for dear life. This time, he was careful not to let the stick hit something to bend it. He was also trying to do this quickly to protect the animal. The use of these capture sticks can be tricky. You have just a few seconds while the noose is tight enough for the animal to not get away to do what you need to do, or you can kill or permanently damage the animal. A New Mexico wildlife officer taught Dennis one time that the two carotid arteries in the neck supply 90 percent of the oxygen to the brain. If both are shut off, death or severe brain damage can occur in as little as seven seconds. The animal can die in under a minute.

Adult badger relocated.

So we had to be quick. Denise got the pet carrier positioned and then Dennis asked her to back away. He slipped the noose around the animal's neck and one leg so he couldn't get away from him, and they don't choke as easily (they don't have much of a neck, and it is well protected with a collar of thick fur). It took some patience, and he was trying to bite the loop and lunge at him the entire time. Once the loop was on the badger, Dennis quickly pulled the badger to himself, swinging him around, and stuffed him into the carrier in one swift motion. Then he turned the knob at the end of the catch stick to release the noose and latched the door shut. He was captured and subdued, kind of . . . he was lunging at the door, but it seemed to hold for the time.

We lifted him and the carrier into the back of our truck. It had a camper shell on it, so we closed him up and headed to Fort Bayard, a game refuge nearby and our chosen release site. About halfway there, we heard some banging in the back. Denise looked and said, "He's loose! He's running around back there like crazy."

Sure enough, he was so powerful that he broke the carrier's door down, breaking the plastic on a tough carrier like it was Styrofoam. He got out—just like Denise had wondered was possible. If we had brought the SUV to do this job, we would have been in trouble. Like Dennis said, lesson learned that day. He is now much better at listening to his wife!

Orphaned badger found in middle of highway.

The baby badger that came in was incredibly adorable, one of the cutest babies we have experienced. He was about the size of a baseball, probably just weeks old. The strange part of this guy's story was where he was found. There was a large highway construction project north of Deming, New Mexico, and the workers found this tiny fella curled up and frightened between the two yellow stripes in the middle of the highway. They said he was watching cars as they went by with this sad forlorn look on his face. They ran to save him before he was run over by traffic or construction workers.

Orphaned badger found in middle of highway.

Orphaned badger.

Even though he was that tiny, he was very aggressive, trying to bite constantly and growling and spitting. It ended up being a sad story because he never did feed very well and seemed to have other things going on such as internal damage. A couple of days later, he was found dead curled up in a pile of wood chips.

Beautiful Vultures

We realize this is a contradiction to some people. A beautiful vulture? Looking just at the head, most would think it unsightly. The plumage of feathers on the body though is amazingly beautiful. Compared to the other raptors that we care for, vultures are completely different from hawks, owls, and eagles, but are still considered raptors. Recent DNA analysis has shown New World vultures to be more closely related to storks than hawks and eagles, where they once were placed, so now are in an order and family of their own: order Cathartiformes and family Cathartidae. They are also surprisingly not related to the Old World vultures of Africa and Asia and are an example of parallel evolution due to similar feeding habits.[28] Vultures

Turkey vulture.

are meat eaters, but as everyone knows, they specialize in eating carrion. One of the few birds with a well-developed sense of smell to find rotting meat, they are highly successful but at the same time generally venerated birds. Usually associated with death, they play a crucial role in food chains in returning nutrients to the cycle by cleaning up dead carcasses. Although these birds are very common here in the late spring, summer, and early fall, they rarely get injured and are rare for Gila Wildlife Rescue to care for, so are included in this chapter on unusual animals.

Turkey vulture wing.

We have grown to admire them greatly. They are gentle and shy, and often get so upset they vomit. This is an adaptation to allow them to quickly get airborne and away from harm. Carrion can be scarce, so when vultures finally find food, they gorge themselves and sometimes eat so much it is difficult for them to get off the ground due to the excess weight. When they are disturbed, they do a very ugly but useful thing to get in the air quickly. They regurgitate their food and are instantly lighter to escape.

Vultures have the most beautiful plumage that has an amazing iridescence to it when in the right light. Every feather is perfect and perfectly in place. More brown than black, the body of a vulture is striking. But then you get to the head. The featherless skin (an adaptation that reduces rotting meat from sticking to it and spreading disease), the odd red color, the lethal-looking beak, and the beady little eyes gives you an ugly bird. It is too bad the head ruins it all because the rest of the body is gorgeous!

Video Link: VultureFlightCage

One vulture case stands out as the most interesting out of the dozens we have cared for. Many animals we care for speak to us, telling us, for example, that they are ready

Turkey vulture preparing for release.

to be released. They can tell us they are ready to be released by becoming more active, for example. They show us by their demeanor that they are sick. We sometimes can feel their pain. The vulture we are referring to told us to not give up on him.

The call was from a man that had a large vulture in his front yard. We captured the bird and found an old injury, partially healed, on his left wing. Old injuries frequently have healed incorrectly, leaving the bird un-releasable, but this one had a chance of making it. Because they have a wingspan of over six feet, we placed him in our large

Turkey vulture.

flight cage for eagles and left him to recuperate. He gained weight and regained his full health after being down on the ground for so long, but he still could not fly. We considered putting him down and even were capturing him to do so when something happened. As Dennis was holding him with his eyes locked with the vulture's, he could feel him. He could feel a spirit that had not given up and even felt him telling him, "Don't give up on me yet." If the wrong decision is made, the animal continues to suffer for a longer period when it could have been euthanized earlier, ending their misery. It is always a tough decision to make.

So Dennis listened and didn't give up. Sure enough, just a few days later, the bird lost two or three large flight feathers in the injured area, indicating it was healing, and he started some new feather growth. A month later he was starting to fly, and a few weeks after this he was ready to be released. We almost gave up on this guy, but he told us not to. We now had another problem, though. Turkey vultures migrate south each winter, leaving and arriving at about the same dates each year. In our area they leave on or near the fall equinox and return almost exactly six months later on the spring equinox. Dennis and a friend of his had been documenting this for years to determine if the rumor was true that you could predict an early or late spring based on the vultures' return date. It was supposedly a Groundhog Day type of thing. So far, the data shows no correlation in predicting this. They commonly return on the exact same day to our area, on the spring equinox.

This bird was still with us in early November. We had two choices: to keep him until spring, which increases his chances of injury or problems in captivity, or release him farther south. We consulted Dennis's old ornithology professor, and he advised us that we could take him south to the Mexican border in Southwestern New Mexico, which is the northern extent of their winter range, and he should do fine. We took his advice and traveled south with the vulture for release. This was kind of a surreal trip, driving a bird down its migration path for him, but we have always used a variety of methods to care for our charges.

We were blessed a couple of times to be able to raise nestling turkey vultures. The first was within weeks of fledging. Beautiful, yet ugly, even as a baby. It had the most unusual plumage, and the behavior was bizarre as well.

Video Link:

VultureRelease

Fledgling turkey vulture.

Fledgling turkey
vulture.

The second was much younger and about four weeks from fledging. He would flap his big wings and stretch them, but it was a while before he was airborne. As with other raptor species, this guy did the ugly duckling transition to a beautiful bird by the time he was released. It was fascinating to watch the typical method of helping to cool their bodies by defecating on their feet, so the white color keeps them cooler.

Pronghorn

A misunderstood and mysterious animal that you normally don't see except from a long distance, pronghorn are the speedsters of the animals in this area and have amazing long-distance vision. Correctly called pronghorn, but commonly known by their totally incorrect name of antelope, these mammals are from a group of ancient creatures making them more closely related to giraffes.[29]

Pronghorn

They actually have a unique family of their own. The antelope family all have horns that are permanent structures made of a keratin-like substance and found on both males and females, as opposed to the deer family that has antlers only on males (except caribou). The pronghorns' horns are a soft calcium structure that falls off each year and grows back larger. Their head growth is neither horn nor antler but something else entirely.[30] Similar to the way a rhinoceros horn is formed, this structure grows from a bony core and is made of densely packed hair follicles forming a hard structure called a prong. Thus, the name pronghorn. The prong falls off each year, leaving the bony core—the horn—exposed until it regrows a bit larger.

We have rescued pronghorn adults after being hit by cars when they cross under fences bordering the highways, and one that was tangled in barbed wire, but just like with deer, we have primarily cared for fawns at our clinic, the adults being too skittish and stressed to care for without causing their death.

Video Link: Pronghorn

By the way, Gila Wildlife Rescue has never cared for any bighorn sheep, although Dennis hazed this group off the Grant County Courthouse parking lot a few years ago, and these videos are of them established successfully on one of our local copper mine properties.

Video Link: BighornSheep   BighornSheep2

Pronghorn

We have successfully raised pronghorn fawns and introduced them to the probable herd they came from. The toughest one was from Mule Creek, New Mexico. This area west of here has always had a small pronghorn herd. One spring, we had a rancher bring us a fawn he had found with a broken leg. We had our veterinarian put a cast on her and continued its care.

Once weaned and old enough to release, we transported her to his ranch and released her with the herd she came from. To our horror, we got a call just when we arrived home that this poor thing had run off when the herd was startled and ended up down on the ground again. She had broken two other legs. They asked if we wanted them to bring her to us, and we told them to put her down. Worried that we did something wrong, we did some research. We found that there can be a genetic

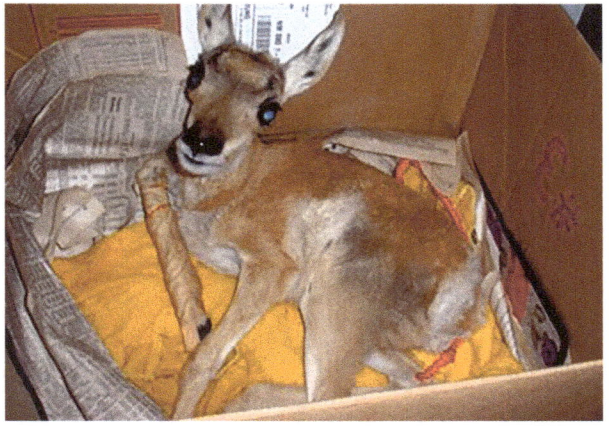

Pronghorn fawn with leg in cast— unexplained calcium deficiency.

Pronghorn
adult

problem in pronghorn that prevents them from absorbing calcium correctly, thus making their bones very brittle.[31] The cause is unknown, but luckily, we have never had a case like it since.

Pronghorn adult

Raccoon Relatives

There are two other very unusual desert animals that we have cared for, ringtails and coatimundis. Both are relatives of raccoons and have a mask and a ringed tail.

Ringtails are rarely injured, but we have trapped and relocated hundreds of them. Rarely seen and much misunderstood, they are very cute creatures that have beautiful and delicate features. They possess a typical raccoon mask, and a large, fluffy, black-and-white boldly ringed tail. About the size of a small cat, these animals are somewhat solitary, living in small family groups, and are secretive and nocturnal. The misnomer for this animal is a ringtail cat. They are not cats at all. Back in the day, they were commonly kept around here by miners to place in shafts, like a canary, to be an early warning system for poisonous gases. Thus, another name for it—the miner's cat.[32] They are very delicate and petite animals, unlike their close relatives, the coatimundi and raccoon, which are both larger and more robust.

Ringtail after
release.

We commonly catch ringtails at the large copper mines in our area. They get into lunchrooms and raid food, take up residence in sheds and abandoned buildings, and tend to commonly get into switch boxes and electrical substations. They not only get killed when they short out the electricity but also shut down operations for a while. As soon as they are sighted and reported, we trap them and relocate them far enough away so we can be assured they will not come back and are away from the danger.

Ringtail from mine in trap.

Video Link:

RingtailRelease

The distance wildlife must be taken for relocation depends on the animal. The goal is to get them far enough away so they don't return and cause another problem. Our theory is that if you not only take them the necessary distance but also release them in a place that is far better than where they were, they don't even want to return. We take most animals at least twenty miles away, including skunks, ringtails, coatis, bobcats, and raccoons. We take many of ours thirty miles away to the Gila River where there are many wild areas and where they can find plenty of food and water. At the mine many years ago, they had a number of ringtails the workers caught and released, taking them four or five miles away. After a while, they wondered if this was the same animal coming back again, so they sprayed a small florescent paint spot on its tail. The next morning, the same animal was caught. Their problem was only one animal, but they had just not taken it far enough away!

Ringtail release—like a bullet out of the trap.

A ringtail ended up being trapped inside our local Walmart one time, and we had to go rescue him. When we got the call, we envisioned it running around in the store wreaking havoc. Upon arrival, we found out he was in the back storage area of the store and not jumping on customers and biting them as we had imagined!

Relieved, we listened to the manager tell us that they called Gila Wildlife Rescue because the dog catcher tried for hours with

Ringtail captured in Walmart.

no luck. The dog catcher told them that there was no way anyone could catch it. As we were trying to get a catch stick on him, we noticed he was running back and forth to escape us along the same route behind a row of huge boxes of produce. So we set a large live trap along this route. At first, he just jumped over it, but eventually shot through the trap, which had doors open on each end. He thought it was an escape tunnel, but he tripped it, and we caught him . . . in just a few minutes. They should have called the wildlife people in the first place!

Coatimundis, on the other hand, are a whole different animal. They may be related to these other two, but the only similarity is a faint mask on their faces and faint brown and tan rings on their skinny but long tails, which they hold upright like a banner. They are much larger and taller, weighing normally around eight pounds, but reportedly reaching twenty pounds.[33] Ringtails are much more diminutive, almost petite, weighing under two pounds. Coatis have a long snout that is somewhat flexible, giving them piglike features. They have bearlike paws on double-jointed feet that allow them to go down a tree headfirst. Coatis are more diurnal and are gregarious, living in large troops of as many as thirty animals.[34]

Their name is a bit confusing with many different names for the same animal. When researching the discrepancies in names, we discovered that in South America where they are far more common, they can all be called simply "coatis." A large male that is roaming around causing trouble is called a "coatimundi." Mammologists refer to them as coatimundi, but many people call them coatis for short.

Coatimundi reported as monkey—left front paw injured by dart.

Unlike much of the wild-life we have cared for where it is primarily young animals, all our experience with coatis has been with large adults. They are aggressive, powerful individuals that seem like a miniature adult bear in disposition. Santa Clara, a small village east of us, seems to be where most of our calls for coatis have come from. Our first experience was reported to us by a New Mexico Game and Fish officer. He related that someone had reported a monkey in the area, and he thought that was more Gila Wildlife's bag than his. We frequently help each other, so we were accustomed to occasionally covering calls for them. When we arrived, it was "just" a coati, but since it had scrambled up a flagpole so easily and most people have never seen one, the people reporting this decided it must be a monkey.

Coatis are strong, powerful animals that we equate with wolverines. When we go on an eagle call, Dennis gets excited as we have described; when we go on a coati call, he gets excited too . . . but in a much different way. These guys are a handful! It seems like every part of their body is a weapon, including their tail. Once captured on a catch stick, they will thrash around much more violently than any animal we have ever handled. And you can tell that they are mad as hell. These guys get really pissed off when you invade their space, much less capture one. This animal in Santa Clara was no exception and was twenty feet high up on a pole.

Released coatimundi showing faint rings in tail.

We ended up having to ask the wild-life officer to meet us there anyway. This "monkey" would not come down, so he needed to be tranquilized. The officer came out and darted him, but the dart hit the bone of his front paw, leaving him with a bit of a limp. We took him to our clinic and examined the paw, but found no major damage yet, so we placed him in our large flight cage to observe. The next morning, he was fine and was released. Capturing him for transport was wild! Gnashing his teeth, snarling, and spitting, he fought like a Tasmanian devil once on the catch stick! When we released him, he ran up a tree, then came back down, headfirst, and growled and barked ferociously enough that we had to scramble back into the truck!

We were asked to trap coatis one time at one of our local mines because a group of them had been coming into the lunchroom and challenging the workers for their lunch. Probably at first encouraged by getting fed, they eventually became very bold and aggressive, so they called us to trap them. We had a large wire mammal trap, so we set it up. The next morning, the entire door was knocked off its hinges! The trap was busted! We next brought our trailer trap, and eventually captured them that way.

Coatimundi mistaken for a monkey.

The other crazy coati case was the call we got about one that had killed a pit bull. The animal was feeding on trash and a dog tried attacking him, but according to the owner, the coati rushed up to the dog, flipped himself upside down, grabbed the dog by the throat, and ripped it. He said the dog was dead from blood loss in seconds. The coati, meanwhile, a large aggressive male we should call a real "coatimundi," ran up a power pole and was very vocally telling everyone all about it.

When we arrived, we realized we couldn't reach him. The police were there and had called in the fire department to get a ladder truck for us. Dennis walked out on a surprisingly unstable ladder on this huge truck and tried to reach the animal, but quickly turned around and climbed back down. He recognized that if he grabbed the coati with the metal catch stick, the animal would immediately thrash around and pull the metal pole into

Coati causing mischief at local mine.

live wires. He was not willing to take the risk to himself or the animal. The coatimundi was not easily able to touch two live wires where it was, so we advised everyone to leave him there and let him find his way down that night. The report the next morning was that the animal was gone, and no more dogs were mysteriously killed.

Here are some coatimundi videos:

Coatimundi showing aggressiveness after release— barking from a tree and growling.

Video Link:

CoatimundiVideo

CoatimundiRelease

CHAPTER EIGHT

Un-releasable Wildlife

Coyote pup "Taz."

The purpose of Gila Wildlife Rescue's entire program and the only reason we are allowed to be permitted is to release animals back into the wild. This is not only our goal, but it was made very clear when we were first permitted that we would not keep any un-releasable animals. Zoos and breeding facilities are the only option besides euthanasia. The exception to this is an educational permit that is issued for keeping captive wildlife for just that purpose. We have never kept any educational animals. We have observed how strong and important a wild animal's spirit is to them. A healthy but non-releasable hawk or owl with a broken wing that has not healed correctly, and cannot fly, would live in captivity for educational use for five to ten years in most cases. In nature, a healthy raptor would live for fifteen to twenty years. So why the difference even with the bird's needs totally provided for and being protected?

It is their spirit. The longer they are in captivity, the more we see their spirit slowly die. Most of this is caused by not being able to fly and be free. Freedom to fly is the fuel for their spirit. Some captive birds have lived longer than this, but usually these birds are also captive bred, so have never experienced freedom.

We frequently have observed birds in longer-term care start to lose their spirit and become depressed, particularly when they cannot fly. When they start to improve, we see that spirit building back up to the extremely high-spirited birds that they normally are. This spirit is absolutely necessary for their survival. A fully spirited, alert, ready-to-release bird is feisty, very aggressive, and has a wild look in its eye that is easily recognized as a spirited healthy bird.

It is difficult to put any animal down. When the animal is suffering and the injuries are not recoverable, then it is not quite as tough because you know you are helping the animal by ending its suffering. Often, the animal has already been suffering for a long period of time, so the mercy killing is a bit easier. When an animal has recovered from injury, but the injury has left them with permanent damage, then this mercy killing is much more difficult. To put down a healthy animal at first seemed backward, and it took us a while to realize its importance. They are not healthy. They cannot survive on their own in the wild. They can't fly, or they walk with a limp, or have a damaged eye or a few other situations where they are alive, but only because of our direct care. They would not survive in the wild and would slowly suffer and die if released.

Out of these two choices, either euthanasia or permanent captivity in a zoo or breeding facility, in most cases the best choice for the animal is euthanasia. To the inexperienced this may seem cold and cruel, but our experiences early on taught us the importance and the need for euthanasia. If the bird never heals and is not able to fly, that slow fading of its spirit continues, and it is eventually snuffed out completely. The bird dies of no apparent cause, save the dying of its spirit.

Our other choice is to place the animal in a zoo or breeding facility. We have strong opinions about placing animals in some of these settings, but we also recognize the

Osprey on intake with barbed wire lacerations.

importance of education to help protect them in nature. Unfortunately, most of the animals we care for are common species that zoos have easy access to and don't need help with breeding.

One of the few experiences we have had in placing an animal in a breeding facility of a zoo was with an osprey. The bird had been caught in a barbed wire fence along one of our local rivers and brought to Gila Wildlife Rescue by a farmer who lived nearby.

The people who brought it to us had the presence of mind to simply cut the wire on either side of the bird, and not try to untangle it from the bird themselves. After a close examination, it was obvious that this bird had been hanging from the fence for quite a while, and he had lost a fair amount of blood. One barb had embedded in the wrist joint of the right wing. The procedure to remove the wire was slow and tedious but it was successful. He was placed in a cage in the clinic where he could be observed closely. After approximately five days, he was moved to our large flight cage for rehabilitation. The x-rays that were taken by the local veterinarian showed no broken bones in the wrist, but there was ligament damage. This rehabilitation was going to be slow and may or may not be successful.

Our catch of the day for the osprey.

An osprey's diet consists of fish, so since he was brought to us, we "had" to go fishing every week to supply him with the proper diet. When we first fed the osprey, we would put a fish on the ground in the cage and he would not eat it. Having a similar experience with a pelican, we tried putting the fish in a tub of water and he began to eat right away. Since they catch their prey in water, his instinct was always to get it out of water, or it might be bad to eat. He didn't feed until he found it in water, even though it was dead.

Interestingly, he ate the head-first, tearing small pieces at a time, and then worked his way down to the tail, leaving nothing but the guts and the base of the tail. During its care,

Osprey

we were very fortunate and blessed, because every time we went fishing, we caught our limit of trout. How cool, to *have* to go fishing! It was one of those "tough jobs, but someone has to do it" type of things. Fishing just happens to be one of our passions in life, among other things, so it was very pleasurable for us to do that. The osprey was well fed, to say the least.

The osprey was very vocal as he communicated with us in a series of loud, short cries followed by a guttural sound. If we were outside, he would do the same as if he was saying, "Hey, I'm hungry in here!" He wasn't imprinted but was one of those birds smart enough to figure out where his food was coming from.

As we observed him throughout his recovery, although he had a great deal of spirit and feistiness in him, it slowly became obvious that the ligament damage to his wrist was not going to heal. He was never going to fly well enough to be free again. This osprey, though, was a rare bird in our area and was otherwise healthy. His wing injury did not cause his wing to droop and because of this, he looked fine; it just could not take the wing loading necessary to fly.

We wondered if there were any breeding programs, because ospreys are a raptor that has been extirpated of much of its previous range, particularly in the northeastern US, and efforts were being taken to reintroduce them. We made the decision to at least explore the possibilities before we made up our minds. We did not want another incident like Taz, which is the next story.

Osprey ready for transfer.

After a couple of months of rehab to fatten him up and get him healthy, we made a couple of calls to the three larger zoos near us. We contacted the Albuquerque BioPark, the Arizona-Sonoran Desert Museum in Tucson, and the El Paso Zoo. We did not necessarily want to have the osprey placed at these zoos but wanted to find out if there was a network of zoos and breeding facilities that we could put out a call to see if anyone could use this fairly rare bird. Sure enough, the Albuquerque BioPark is the one who contacted us. We worked with their zoo veterinarian to put our osprey on a special listserv that zoos, breeding facilities, and research facilities use to obtain animals. We still had reservations about a zoo setting, especially with a raptor spirit that is so delicate. The veterinarian from the Albuquerque Zoo received only one response and that was from the Bronx Zoo in New York City.

This was one of those things that were just meant to be. The woman who responded is the head curator of birds at the Bronx Zoo and did her PhD dissertation on ospreys, so she was very interested in this bird. Through a series of emails, we communicated the details about the bird. The thing that excited us the most was that she wanted him not only for display, but for breeding purposes to eventually release his offspring into the wild.

We had to get permission from the New Mexico Department of Game and Fish and the U.S. Fish and Wildlife Service for the transfer. We were required to get a statement from the local veterinarian to confirm that the bird was un-releasable. We also needed a "veterinarian health certificate" stating that he was healthy and had no diseases that could be spread to other animals or humans. The animal shipping specialist from the Bronx Zoo sent us an animal crate along with the needed labels and made all the arrangements to get him to New York via air freight.

Transport cage from the Bronx Zoo.

We woke very early the morning of transport, put all the shipping labels on the cage to get it ready, and then went into the flight cage that had been this beautiful bird's home for the last five months. We caught him easily and Dennis carried him outside the cage so Denise could take some last photos. We watched him as he looked around the yard, flapping his four-and-a-half-foot wingspan in the air. We could easily see the deformity in his right wing, although new feathers were growing in. Our feelings then were a bit bittersweet, similar to how a parent feels when their children are moving out. A little weird of us, we know, but real all the same. We took several photos of him and then put him in the shipping crate. This crate is a pet carrier, containing a perch inside and burlap that covers the openings on the sides and the door to keep it dark. This darkness helps to keep the bird calm and quiet (like a falconer's hood) and offers him privacy but still allows a flow of air.

Osprey before transfer.

We were praying that the people handling his crate would be gentle. We drove down to El Paso, the closest major airport to us, and put him on the plane to New York City. About ten in the evening our time, midnight in New York, we got the call from the zoo veterinarian. The osprey was not only received in healthy condition, but took to his new temporary cage right away, where he was to wait for his permanent display to be completed. He will be well cared for and may help populations of osprey increase in the eastern United States. Live long and reproduce!

The last story in this section is about Taz. He was named after the Tasmanian devil and one of the few animals besides eagles that we ever gave a name to. The call came from an elderly rancher that ran a livestock feedlot in Deming, New Mexico. He normally would shoot an animal like a coyote that was anywhere near his feedlot, but when a tiny and very cute five-week-old coyote pup appeared on his doorstep, he said it was so cute that he couldn't kill it.

We started the process of raising him, which was going to be challenging because he was not with other coyotes. A few days later, we were contacted by the New Mexico Department of Game and Fish who had heard we were caring for this little pup, and they determined that we should raise him to young adulthood for six months and then turn him over to the Alameda Park Zoo in Alamogordo, New Mexico, for a display animal. They asked us to purposely imprint him on humans so they could clean cages and treat him with less stress and danger. When we asked the Department of Game and Fish if we had a choice they said no, and we assumed that this meant our permitting would be in jeopardy if we did not comply.

It was an amazing and surreal experience because for the first time ever we petted and talked to one of our animals. We let him play with our dogs. We were interviewed for a press article while Denise was holding him, and he loved the attention. Pack animals like this have a hard time being raised alone and need some interaction anyway. He responded quite well, but every once in a while, he would suddenly show his true wild colors. When we held him, he liked to suckle on a finger and was normally very gentle and it was not a problem. Suddenly, with no warning, he would go crazy and bite hard and scratch and struggle away from us.

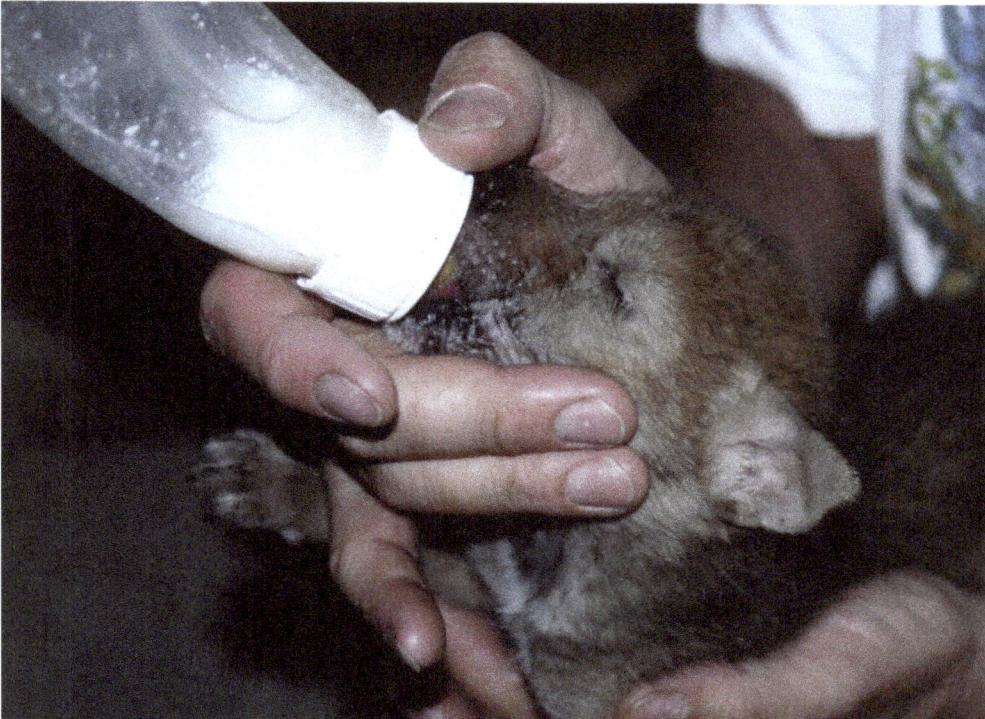

Taz just after intake—he was starving.

Coyote pup Taz, Denise, and our boxer being interviewed for a news article.

Taz and Denise posing for photo and the "devil" comes out, resulting in a scolding.

Thus, the name Taz was given to him. He was a very spirited animal that was full of mischief. No wonder Native Americans called coyotes the "trickster." We transported Taz to the zoo ourselves. It is about a three-hour drive and the transfer went well. We were assured by the small staff that they would take special care of him. Denise said one last goodbye and we drove off.

Taz in zoo enclosure.

Six months later, we returned to the zoo to see how he was doing. We walked up to the cage and didn't see him at first, but then saw him lying down, curled up behind a log. Since he didn't get up as we approached, Dennis called out to him, "Taz!" and he lifted his head with a curious look on his face, like he should have recognized that voice, but didn't. What was so disheartening was to see his eyes. Denise started crying when she looked into them. There was an emptiness in his eyes, despite the best of care from caring zoo employees. The next time we are asked to do this, we may hesitate. . . . We would much rather remember him like this:

Taz

CHAPTER NINE

The Things People Do

Great horned
owl after surgery
from barbed
wire injury.

Each year Gila Wildlife Rescue has cases where we have had to deal with the not-so-kind acts that some people inflict on wild animals. We have experienced humans doing everything from killing animals for no apparent reason, to stealing babies out of dens for pets, to loving them to death by feeding and attempting to tame them. Some of these are malicious acts and others occur out of ignorance or a misdirected sense of caring. Fortunately, a great majority of people in our area are informed and are careful to deal with wildlife responsibly.

Sometimes people do things to control nuisance animals and inadvertently kill the wild animals that they like and end up facing possible prosecution. A very sick great horned owl was brought to us one day, having been rescued near downtown Silver City. She was standing, but just barely, and was a bit wobbly. We say "she" because this bird was so large. Female great horned owls can be a third larger than males, which is also true of most other raptor species.[35]

This new acquisition worried us because she was displaying some very strange symptoms. Her head would slowly turn to one side, then jerk back to face forward, over and again, similar to symptoms of a concussion. She was slightly shaking, as if she had tremors. Her pupils were constricted even in low light but responsive. Concerned that we may lose her, we were about to take her to the vet and get a blood sample when she lifted her tail and shot out a bright green stream of feces. We recognized this right away and knew what to do. She had been poisoned, probably with strychnine, commonly found in rodent and nuisance bird poisons.[36,37]

The person that reported her said the owl was eating a pigeon when they found her, and she had a full crop when we got to her. Based on the symptoms, we ascertained that this pigeon had been poisoned, and inadvertently the owl had been poisoned. The ever-present pigeon problem in town was dealt with by someone who doesn't understand what happens once they kill the unwanted animal. Anything that eats the carcass will also be poisoned.

This very sick owl was given a charcoal solution, similar to the treatment used in humans, to help absorb and pull the damaging chemicals out of her body. We administered this with a stomach tube. This is a long flexible tube that fits onto the end of a syringe and is carefully placed in the bird's mouth, into the throat, through the crop and gizzard, and into the stomach. This process binds the toxins to the charcoal and is eliminated out of the body through feces and urine, occasionally forcing vomiting, which helps rid it from the body as well.[38]

This poor owl had so much food in its crop, and some of it recently ingested, that when we administered the charcoal solution she immediately threw up. We administered a bit more charcoal to pull the rest out and she was fine a day later. It was close, though. For a full day after the treatment she was shaking and turning her head and looking very forlorn. She suffered but survived and was released in a safer area away from town. We informed the public via newspaper articles in the area about the dangers of using poisons and how it can affect other animals that people may like and want around, like their pets or owls and other predators.

On another occasion, we had a report of an adult bobcat that had a spring trap on its foot, but the leghold trap had gotten loose from its anchor. Once the cat climbed up a tree, the chain got stuck and he couldn't get down. It was a sad situation as the animal had been stuck in the tree very close to someone's house for a few days before we got the call. This trapping was illegal because it was not trapping season, and the trap was not adequately anchored down and had no identification tag.[39] It was obviously someone without experience who put out a trap and did not know the consequences of not trapping the proper way.

Large adult bobcat with trap on foot trapped in tree.

When we arrived and inspected the situation, we were surprised to find the largest bobcat we had ever encountered. Snarling and spitting while Dennis used a catch stick on him, he removed the chain off the branch and hauled him down from the tree thrashing and slashing. He was like a little tornado. Dennis struggled to quickly get him into a carrier to prevent harming him and we swiftly shut the door. Dennis had to keep his protective gloves on while latching the door because the entire time he was trying to scratch and bite.

Spring trap removed from bobcat's leg.

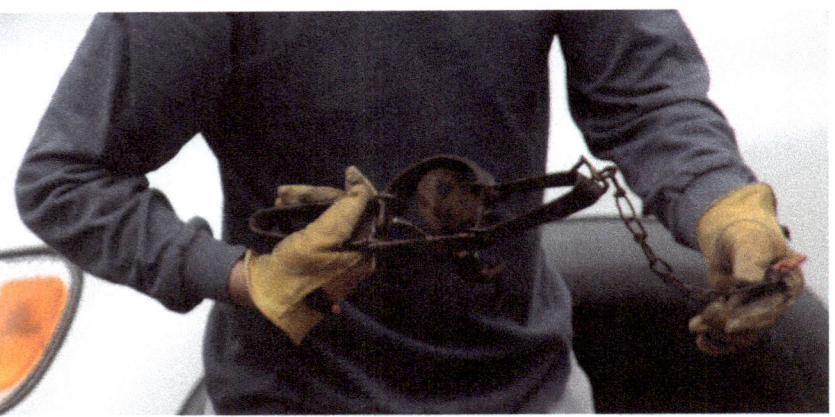

We transported him home, trap still attached, and called one of the game officers that helps us with wildlife to assist with removing the trap. Being careful to not use the tight noose on the catch stick for too long and cause brain injury or kill him, Dennis pulled him out of the carrier while the officer tried to get the trap off. Using gloves as well, the officer quickly grabbed the dangling end of the chain on the spring trap and pulled on it. He stretched the bobcat's back leg out and out of the way of slashing claws and teeth, then reached up and grabbed the spring trap, hastily opening it enough to get the trap off the cat's foot. Then it was Dennis's job to get the angry critter back into the carrier. The whole thing took less than five seconds. Denise was trying to take photos, but it was all over before she could take a decent shot.

The trap had not damaged the leg extensively, as they are designed to do. We looked closely and observed how he put weight on the paw and concluded that we could release him right away, which we did in a remote area shortly after. This was definitely an adrenaline producer for all of us!

Very angry bobcat ready to release.

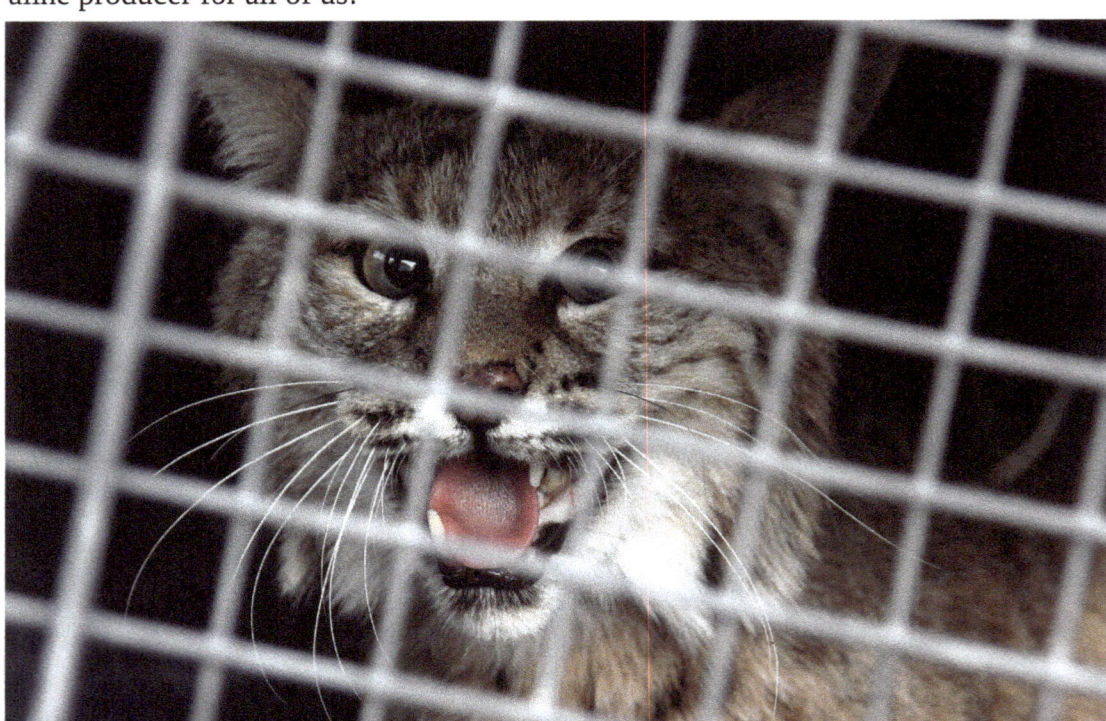

Wildlife as Pets

It is an extremely selfish act to keep a wild animal in captivity apart from zoos and breeding programs. The spirit of a wild animal is fed by its freedom. This spirit is necessary for survival. To take their freedom away is cruel and ruthless in our opinion. We see this in animals that must be with us long-term, how their spirit slowly starts to wane. As they recuperate and become healthier, their spirit slowly returns along with their "wildness."

We have treated fawns that when accidentally trapped in fenced areas, have continually hit the fence trying to get out. Confused and disoriented, they don't see the wire as a barrier. We have treated torn faces, damaged eyes, and concussions from being caged. The capture myopathy of this trapped animal is its worst enemy at this point, producing lethal levels of lactic acid and adrenaline coursing through their veins.

The ones that survive capture that are made into "pets" and get habituated to humans are placed in a dangerous surrounding full of unnatural hazards. A wild animal like a bobcat will treat a house just as if they were out in nature, including climbing, tearing, and chewing everything. Problems eventually arise with being bitten, clawed, or gored

Bobcat taken from mother for a pet.

by this "family pet" that still is a wild animal and turns on its "master." Hand-fed deer will commonly gore their provider. Diseases can be spread to the family dog or cat and eventually to owners. Treatment of this "pet" by a veterinarian is illegal in most states. State and sometimes federal laws are broken. Eventually, all this leads to the person either just releasing the animal, which leads to certain death now that they are habituated to humans, or to the animal being brought to a rehab center for rehabilitation. The process of getting an animal like this back to a wild state is extremely difficult, but with our methods of no contact and patience, most get there.

Bobcat given to GWR after it killed chickens, cats, and tore up the house.

We were contacted about a mule deer fawn one day by a woman who said she needed help raising it. Concerned she was trying to do this herself and may get in trouble, much less being worried about how the fawn was being raised, we immediately drove out to her remote house. She had all sorts of questions about how to get this large fawn out of her house and away from her yard. It turned out she had attempted to make a pet out of a fawn she had found, treating it like it was her dog and even had a bedroom set up for it to live inside the house. She contacted us only when she realized that this nearly adult-sized deer was a problem inside her home, and when she tried to get it out and keep it away, it kept returning.

Frustrated and exasperated, we explained how many mistakes she had made and even laws she had broken. She honestly had no idea that it was wrong both legally and morally. Once hearing the facts, she was a bit devastated and showed remorse. The deer was transported to a very remote location as far away from people as possible and released.

A bobcat kitten was confiscated by the Department of Game and Fish from someone who was trying to keep the animal as a pet. Just days after arrival at Gila Wildlife Rescue, he mysteriously died. We performed a necropsy (autopsy for animals) and discovered a small hair band for a child's hair lodged in her intestines and blocking it. The people were treating it like a domestic cat and letting it play with anything in the house, but like with any human baby, they also swallow things. We are always very careful about what is in a pen we are raising babies in because of this. Raising wild animals as if they are dogs and cats and inside a home is as criminal as placing a small child in

Hair band removed from intestine of bobcat kitten during necropsy.

a workshop with nails, screws, and power tools and way too many dangers. This case prompted a phone call from Dennis, and he let them know exactly what they did and whose fault it was that the animal died.

One of the best examples of this problem of keeping wild animals as pets are people who want to keep a skunk. Why? It just boggles our minds. Skunks are wild animals that bite, scratch, and spread disease. Not only that, but they have the worst smell. In New Mexico it is illegal to keep a skunk as a pet and for a veterinarian to treat it. Most people want to get a cute baby, raise it to be acclimated to humans, and get a vet to de-scent it. This is illegal, but it is not a New Mexico Department of Game and Fish statute—it is a New Mexico Department of Health statute,[40] which shows how much of a health risk these animals are. The reason for this is rabies, a disease that is 100 percent fatal once contracted, and the department's duty is to protect the public from any disease.

Skunks are well-known to have a high rate of rabies, causing some of the highest risk to humans of any animal.[41] Some animals can be carriers and not show signs of the disease but are continually spreading it. Skunks found in urban populations tend to have a higher rate, and populations of skunks in cities are unusually high due to humans providing them with pet food and garbage. We will not care for a skunk at Gila Wildlife Rescue because of this disease. Recently, the New Mexico Department of Game and Fish confirmed our concerns and have since made it illegal for rehabilitators in our state to care for skunks. This frustrates people at times, particularly when they find babies. All we can do is tell them that we cannot take them in and that it is illegal and dangerous for them to keep them. We advise releasing them in a wild area and letting nature take its course.

Spotted skunk

Some people just don't listen when we explain the dangers, which is a mistake that could be fatal. A woman contacted us one time about keeping a skunk as a pet and after hearing all this, she went ahead and tried to catch a baby. She ended up having to go to the hospital for burning eyes and vomiting, having been sprayed directly in the face. Dennis experienced this himself one time having discovered that a litter of babies had been born under the bedroom of his house. When the phone rang in the middle of the night, it startled everyone, including the babies. The smell came up through the floorboards and drove him out of the house.

One night he woke up vomiting. They had sprayed while he was sleeping, and he had breathed it in for a while. Being driven crazy by this for quite a while, he patiently waited for the babies to get old enough for the mother to take them out on her nightly forages. Once she did, he put a rock in the opening where they were getting under the house. The next morning the rock was moved, and he had no doubt the skunks were still there. After they left the next night, he put a large cinder block with the rock on top, and the next morning he saw that she had dug around it and was under the house again.

His next choice was to start trapping them alive and relocating them. Catching one baby at a time, he eventually got all five of them, by this time old enough to fend for themselves and be released. The mother, though, would never get in the trap. He tried everything, but she still insisted that this was her house, not his. In a fit of insanity one night, he waited by the opening for hours until she came out and shot her with a shotgun. The wildlife rehabilitator did what? The county jail was just up the street from his house and, of course, they came quickly to investigate, but when the sheriff's deputies arrived, they didn't cite him because once they heard the story, they were laughing so hard. Okay, so Dennis was in his early twenties and he was young and stupid.

We had a case called in where a woman was yelling, "There's a skunk in my kitchen!" As she was talking to me, she calmed down and decided it was cute. It was a spotted skunk, not a striped skunk. This rarely seen species is smaller and without the obvious white stripe, having a white spotted back instead. They have learned to advertise their potential danger by doing a handstand to clearly show the spots. The animal was doing this as we talked, and the woman thought it was adorable. Dennis gave her advice not to touch it, explained the dangers, and encouraged her to just open the outside door, to close all other doors to the kitchen, and just wait him out until he left. We got another call from her a few minutes later, this time asking what the skunk formula was that he had mentioned to her earlier. Yep, she didn't listen to him and tried to get closer.

Here is a video of a spotted skunk being released and doing his "handstand."

Video Link:

SpottedSkunkRelease

The "skunk formula," discovered by a biochemist,[42] is a mixture of some household products that can be used to eliminate skunk odor. Safe enough to even wash a pet with (or yourself), it works so well that if you still smell skunk, you just missed a spot with the formula. Mix one bottle of hydrogen peroxide, one-quarter cup of baking soda, and the magic ingredient—one teaspoon dish detergent. We just put it in a spray bottle and spray anywhere the odor is. This stuff works great. Doing all the crazy things we do, we keep the ingredients in the truck ready to go.

After decades of caring for wildlife, with many of the local residents and thousands of former students aware of our experience, we get calls almost daily just asking some wildlife or biology question. We remember one time even being called by someone in a trivia game, music blasting, wanting to know if we could confirm some fact for them and when we did, you could hear loud cheering from one side.

One day, we received yet another call asking about skunks as pets. The call came from a woman who had already caught a little baby skunk and was holding it and feeding it, basically treating it like her pet. We gave her the standard warning, including information about the illegality of veterinarians de-scenting them. She called us back the next day and a bit defiantly said, "You can, too, get them de-scented! I have an appointment tomorrow morning to get it done."

We explained that the vet was doing something illegal as well, but she didn't believe us. The next day she called again, a bit contrite, and told us that when she got to the veterinarian's office, they wanted eight hundred dollars up front. This is ten times more than what would be charged for a dog or cat at the time. She ended up releasing the baby, regretfully, after it had sprayed her several times. She also learned about the skunk formula!

Particularly sad to us is when someone tries to keep a hawk or other raptor as a pet. Luckily, most people know how illegal this is,[43] so it does not happen often. Not only is it cruel because it kills their spirit and eventually the bird, but it also takes one more important predator out of the ecosystem. It is obvious when a bird that comes to us has been cared for by someone that has experience with captive birds, because all their flight feathers are clipped to prevent escape. It can take up to a year for the feathers to be replaced through molting in order to release them.

It is a sad time we live in with respect to how wildlife is sometimes treated, as some of these examples show. Unfortunately, the animal is killed or suffers needlessly. The New Mexico Department of Game and Fish is tough on keeping not only wildlife as pets, but also on exotic animals being brought into the state as pets.[44] For example, no one is allowed to bring a tiger into New Mexico as a pet. No native wildlife can legally be kept as a pet except for small reptiles like snakes, turtles, and lizards.[45] Jackrabbits and cottontail rabbits have no protection either, but they are not commonly made into pets due to their dying of fright first. Most other mammals are considered either a big game animal or a fur-bearing animal that requires permits to hunt or trap and that makes it illegal to keep them as pets.[45]

We applaud and support the New Mexico laws that prevent keeping wildlife as pets and bringing in exotic animal pets like tigers into the state for pets. We were even instrumental in getting a law enacted to protect reptiles and amphibians from being caught and sold for profit, the last group of wildlife with no protection in the state. As described earlier, we see firsthand what captivity does to these highly spirited wild animals. No matter what good feelings the "pet" may generate in its "owner," the torture of the animal does not justify it at all. We encourage federal laws that would make the entire nation have wildlife laws like New Mexico. Wildlife should stay exactly that . . . wild!

Ecological Morality

We received a call one evening during our annual summer monsoon season about a great horned owl. It was tangled in a barbed wire fence in a housing development out in the country. The call happened to be from a physician at the local hospital and he said that when he went to work at six in the morning the owl was there and when he came back at five that evening it was still there, so he decided to call us. We were confused as to why the call was not made that morning, it seemed like it was an obvious emergency. Sure enough, when we got there and cut him out of the fence, he was almost dead.

He had been in the fence all night, all the next very hot morning and afternoon, and then through a torrential downpour a few hours before we were finally called. He had to be put down, because his injuries were so extensive, and he suffered for hours and hours before we got to him.

This leads us to a discussion about the impact that humans have on wildlife and what our responsibilities are as a part of this life here on earth. This bird would not have been injured if not for the barbed wire fence. This was an "accidental" death that was not malicious or purposeful, but still human caused. Thousands of birds and other wildlife get hurt this way every year.

Extending the period of suffering was unnecessary and directly contributed to the bird's eventual death. Sometimes malicious acts are due to ignorance, sometimes due to a lack of caring and compassion, and sometimes due to an attitude of superiority that humans are better than other life and that other life doesn't matter. Whatever the reason, in our opinion it is wrong.

Ignorance is certainly no excuse. That owl was obviously in trouble and needed help. No one can plead ignorance in a situation like this. This was more due to a lack of compassion and likely that superior attitude. Many people would be angry and shocked like we were with an incident like this owl. Others may think, "What's the big deal? It is just a bird." There would be no legal ramifications, but we feel the moral obligations to help another living thing and to stop its suffering are just as important as if this were a human patient.

Great horned owl caught in barbed wire fence.

Birds and other wildlife are highly protected and if a person kills a bald eagle for example, they have broken several laws including the Migratory Bird Treaty Act,[46] the Eagle Act,[47] and the Endangered Species Act.[48] They can pay tens of thousands of dollars in fines and may have to spend a year or so in prison. If someone kills a bird like a raven, there are still substantial fines because of its protection under the Migratory Bird Act, which protects all native birds in the United States. The only birds that are not protected in our area are nonnatives like English house sparrows, European starlings, Eurasian rock dove (common pigeon), and the Eurasian ring-necked turtle dove.[49]

Despite these strong laws, the protection is only at the level of killing the animal or having the animal or parts of it in your possession. There are no laws that say you must report an injured and trapped owl in a fence, but aren't there some moral obligations? It is illegal to pick up the molted feather of a native bird and keep it, but it is not illegal to let an obviously suffering animal remain unreported. Things are backward here. The law shouldn't even be the reason, a person's sense of right and wrong should be.

Moral obligations are also present on a larger scale, an ecological scale. Morality should be a concept applied to environmental and ecological issues as well. We have an imperative moral obligation to the other life on earth we live with and to the future of our planet. Humans are the only organisms on earth that have the ability to destroy this planet through nuclear weapons, mass warfare, environmental disasters, and slow destruction like global warming, pollution, and habitat destruction. If humans have the power to destroy the earth, it also makes us the only organisms on earth that can save it. Due to this obligation and this amazing power, we must have a moral obligation to the future of the earth.

We strongly encourage everyone not to be ecologically immoral. There is an obligation to all humans to be stewards of the earth. This includes offering help, protection, support, and care for wild animals whenever possible. To most people this is a natural response. To others, guidance and education may be needed to make them aware of how their actions affect not only wildlife, but eventually humans and themselves. Most humans feel that we are all in this together, this battle to keep from destroying the environment, but we also need to remember that the other living things here on earth are part of that team too.

As we conclude this chapter, we would again like to point out that a great majority of the people we deal with are caring, intelligent, and have common sense. We would also like to point out that the minority, most lacking these traits, can drive us crazy and frustrate us to no end. We have often said to each other, "The more we work with animals the more we dislike people!" We are joking, of course, but it's kind of like the apple that spoiled the barrel type of thing. We hope that the future brings all of us more ecological morality.

CHAPTER TEN

The Problem with Deer

One of the most heartwarming animals to save, and at the same time one of the most heartbreaking to care for, are deer fawns. They are so cute and innocent. But they are also animals that have a delicate digestive system that tends to not transition well between mother's milk and formula from a rehabber. In over forty years of doing this and hundreds of deer fawn cared for, we still don't feel totally comfortable with our formulas and medicines to treat this problem. We have had many fawns that did not make it. Each one lost was sad and painful.

You will once again notice that we discuss only caring for young animals. It is impossible to care for adult deer because the capture and treatment by well-meaning humans,

Mule deer doe after release.

including us, causes so much fright and stress that they do not survive. Adult wild deer often will hit the side of a cage repeatedly, trying to find a way out, until they have a concussion. The biochemical changes in their bodies because of the stress of being captured can also kill them as we have described earlier with fawns. Adult deer tend to get injured by big things like automobiles, guns, and rogue arrows. As a result, their injuries are either so severe that they do not survive long enough to even be transported or are so minor that they can be treated at the scene and released. There is usually no in-between, and if there were, they would likely die anyway due to stress.[50]

Mule deer fawn.

What makes fawns so difficult to raise is that we have four challenges to fight. We must find the proper milk formula, deal with the fright caused by capturing the fawn and keeping it captive, prevent imprinting, and the fourth is how to deal with the lack of parental bonding.

Concerning the formula, if they do not get the correct mixture, they develop one of a handful of infections that all cause the same symptom and can lead to death very quickly by scours.[51] As described earlier, the term scours is used for animal dysentery. Some forms of it are close to what we experience as humans and are not life-threatening.

Other forms, particularly those contracted by fawns, can cause such severe dehydration in a short period of time that the animal will die in less than twelve hours. Since this progresses so rapidly, we must always be vigilant. In addition, it may not be the formula causing the problem but something in the environment that is beyond our control, or the stress from being captured, which is another source of frustration as well.

We experienced this firsthand in a horrible series where we lost almost every fawn that came to us for about three years in a row. Not only were they having a problem with scours, but we also started noticing that they were having a problem suckling. Thinking

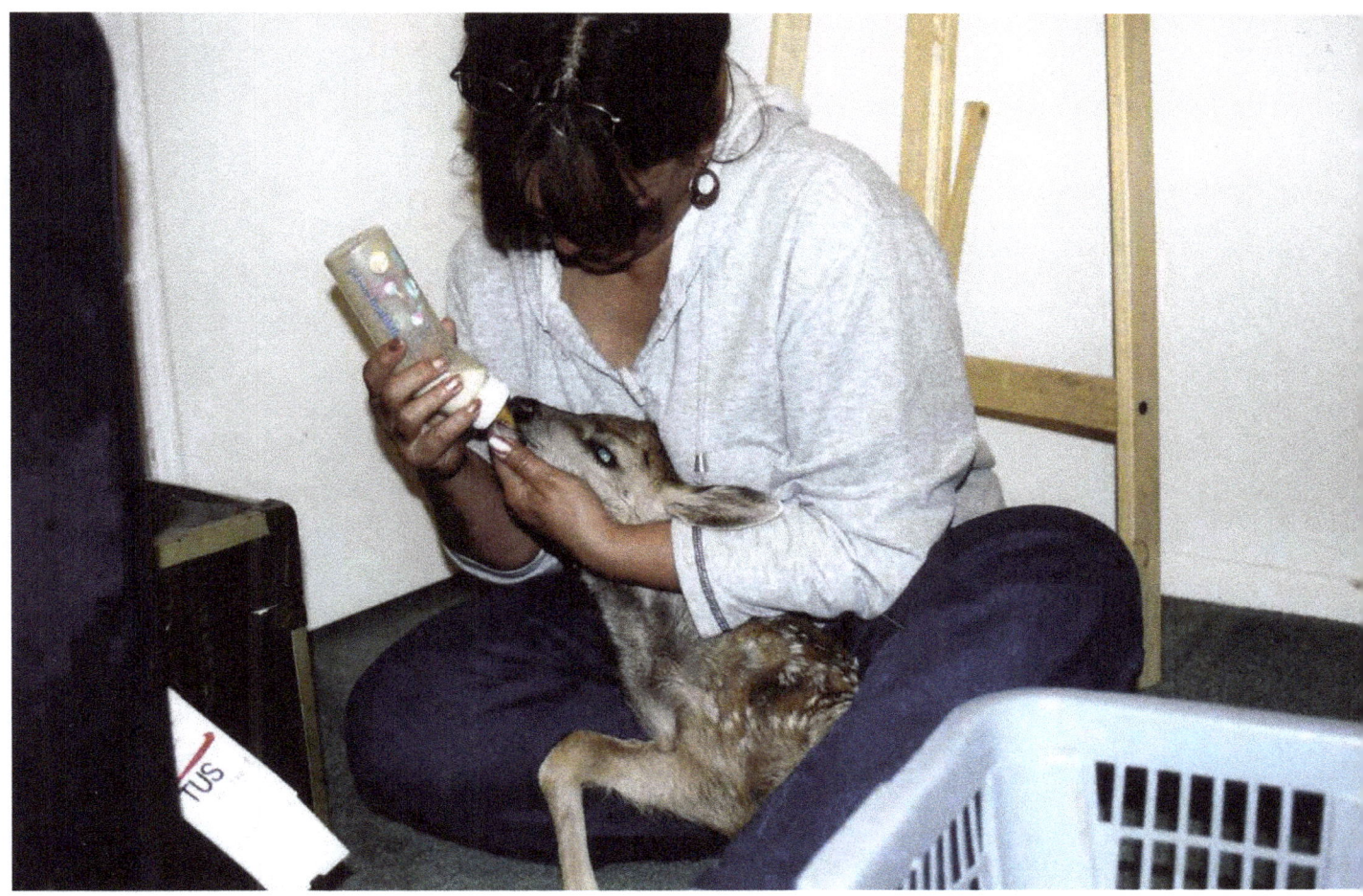

at first it was just weakness from the scours infection, we soon realized we had another serious problem to deal with.

Force-feeding a fawn that could not suckle due to lack of selenium in diet.

While examining a broken bone on a pronghorn, one of our volunteer veterinarians listened to our frustrations about the problem. He explained that ranchers for the last few years had been describing similar problems with calves not being able to suckle and they discovered that a mineral, selenium, was mysteriously missing from their diet. The vets and ranchers working on this problem theorized that there was a plant that had previously provided selenium and was no longer available or not as common. This made sense. It remained a mystery. Fortunately, the problem eventually resolved itself.

Challenge number two is that deer are normally very skittish and frightful creatures. They do not want to have any interaction with humans. We constantly scare them with our automobiles, guns, and noises. Humans are their enemy and shoot and kill them. To have a well-meaning human come up to it and touch it and pick it up is the ultimate fright. When animals like deer fawns get frightened like this, every muscle in their body tenses in preparation for a quick escape. This continues until the stress is removed, which could be hours or even days.

Mule deer fawn showing classic capture myopathy sign of curved back and swollen joints and muscles.

Adrenaline courses through their tiny bodies, and in just a few minutes they can have a chemical called lactic acid build up to fatal levels. This condition, called capture myopathy or lactic acid acidosis,[52] is also caused when an animal runs and is chased. Lactic acid is the substance that causes pain and fatigue in muscles when they are overworked to the point they run out of oxygen. Muscle cells can still function without oxygen by

Opposite page: Healthy mule deer fawn.

switching to another metabolic process called anaerobic respiration that does not require oxygen, but it causes a by-product of lactic acid. The burn that everyone feels when doing something like lifting weights, or bicycling, or using any muscles heavily is caused by lactic acid. Imagine this building up silently inside a poor newborn fawn and the pain and stress that it must cause, sometimes leading to death.

The initial treatment for a fawn is to reduce stress as much as possible by having minimal contact with them. Early on, from when they are captured to when they are finally feeding well and are free from scours, it is imperative that the animal is not talked to, and handling and touching be kept to a minimum. For example, quickly picking up a fawn and putting it in a box or pet carrier, then transporting it, is better than slowly walking up and picking it up and petting it and holding it in a person's lap to transport. Petting the fawn at this point may seem to calm it but in reality, it is not moving because muscles are tensed due to the invasion of human touch. The lactic acid builds up from these tensed muscles and eventually can reach toxic levels. And from our experience, once this has occurred, the animal will not survive. It may seem healthy and even start feeding well, but a few days later it is "mysteriously" dead. Capture myopathy is the culprit, but what was the cause? Humans with a soft spot in their hearts who think they are helping are in reality killing them.

The third challenge is imprinting. As described before, this is where an animal basically thinks you are its mom. You may recall the famous research by Konrad Lorenz where he showed that the very first living thing a goose or duck sees will be their imprinted parent, and it is so strong that it cannot easily be undone.[53] Once a fawn has survived the first few weeks of stress, and it gets accustomed to its new home and the food being provided, the fawn will latch on to whomever is the caregiver as if she or he were its mother. Luckily, this is quite easy to prevent, but what you must do to prevent it can be quite difficult. The nurturing drive in humans is tough to control, but it is imperative that there is always only a bare minimum of contact. Everything must be done to make sure they do not ever associate you with food. If food and attention are given, even once, the damage is done, and it is a long road ahead to undo this. If we have just one fawn at a time to raise, this becomes even more difficult. With a second fawn ,present, they will interact with each other instead of a human. Imprinting can be reversed, but it takes a long time. We have successfully "un-imprinted" quite a few deer, bobcats, and hawks using this method. After many months of no contact, no food associations, and a quiet outdoor pen to live in, they eventually become wild again and lose their imprinting. We sometimes purposely make noises to slightly scare them when we have to be around the cage they are in. We want them to fear us, not like us. It seems cruel but this is necessary for their success once released. To keep them safe, we must ensure that before being released they see humans like any other wild animal, as their enemy. Most humans would at least be fearful if a wild animal walked or flew up to them and wanted food or attention. Other humans would take advantage and poach or otherwise hurt the animal.

The last challenge when raising deer fawns is also quite a difficult task. This very delicate animal that totally depends on its mother for everything has a bond with its mother that is important in its development. Without this bond they can survive, but it certainly puts stress on them, which coupled with other factors is sometimes fatal. A mother's touch, caress, lick, or even look can be very soothing and is important in bonding with its mother and learning how to be a herd animal. But just like a human who has been raised in a closet or without much attention and love has terrible psychological damage, wild animals can too. We must be careful about not anthropomorphizing here, but wildlife has similar needs as humans to be close to a parent or a group and receive support, attention, and affection. We see this more commonly in deer, raccoons, and bobcats. Raptors do not seem to need bonding and are content to lead more solitary lives, possibly an instinct to reduce competition for food.

Mule deer fawn being kept wild.

Dealing with this challenge is tough, not only with deer fawns but with all orphans we have. Raising more than one together at a time is the best way because they usually use each other for that parental comfort, even though it is just a sibling. Keeping them wild but providing things for them to do to keep them occupied helps a great deal. We place logs and ropes and branches in bobcat kittens' cages, for example, to give them a jungle gym to play on. We provide live food throughout their "training to hunt" period to stimulate the wild hunting instincts that the parents would normally be teaching them. What we do not do is interact with them in any way to give them that affection and attention. It would immediately cause imprinting problems.

So you are beginning to see why we describe deer as one of the most challenging animals we care for. One of the tricks we have learned to improve fawn care and to keep deer from being imprinted has proven to be incredibly effective. Holding a bottle for the fawn to suckle clearly imprints you as caregiver and food provider. Instead, we place bottles in a rack outside the cage with only the nipple appearing in the cage.

Feeding rack on cage for orphaned mammals.

Once a bottle is placed in the rack, the rack holds it tight, and the fawn can feed without human contact and break their association with food. The bottle magically appears, and they get full and are satisfied. Some fawns smell the milk and find the bottle on their own, others must be shown it is there and be encouraged to drink. Soon, they are feeding voraciously and are much less stressed. This method has been astoundingly successful. It is something so simple, yet so effective. The first year we tried this method, when we walked into the cage to administer injections, they immediately ran from us like they were wild deer. We eventually observed that it was harder to catch them for release because they were much wilder acting and afraid of us, and when they were released, they shot out of the carrier like a bullet. It now is a major factor in keeping our deer wild and giving them a better chance of survival when released.

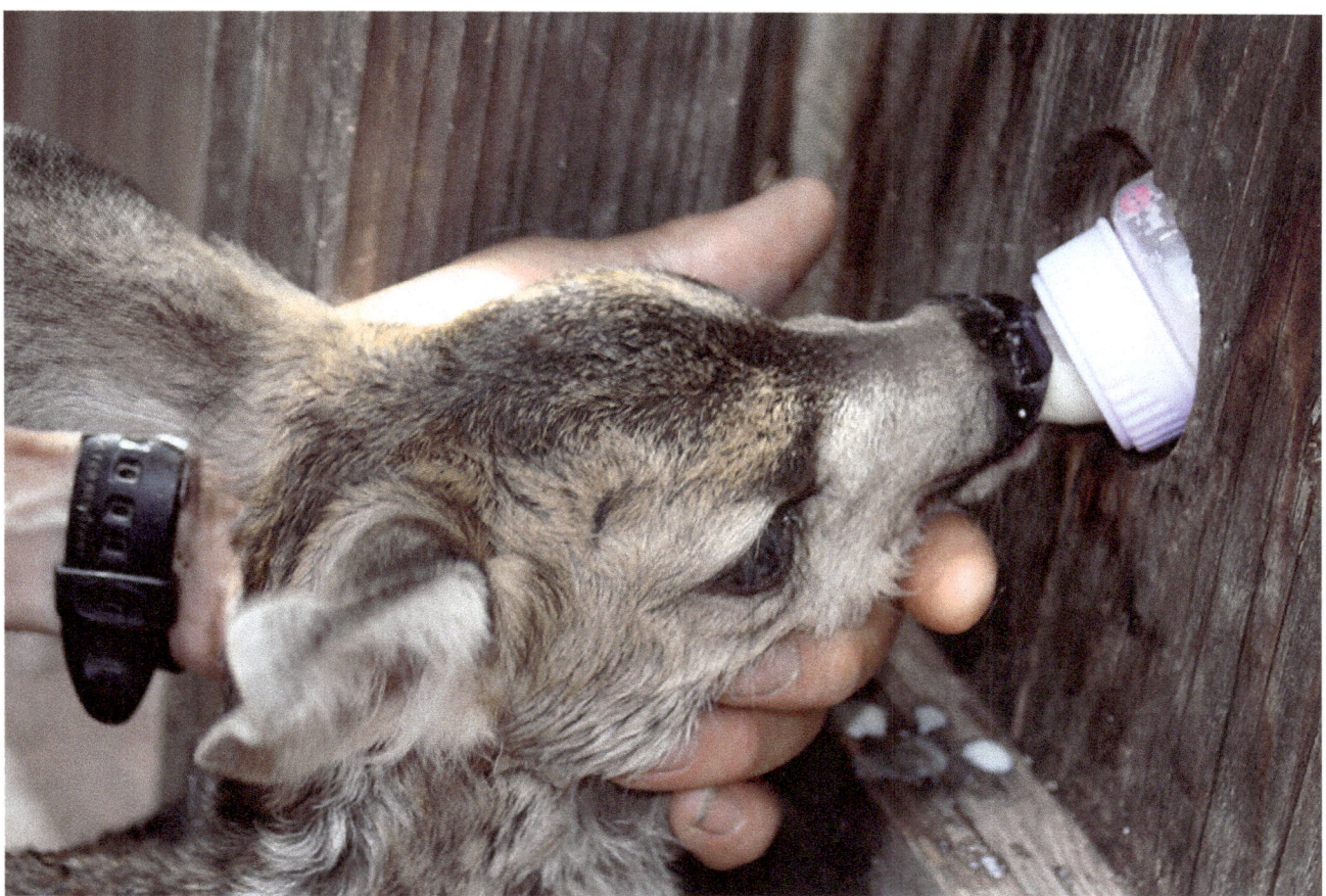

Some fawns need to be shown where the milk is.

"Rescuing" Deer Fawns

What is sad and frustrating about fawns is that most of the time the deer should not have been picked up in the first place. The fawn was fine, healthy, and being cared for by mom. On each of the calls we receive where someone has already picked up the fawn, we try to get the person to take the animal right back to where they found it, or to just leave it alone if they haven't picked it up yet. We explain the same thing over and over, each time hoping that the word will get out and people will stop this. Here is the basic problem. Deer *do not* abandon their healthy young.[54] If a person picks up what they think is an abandoned fawn, they are not only stealing it from its mother, but they are writing a death sentence for it in most cases. Meaning well, people also do this for a selfish personal reason of wanting to be the animal's savior. They often cause the fawn's death.

We get dozens and dozens of calls each year, starting in July and ending in September, during the fawning season. Most of them are from someone who has already made the serious mistake of picking up the fawn, a mistake that will more than likely kill the animal they were trying to "save." Capture myopathy, a condition caused by the fright of being caught, is commonly fatal and not easily treated, once taken hold. Some people call and have not picked the fawn up yet, just to double check. We encourage this because some circumstances are different than others.

Healthy mule deer fawn.

Fawns are born with a neutral smell to help keep predators from finding them. Their mothers have a strong smell as an adult, but after the birthing process, they have even stronger odors that attract predators.[55] She moves the fawn away from the birth area and leaves it somewhere safe. She then moves away, staying in the general area and occasionally coming back to feed it, but keeping her distance and keeping her scent from

endangering her newborn. The fawn has an instinct to lie down on the ground and stay still, so much so that often you nearly step on it before the fawn will move. Their coats are spotted at this stage to keep them successfully hidden.

Mule deer fawn in instinctive hiding position.

The mother will regularly move the fawn, but each time leaving it in a safe place and not staying right there with it. With this occurring in urban areas, safe places are sometimes difficult to find. Unfortunately, well-meaning humans who are ignorant of these facts and imagine themselves a hero, will pick up the fawn and have in reality stolen it from the mother.

We always try to return fawns to their mothers when possible. We have observed that they overcome myopathy problems quickly when back in mother's natural care. In our care, their chances are fifty-fifty depending on the degree of capture myopathy. To be honest, those that have been picked up, held, petted, and have scours from drinking the wrong milk have almost zero chance of survival by the time they are in our care.

We work with each one and help it try to fight for its life. We are spreading the word trying to educate the public and because of this, we are seeing signs of improvement.

To illustrate this further, one summer we had a busy fawning season with our monsoons coming on time and lots of feed available. The call came from a friend that had found a fawn at a park near the outskirts of town and edged by a creek. He had found the baby and knew enough to call first. We told him what he suspected, which was to just leave it alone, and that the mother would be back for it. He said that it was in the back of the park near the creek and not visible from the road. He left it there, but an hour later someone called us who had picked up the same deer and taken it home. So we went through the spiel about how they stole it from the mom and now they need to take it right back. They did, but three hours later we got another call. Another person had picked it up! They had it in their car but were still at the park.

Again, they were told to put it back and why. Late that afternoon, the last report came in. This time from someone who left it alone but called to make sure they were doing the right thing. Dennis assured them they were, but he could tell they were skeptical. They lived nearby and could watch from their house, and similar to what has happened many times with those who don't accept our advice at first, they eventually called us back, very excited, telling us about how the mom came back and took the fawn up the creek. That poor fawn was so stressed from all this; the only chance it had was with its mother.

We have regularly submitted articles in our local newspapers and have posted the same information on our Gila Wildlife Rescue page on Facebook in hopes that people read and learn. On Facebook alone, fourteen thousand people have been reached in the post about deer fawns and have responded in a positive way. The best thing to do is to err on the side of caution, which in this case is to let nature take its course and leave the fawns alone.

Feeding Deer

This chapter on deer cannot be complete without a discussion about feeding them. The information here can be applied to any wild animal that is fed by humans. It is always wrong to feed wildlife with the exception of songbirds being fed, which does no ecological harm and helps those populations in a healthy way as long as their spillage is kept away from other animals. Feeding wildlife habituates animals to depend on humans for food. Wildlife should be out in nature, interacting in their own food chains and ecosystems, not being totally provided for artificially by humans. Feeding deer can make them malnourished and can kill them, which is a surprise to many people when they first hear this.

It turns out that deer have been interacting in the ecosystem for so long that their digestive enzymes change a few times throughout the year as seasons change and the plants they eat are replaced by others. One enzyme may be needed for digesting fresh green grass that appears abundantly in the spring and summer, but another enzyme is needed for digesting mountain mahogany, a staple for deer in our area during the winter when grass and other foods are not available. A deer's body is genetically programmed to change the digestive enzymes it produces, timed perfectly with the change in seasons and the natural changes in the plants that are available for it to forage on.[56]

So think of a person who is feeding deer. Most people don't know these dietary facts. The alfalfa that they are feeding can be digested during one time of the year, but at other times they cannot get much nutrition from it because they don't produce the enzyme that will digest it. Deer are not very intelligent, so they eat what is provided for them. When there is nice lawn grass or garden vegetables available to eat that are easy pickings and in an area that (at least at first) is without many predators, wildlife will come to it, even if it means compromising their innate fear of humans.

Nature provides them with food, but the food changes seasonally. Nature doesn't fail them, but a human can by providing food that their digestive enzymes can't break down. We commonly see deer in our area that are emaciated and look like they are starving, yet they come to a feeder daily and eat their fill. Consequently, they can lead a shortened malnourished life as a result.

Feeding wildlife is dangerous to humans too. Feeding them attracts them to urban areas where people live, and they become a serious danger for traffic. How many times have you had to slam on your brakes in your community inside the city limits because a deer has jumped in front of your car? This problem is more common around the country than most people know.[57] It is certainly a problem in this part of New Mexico. We have had serious damage to our vehicles by hitting deer and now have brush guards on them to also act as "deer guards."

Massive damage to our own vehicle occurred one time after it collided with a very large buck. Along the highway where he was hit, a man had been feeding deer for years. The area was well-known for having deer and car collisions, partly because of deer crossing the highway to get to this man's handouts. After Denise hit the deer, Dennis went with one of our local wildlife officers to talk to the gentleman. Dennis warned him that if he did not stop feeding that he would file charges against him, and the Department of Game and Fish would back him because he has caused such a problem for a long period of time. The man was belligerent at first, but once he

Damage to our vehicle from hitting very large buck.

understood the danger he was putting his precious deer in, he stopped feeding them. That area is now much safer for everyone.

Hitting a deer with a vehicle is obviously dangerous. Often, the deer gets thrown onto your windshield and can end up in your lap along with your windshield. Collisions and near misses with wildlife are common. They are not the animal's fault, but it gets the blame. "Damn deer ran right in front of me and caused five thousand dollars worth of damage!" We hear this often. Whose fault it is, particularly with collisions in urban areas, is usually some "animal lover" who is feeding deer. Come on! Don't love them to death. People should start looking at the facts and using common sense, instead of feeding their own desires and egos. Don't be ecologically immoral!

It turns out that New Mexico, like many other states, does not have a law that makes it illegal to feed wildlife, even though most people agree it needs to be in place. We have laws preventing "baiting" wildlife to hunt them, but the only other law in the Department of Game and Fish statutes to prevent feeding is totally ineffectual. There is a law that says it is illegal for a person to "cause a nuisance" with wildlife.[58] If a neighbor is feeding deer and the deer are getting into your yard and causing problems, then the neighbor has caused a nuisance by feeding. But it is *not* illegal to feed them.

In one case where a person was charged with causing a nuisance and Dennis was lined up to be an expert witness, the judge threw the case out of court, saying that the New Mexico Department of Game and Fish did not have the right to tell people they cannot feed wildlife. The statute had clearly been broken, but that is the mentality we are dealing with. It is frustrating to have not only some of the public being ecologically immoral, but an elected official not enforcing a law due to his personal bias? By the way, the first judge that was to hear the case had to excuse himself because he was well-known in the community for feeding deer!

We hate to bring this one up, but that danger can be directed to humans, too, and can lead to tragedy. We have had incidents all over the country, including many here, where humans have been injured by wildlife, usually the fault of the human. Vehicle accidents are very common with either deer jumping out in front and colliding with the vehicle or swerving to miss deer and colliding with other vehicles, causing 1.9 million accidents nationwide annually.[59] Deer that have been tamed to the point of being hand-fed have also turned on their providers and gored them once antlers have formed and reproductive hormones start flowing.

We have had numerous calls, and the numbers are increasing, about mountain lions being spotted in neighborhoods in this area. Where there is prey, predators will always follow. What makes it worse is that all this interaction with wildlife has slowly made these predators more accustomed to humans and to being around them. They start to lose their fear of humans, a fear that is mandatory for their survival, and for humans' safety. If a deer loses its fear, few people are concerned and many like it. Now they can be petted and fed and be treated like pets. If a mountain lion becomes more accustomed to humans, like this deer has, the public now is very concerned. The lions walk right into towns and neighborhoods and predate right in front of everyone, and many times find other much easier prey to catch such as dogs, cats, and yes, humans.

In order for lions to come into town and predate on deer they follow into urban areas, they must also lose some of their fear of humans. A couple of years ago a man was killed and partially eaten in the village of Pinos Altos, New Mexico, just nine miles north of Silver City, and in an area with many people living nearby.[60] Some of the people living there were feeding deer, and one in particular was feeding very heavily. This practice acclimates deer to that area and being around humans. When a mountain lion shows up and observes that these deer have no fear of humans, it is influenced to not be afraid either. This usually is a gradual process that can slowly acclimate wildlife to be less afraid. In this case, the lion was in town hunting and was acclimated enough to take a human as prey, something its instinct would never have allowed it to do previously.

What made everyone even more angry was that it was discovered that one of the residents in PA, as we call it, was actually feeding this lion, baiting it in with meat to get photos of it. Once again, who was at fault here, the lion or the people who are feeding wildlife? Someone was getting the lion used to humans and losing their natural fear. Then it killed an innocent, gentle, kind man who was mentally challenged. Dennis reported the photos posted online to the New Mexico Department of Game and Fish officer investigating the incident when he heard this on social media. They investigated, got a warrant to search, but all they found were wiped-clean hard drives on the photographer's computer, so there were no consequences for this man. By the way, it is believed the offending lion was killed, but not before two other lions, a bear, some javelina, and somebody's dog also were killed in traps meant for this lion.

Mule deer at age ready for release.

Remember that a great deal of feeding wildlife is indirect feeding, not direct. Although some people put out food for wildlife on purpose, most feeding is accidental. It occurs with the spillage of bird feeders, feed put out for pets and livestock, growing plants that attract wildlife, and a multitude of other ways. The most common method in most areas are bird feeders and dog and cat food. Pet foods usually attract a whole group of nuisance animals that will be a problem. We work hard for many months to keep these young deer wild, and the results show when we have to capture them for release. It can get very challenging to capture one that is ready to be free. Releases are usually quick, the animal sensing freedom and running off from us right away. More times than not, they will stop and look back at us, then continue on their way. We are not sure why it occurs, but a majority of the time when we release not only deer, but raptors and even mountain lions, they will run off and then stop and look at us or fly away from us and then quickly circle around and fly directly over again. We like to think they are saying thank you.

As cute and as beautiful as most people consider deer, they are at times a serious problem for humans, and they are having all sorts of problems themselves.

And so the problem with deer in reality is . . . ***people***!

Mule deer after release, saying, "Thank you."

CHAPTER ELEVEN

Frustrations and Heartaches

White-faced ibis hit by golf ball.

As one can imagine, wildlife rehabilitation can have its share of frustrations. Some of these are easier to deal with because they are related to our direct care and interaction with animals. The frustrations in getting deer past the weaning stage without having diarrhea complications or the frustrations with dealing with an un-releasable animal are commonplace in our venture so we are accustomed to it. The one area that bothers us the most, though, is where human actions have caused wildlife to suffer and be harmed. Humans should have a strong obligation to care for other living things around us, not destroy them, torture them, or harm them in any way unnecessarily. As long as the animal is used for food, we even support hunting, which Dennis did quite a bit of when he was younger.

Certainly, there are animals that need to be controlled, such as flies, mosquitoes, cockroaches, rats, mice, skunks, etc. Most wildlife does not cause a nuisance or spread disease to the extent these do. Wild animals not only need to be saved and cared for out of our sense of morality, but out of common sense in the realization that we are all connected. The success of ecosystems where many different living things interact is paramount for any life on earth to survive.

Species protection in general is a misunderstood subject but directly connected to this concept. Often, negative views occur when it is not clear why a small fish or plant is protected, especially when it sometimes halts human activities. The Endangered Species Act's primary goal is not to just keep the rest of life on earth from disappearing and causing a major environmental catastrophe, but to prevent the ultimate extinction of humans. The bigger picture, considering food chains and ecosystem balance, is what must be appreciated clearly. What place did that fish or plant occupy in the food chain? In the long run, what would occur if this species was extinct and how would that affect the other members of the ecosystem it is interacting with? It took humans a while to realize that if we destroy other life on earth, it will lead to our own destruction. Most of the public is not clearly aware of the Endangered Species Act's goal and justification for protection.

There are many examples of humans accidentally, unknowingly, or purposefully harming animals, and some are described later in this chapter, but the big one, the widespread issue that is causing major problems in many areas of our country, is the taming of wildlife. The better wording is the "attempt" to tame wildlife, because the wildness is innate and cannot be completely removed. When wildlife becomes accustomed to humans, it will always cause harm to the animal and eventual problems for people. There is no way around this.

The most important concept when we are caring for wildlife is to keep them just that, wild. In fact, we struggled to decide on a title for this book, but when we thought about what our primary objective is, we decided on *Keeping Them Wild*. We don't know how to impress how important this is or how paramount of a goal this is at any time when we are dealing with wild animals. The only way to successfully care for wildlife, to get them to the point they can be released and be successful once back in the wild, is to keep them wild. If we tamed these animals in any way, it would jeopardize their success once released. Once people understand our ultimate goal, they can clearly see why we do not allow visitors and why we would never keep an un-releasable animal.

This concept of keeping wildlife wild and not taming them is important for the public as much as it is for those who rehabilitate. Yet many out there are doing the exact opposite, they are trying to tame them. The worst thing for the animal is to become accustomed to being around humans and to trust them. Just as most of these animals all look alike to us, we all look alike to them. If someone is nice to them, gives them food and attention, then they assume all humans will do this and that our cars are safe to be around, and our fences, and our guns.

The "taming" of wildlife, trying to get animals to be accustomed to humans, is a serious problem nationwide. People are finding out the hard way that they can create many more problems by attempting this. Some are not even aware that their actions are causing wildlife to become less afraid of humans. This is often done through ignorance and not maliciously. Putting bird food out but not fencing the deer out that eat the spillage, or not fencing a garden that invites deer to feed are common examples of this. These frequent visits slowly get them acclimated to being around us.

Humans' own reactions to these wild animal encounters can put the animals in peril. Talking to them or trying to get closer to pet them or to feed them by hand is a common goal of some people. This just familiarizes animals even more to humans. We are always amazed at how most people treat wild animals. They either treat them like they treat their pets, or like they are humans. Anthropomorphizing, or falsely identifying human behaviors in animals, is so easy to do, and unfortunately leads to terrible mistakes in dealing with wildlife. The following are some examples of some of those mistakes.

A woman called us about a baby hawk she found in her backyard. Even though we told her we would be there in ten minutes and not to feed it, she stuffed at least a tablespoon of birdseed down its mouth. The bird was almost choking when we arrived. As most of you know, hawks, even as babies, eat mice, other rodents, lizards, and snakes . . . not birdseed! The woman told us that it was crying for food and was starving and had to give it something. It was probably crying in alarm. Luckily, the baby hawk survived.

A family who lived near Fort Bayard, a historic hospital near Silver City and a game preserve, picked up a newborn white-tailed deer fawn and called us three days later when it became a burden. This historic old hospital has a large, well-known herd of white-tailed deer living there. Walking into their house, we found the fawn on their laps being petted and fed milk for humans out of a bottle. They had assumed the mother had abandoned it and thought they were "saving" it. When Dennis explained that they had stolen it from its mother, and only if the mother is dead do we ever pick one up, they felt terrible. The fawn was returned to its mother five minutes later because she was still hanging around looking for her baby. When asked why they were treating it in this manner, they said they thought that it liked being petted and that it *had* to have companionship and touching with some living thing (any living thing?) and that it was crying because it was hungry when they first found it. It was more likely to have been crying for its mother because it was scared that these people were walking up to it and were stealing it. Luckily, the fawn survived but most of the time being treated and "loved" like this is fatal to these poor unsuspecting animals.

These examples show the mistakes people make who are ignorant of the best way to deal with wildlife, but sometimes a little knowledge can be dangerous as well. We received a call on the day after Christmas a few years back from a man in the Mimbres Valley east of Silver City who had found an injured golden eagle. We were immediately concerned because he said he had hydrated it. Birds go into shock when they are injured or stressed by being captured by well-meaning humans. The shock can cause severe dehydration that if not treated, can kill them within days. But the opening to the lungs is in the very front of the mouth of the bird, just in front of the tongue. If you were to squirt water into a bird's mouth with an eyedropper or pour it in, they will immediately aspirate (breathe) that fluid into their lungs and die. Water should never ever be administered in this manner. We use a stomach tube to provide the large amount of water needed.

 The man who called about this eagle was aware of this fact, and so our initial concerns were alleviated some by him telling us he had a stomach tube and hydrated it in that manner. He said he knew how to do this by volunteering in a clinic in California. As we mentioned, sometimes a little knowledge is dangerous. When Dennis met up with this man, the bird was in a box. Not wanting to disturb it too much, Dennis just transported the box to our clinic before examining him. When he carried the box to his truck, a bit of water leaked out of the corner, which was curious, but thought it was a dish of water that was spilling. As soon as Dennis arrived home, he opened the box and could tell this bird was in trouble. He was hanging his head down, had labored breathing, and was what he thought was salivating. When he lifted the eagle out of the box and laid him on his back to examine him, about a quarter cup of water came out of his mouth and he took two big breaths, then proceeded to die right before our eyes. And there was nothing we could do for him.

Dennis was livid! This man knew that the bird needed to be stomach tubed to be hydrated but did not have any concept of how much to give him. He filled up his stomach and it all backed up into his lungs anyway. Dennis tried draining the excess water out of his lungs by hanging him upside down, but it was too late, the bird had stopped breathing. Dennis does not do this very often, but he called up this guy and gave him a piece of his mind.

Once again, he should have left the bird alone and waited for the people with experience to treat it. His justification was that he found it on Christmas Day and did not want to disturb us. Little did he know, we have been on constant call twenty-four hours a day, seven days a week, for more than forty years. Animals don't care about holidays or your schedule. We are very used to being interrupted and having to rush off to get another animal. If only he hadn't taken things into his own hands and without proper knowledge. Once again, what was his real motivation? Looking good in front of friends? Wanting to be the savior? A true savior would have thought more about the animal than their own ego or image and would have thought about not having enough experience to do this properly. Now you can see why we get so frustrated sometimes with some humans' lack of intelligence.

We actually see this a great deal, where people do downright senseless things, many times against our direct and implicit instructions. A majority of the public is wonderful—a few are not.

We think the reason some people do things like this is total selfishness, but in the name of "saving the animal." In reality, *they* want to be the person who does the capture, treatment, feeding, etc. because it gives them a sense of fulfillment that they helped this poor helpless creature. Believe us when we say, we know this feeling. If a person really wants to be the savior of the animal, they would do exactly what we told them, not the opposite, realizing we are experts with years of experience. If the person truly cares about the animal, their motivation should be purely what is best for the animal.

Denise observing fawn during intake for signs of myopathy.

One summer, someone who had found a baby deer called us and was told to leave it alone and not pick it up because they would be stealing it from the mother. We then found out that this person did pick it up and was carrying the fawn around downtown like a baby doll and showing everyone. They also told people that they were caring for it for Gila Wildlife Rescue! When we heard this, we immediately confiscated the animal. The animal died a painful, horrible death due to capture myopathy.

As you can imagine, most of these examples did a great deal of harm in the long run and the person who was trying to "rescue" the animal has now had a horrible experience because of their direct actions. They caused the death of the very animal they were trying to save. We hope that this book, the many newspaper articles, our website, and the talks we give will help to educate the public on their correct role in dealing with wildlife. Again, we don't want anyone to act in an ecologically immoral manner.

Referring to an earlier statement though, about the change in the makeup of the people in the Silver City area, and hopefully nationwide, we are finding the ignorance

Javelina

described above as the exception to the norm and becoming less common. We see an increasing number of people who are very conscientious and aware of environmental issues and have changed their lives accordingly. We applaud them and do not mean to insult anyone by giving the impression that everyone is as ignorant as some in these horror stories. Keep up the good work and let's all keep learning and improving to play our part in this web of life so that we interact in it, not fight it or do battle with it.

As you can see by just a few examples, sometimes humans who mean well can do more harm than good. They are interacting with that wild animal as if it were a human or one of their pets. We have had many cases in our area where someone who thought a wild animal was "tame" ended up getting severely bitten or scratched due to this.

It is amazing how some animals will, through time and repeated exposure to talking, lose some of their fear of humans. Be careful though, they are still wild animals and are always unpredictable. Losing this natural fear of humans is often a death sentence to them, causing them to behave in ways that will either get themselves killed or cause problems for humans and become a nuisance. Not all humans will be nice to them for example, and a deer that can be walked up to and petted or fed can also easily be poached or be mistreated. Losing their fear and coming into populated areas, causing traffic hazards and problems for people's yards, makes it dangerous for them and us.

We have a healthy population of javelina in our area. They are commonly fed by some folks and accidentally fed by others, as javelina and other wildlife will come in to clean up the bird feeder's spillage or to eat the unprotected garbage or pet food. As people are working in their yards or watching and photographing them, the animals get a bit more accustomed to humans with each encounter. They may give people the impression that they are somewhat "tame" but there is another factor involved that most people are ignorant about.

Javelinas have terrible eyesight.[61] With small eyes on the sides of their heads, they depend much more on their sense of smell and hearing. If someone who thought they were "tame" wasn't aware of this, they may get a big surprise. As a person walks up closer to watch or photograph them, the animals seem to not notice or even care the humans are there. In reality, the javelina actually have no idea the people are there or at least that they are that close, especially if the wind is blowing the scent away from them. Once the person is within about ten or fifteen feet, the distance that their small beady eyes now can focus and see things, they are now highly threatened. You are too close to them now and their typical reaction is to turn and fight, or if they have young ones and babies that need defending, they will defend as viciously as a mother bear will protect her cubs. The slashing tusks of these animals that self-sharpen each time they open and close their mouths can cause serious damage. Once more, it is a grave mistake to think that any wild animal is tame.

Javelina with young—very protective and dangerous at this time.

One of the saddest and most frustrating things ever to happen at Gila Wildlife Rescue with javelina was when Dennis was teaching high school biology. An animal control officer brought him a baby javelina that had been taken away from someone who was trying to raise it as a pet. This animal was severely imprinted and would cry if he were not right next to you. What was so sad and upsetting is that the "owner" of the little baby had some experience with raising pigs and decided to crush its tusks with pliers to prevent them from growing and becoming dangerous. Dennis was shocked! He wanted to use the "an eye for an eye" rule on this guy!

The situation ended up a bit better because the New Mexico Department of Game and Fish found that the Carlsbad, New Mexico, Living Desert Zoo was in need of a javelina for their display, so we were asked to keep him "tame." Needing to feed him every couple of hours, Dennis took him to school with him. The javelina was imprinted so much that he did not want to lose contact with him, so all Dennis had to do was to set him on the ground when he got out of his truck at school, then walk to his classroom. The entire time, the little one was walking right behind him, constantly softly bumping into his heels to make sure he did not lose him. The first time he walked through the halls like this you should have seen the double takes of the students. After that, there was a pack of students following so they could help feed him. We kept him until he was weaned and then transported him to the Living Desert Zoo.

One spring, a red-tailed hawk case made us so angry that we wanted to have someone arrested but couldn't get enough evidence to prove it. The call came in from a gentleman who had a baby red-tailed hawk he needed us to care for. Upon arrival at his house, he explained that he knew this ball of fluff he handed to us was a red-tailed hawk because he saw the kids across the valley from him shoot the mother. We were flabbergasted! To us, an action like that was an egregious act that needed accountability.

We took the bird and called the Department of Game and Fish. An officer went out and interviewed the gentleman and then went across the valley and talked to the kids. They swore they did not do it and there was no evidence for conviction. At least they

Red-tailed hawk nestlings—mother shot by kids.

volunteered to give him something. As he was leaving, one of the kids said that they did have a baby hawk that needed to be cared for, did he want that? The officer was shocked, but just took the hawk, likely the littermate of the one we received the day before. We felt a fine was in order, or the parents be held responsible—or something at least—but it shows how difficult it is to enforce some of these laws. It is illegal to shoot and kill a hawk. It is illegal to keep a hawk or a nestling in captivity. Finding enough evidence to convict is an entirely different story.

Red-tailed hawk shot in eye with BB gun.

This reminds us of another case where kids did an incredibly cruel thing that frustrated us. Only a few years into the program, a red-tailed hawk was brought in, a large mature female with beautiful plumage, truly a gorgeous bird. It was sad and a bit disturbing to see the injury it had. One eye was swollen and infected with puss draining from it.

The other eye looked good and was moving and reacting to motions, so we thought it was still functional. The wildlife officer that brought him to us related how this bird had been shot by a kid with a BB gun. It is frustrating, because here is another kid who was allowed to use a deadly weapon, without proper training and age limitations. This kid said that the bird was flying by, and he shot at him and thought he missed, but then saw him drop down. A few days later, the bird was found in the area with this injury.

We called our veterinarian contact in Española and consulted with her. She had us transport the hawk up to her, a six-hour drive. Upon arriving, we decided to attempt surgery to remove the bad eye and let him try to survive with one eye. There have been cases where large raptors like this have survived with one eye, adjusting to the lack of depth perception that two-eyed binocular vision provides.[62] This case ended sadly and made us even angrier at the situation. Once we removed the bad eye, the BB could be seen through the thin wall of the skull that separates the two eyes . . . and it had penetrated the back of the other eye. We had thought that one was functional, but he was blind in that eye too. The bird had to be euthanized. If we could only have had that kid that shot him look this hawk directly in the eye before the injury and see how noble and impressive these hawks are, maybe the bird could have been saved from this flagrant violation of his right to fly free. Why would someone want to shoot and kill something so majestic and beautiful? It boggles our minds.

Heartaches

People tend to look at what we do in two ways: They either admire us and want to do this themselves, or they think we are crazy for volunteering this much time and effort, and even crazier for actually handling these dangerous creatures. Although this may seem very cool, there are downsides to wildlife rehabilitation too. The elation we feel when releasing an animal is sometimes balanced by those that we lose. The heartaches are obviously those animals we cared for that did not survive. At times, this is a heartache that is felt deeper because we have worked countless hours and worried and stressed, but the animal still dies. We get used to animals in our care dying at times, although it is always difficult. When it is due to another human's selfish and uncaring act though, we are more deeply affected.

The New Mexico Department of Game and Fish, whom we work with almost on a weekly basis, has been amazing. Every officer we have known has been tremendously supportive and helpful to the program. They help with transporting injured wildlife when they can and have helped at our facilities in situations where we needed someone with wildlife experience and experience with dangerous animals like mountain lions, bears, and bobcats.

A good example of this was when the department was an immense help in delivering twin fawns. Due to the severe problem of people feeding deer in this area, deer were crossing the roads all over town and were involved in collisions with vehicles quite commonly. Occasionally around here, usually after a couple of wet years in a row, deer commonly double fawn due to the excess food available. During one of these high population periods, we had observed quite a few twin newborns.

The call came in from a neighbor who lives up the road from us, a great animal lover, but lives on a highway where quite a few deer get hit in front of her house. Unfortunately, she has had to deal with some of these injured animals and has our number on speed dial. The call we got that day was no different.

"Dennis," she said, "I hate to bother you again, but another deer just got hit and it is still alive. She probably needs put down, but it looks like the one we have been seeing around here that is very pregnant."

Dennis rushed over to her house and as soon as he arrrived, an officer from the New Mexico Department of Game and Fish happened to be driving by. Dennis flagged him down to help and he did not hesitate. Sure enough, the doe was very pregnant and going into labor. She was breathing but was not conscious and had an obvious head injury. The rest of her body was without any signs of major trauma.

Looking at the officer Dennis said, "Have you ever done an emergency cesarean section before in the field, or along the side of a busy highway?" He knew his question was crazy because neither of them had ever done this before. He said, "Let's get her up into the back of your pickup and I will get my sharp hunting knife, unless you have a scalpel in your back pocket!"

They got the truck backed up where they could lift her in, then with quite a bit of effort because she was a big mature doe and pregnant as well, they got her into the truck bed and quickly went to work. Swiftly making his incisions, careful not to cut too deep with this large hunting knife, Dennis reached inside bare-handed and felt around for the fetus. He found it and lifted the fawn out. It was not breathing. He wiped its nose, clearing it the best he could and blew gently into the nostrils. The fawn jerked back and sucked in a breath, but Dennis could hear that it was a very wet breath. He then grabbed him by the neck, with his body along his forearm and with his head down and his tail pointing to Dennis's shoulder and swung him and spun him quickly to get the mucous out. Once his airway seemed clearer, he blew in his nostril once more and the baby started breathing, sucking in raggedly at first, then a bit better.

Dennis turned around to where the mother's now dead body lay and reached for the umbilical cord to cut it. He immediately realized that also connected to that cord was another cord, connected to another fawn! Dennis and the officer scrambled to get the other fawn out and breathing. Meanwhile, the first fawn stopped breathing, and the officer tickled the inside of the fawn's nose with a stem of grass and got him to start breathing again. Dennis carefully removed the second fawn from the doe's open abdomen and underwent the same procedure but this time to no avail. This fawn was unresponsive, and the first fawn had stopped breathing completely by now. Both of them started CPR, trying to fill up lungs as best they could, but were having difficulty making connections between their lips and the fawns' tiny noses. They tried for a few minutes but eventually had to give up. They had lost both of them. It was too much to expect that an emergency cesarean on a wild deer that just got killed by a car was going to be successful every time! He was hoping his first one, and so far his last one, would end better. Sorry, no photos of this case.

The only adult mountain lion we ever cared for ended up being a tough case for us to handle, and certainly belongs in the chapter on heartaches. Dennis was interrupted in the middle of teaching an invertebrate zoology lab with a wildlife call from a concerned citizen that he had to deal with immediately. Luckily, his graduate assistant was ready to cover his class for him and he could jump right out to deal with the situation. The call was from a man who had been driving behind another car that hit an adult mountain lion in the Mimbres Valley. The man was distraught and extremely excited, but mostly angry that the person driving the car had hit the lion without even trying to swerve. He said the car never braked, and he thought it might have even accelerated a bit just before the impact. The mountain lion had not run far, and limping a great deal, it had crawled up under a tree a hundred feet from the highway. After a thirty-minute drive, the man was waiting when we arrived, still very worked up. "Can't we do anything about this guy who purposely hit this beautiful animal?" were his first words to us. Then he realized that he had not even looked at the license plate number and the futility of his request.

We processed the situation and quickly decided that we needed to dart (tranquilize) this poor animal and assess what the injury was and go from there. Dennis called an officer from New Mexico Department of Game and Fish who arrived quickly, and we darted the lion. The injury either was too severe, or the stress from the ordeal was affecting him, but he did not run off when shot with the dart like most animals do. The lion slowly crawled up the slope to another tree ten feet away as the drug worked to immobilize him. We had eye drops ready to keep his eyes moist, as under tranquilization they cannot move their lids to blink, and moved up to examine him. Dennis was then able to palpate (using sense of touch to feel for broken bones) his legs, starting with the front legs and shoulders. Finding nothing, he moved on to the back legs. The first leg examined was already swollen and Dennis discovered a broken bone, his tibia, a large bone in his lower leg. Dennis quickly checked the other leg, the torso, and head, and tested for concussions, but found no other injury.

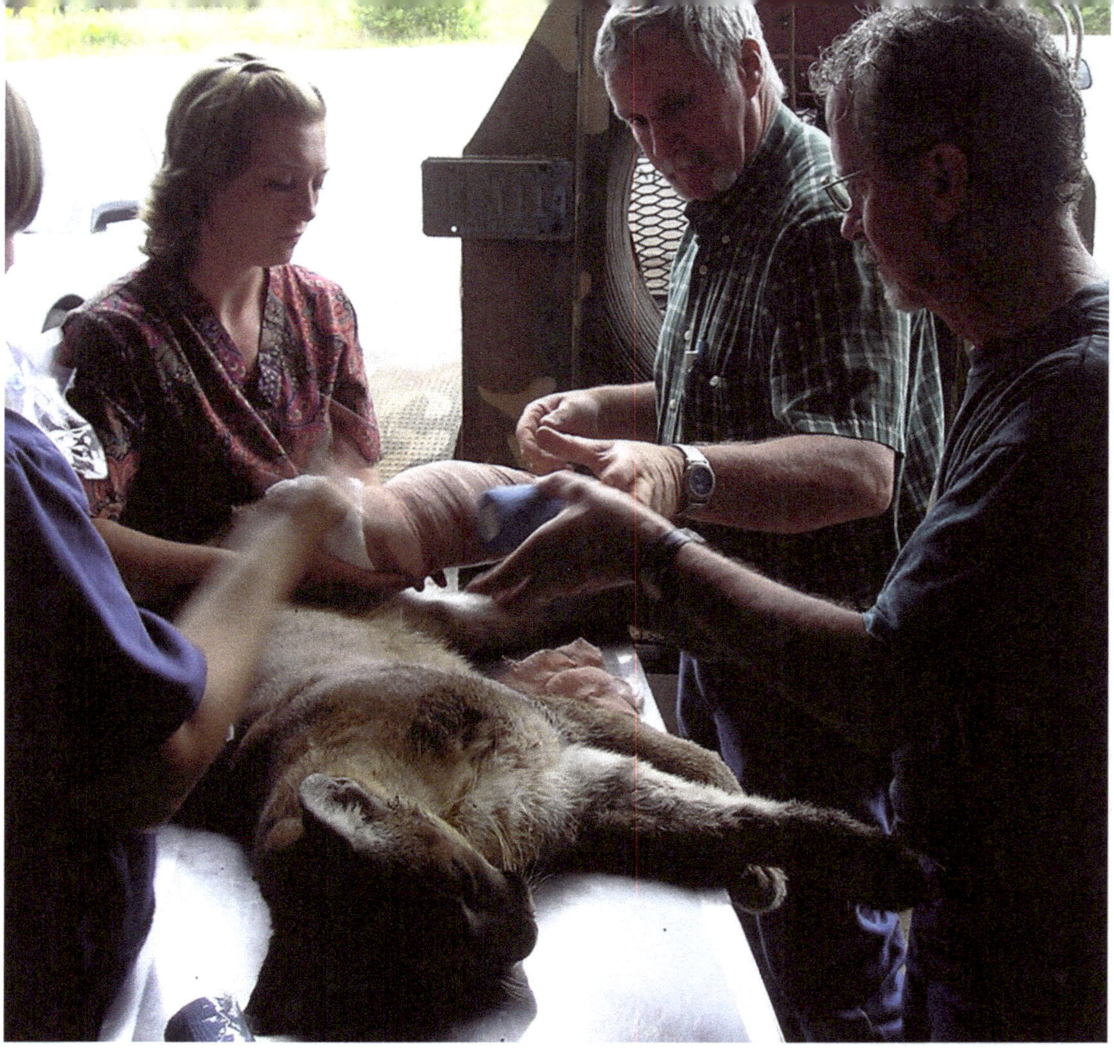

Veterinarian and Dennis wrapping a lion's leg.

Sedated mountain lion in bear tube.

While driving in with the lion, Dennis called our veterinarian in northern New Mexico who handled most of our major surgeries like this at the time. (We now use the amazing expertise of the veterinarians at the El Paso Zoo.) She was informed of the situation and began preparing to receive the animal for its surgery. The game officer that was helping us was able to drive the lion up to Española. The cat was delivered late that evening, but once examining him, the vet was concerned so delayed the surgery and called a friend of hers. Her friend was a human orthopedic surgeon who had conducted complicated surgeries on wildlife with her in the past. He was brought in because of where the break was located on the leg and the discovery that despite weighing 132 pounds, it was still a yearling lion that was growing.

The young mountain lion had broken the tibia close to what is termed the "growth plate." This area, close to the ends of bones, is busy with active bone growth during formative years, and growth occurring here makes bones longer.[63] Once fully grown, this area becomes inactive, and bones do not grow any longer. A break near this growth plate, if not healed correctly, would retard bone growth and cause one leg to be shorter than the other. In a predator like a mountain lion, this handicap would prove fatal. The highly specialized surgeon was brought in to attach a special plate, designed originally for humans, which allows for healing but does not interfere with the growth plate. Six and a half hours later, the surgery was completed, and the patient was recovering.

After three months, we were contacted that the lion was ready for release. We suggested that we use the bear tube from the department to transport him, or use our transport cage, which is a modified trailer and also serves as a trap. The veterinarian did not think that was necessary and put him in a smaller cage that fit inside her pickup truck with a camper shell on the back.

A few weeks before the releae, we consulted with the New Mexico Department of Game and Fish about a release site. With large game mammals like this, the department insists on advising where to release, probably for good reason. We were experienced enough to know ideal release sites, but not all rehabbers have that knowledge. When the officer asked Dennis's opinion, he had already thought it out and told him the McKnight Mountain area, a remote, picturesque place in the middle of the Aldo Leopold Wilderness northeast of us. This area had a large fire back in the 1950s and was recovering nicely with lots of lush plant growth that attracts deer, elk, turkey, and other prey. All the things needed to keep a lion happy and healthy, and remote enough to keep interactions with humans to a minimum. He agreed, and we made final arrangements.

The day of the release was bright and sunny. The vet from up north transported the lion, starting early in the morning. We met her and the wildlife officer near the turn off to McKnight. Everyone got out and we had our first look at our lion since he left here months earlier. In a small wire cage inside the covered back of this truck was a bright-eyed, aggressive lion, obviously ready to go. He had gained at least thirty pounds since we saw him last. The wildlife officer took the lead driving up the road that cuts through the heart of an area that few other roads penetrate, surrounded by wilderness. Soon after we started, we had to stop everyone to tell the vet that the cage the animal was in was bouncing quite a bit and was sliding on the back of the bed of the truck. We told them that we observed the cat being slammed up against the tailgate solidly, and we were concerned about its safety. We were told he was okay and that he would be fine. Despite our protests, we continued.

Mountain lion with damaged eye in transport.

Halfway up the road, the officer turned on a dirt road and stopped. He told us that there was a large stock tank over this ridge and that this would be a good place to release the cat. Dennis protested that it would be better to go farther up the road to the McKnight Peak area, not here halfway between McKnight and the Mimbres Valley. We wanted to keep him far away from humans and their dangers. Dennis reminded him that he asked for his advice, and he had said the burn area. He protested that this was too close to humans. Dennis lost the battle—again—and this was becoming very frustrating.

We went just a bit farther up this side road and stopped. Both of us jumped out to check on the lion. As we feared, the repeated slamming of the cage into the front and back of the bed of the truck caused some ugly-looking damage to his left eye. The entire surface of the eye had tiny red blood vessels spread across it. By now, we were truly angry, but the damage was done. If only we could have transported him in our transport trailer! The vet examined his eye and told us that it would not be any problem, it would heal quickly and would not leave him with vision problems. Again, angry but helpless, we disagreed, but we were outvoted . . . they were supposed to be the experts with more experience than us. We would have called off the release and waited for the eye to heal.

Everyone got in position to release the cat. The vet who brought the lion got ready to lift the door of the cage from above, and Denise, and the officer climbed into the back of his truck nearby. He had a shotgun ready if the lion turned on us (we were praying that it wouldn't, after all the effort to save him). The veterinarian lifted the door. Our lion shot out of the cage, off the bed of the pickup, and ran directly away from us. Then one of those things happened that we see time and time again when we release an animal. He stopped briefly under a juniper tree, surrounded by tall dry blades of grass, and looked back at us. Not sure if this time it was a "thank you" or if it might have been a dirty look for what he had just been through.

Mountain lion release.

Mountain lion eager for freedom.

The release was a success, at least we thought at first. We received a call just a few weeks later. The same officer that had chosen the release site, despite our protests, had to contact us and inform us that the lion had to be shot by the department because it was down in the Mimbres Valley predating on sheep at a ranch. When he examined this poor cat, his left eye was still just as bloody, having not healed at all, and he was obviously blind in that eye, influencing him to be desperate for easy prey, even if it was around humans.

We cannot fully express the feelings we had at the time. Heartbreak, anger, and disappointment were all wrapped up in our emotions because two major mistakes were made with this spirited animal that directly led to his death. This lion's eye was damaged in transporting it in an improper cage despite our alerting them to the problem. The decision to release it halfway to the site we had chosen contributed to it finding its way back to humans and the dangers that are always around them. We learned to be more insistent next time and put our foot down when it comes to these issues. It was, without a doubt, our most difficult heartache to recover from, and we still get angry inside and tears well up just thinking about it because it all could have been prevented and all the time and effort would not have been wasted.

Mountain lion's
last look after
release.

CHAPTER TWELVE

Inspirational Experiences

When a person works with these remarkable and beautiful creatures for long enough, they experience things that are beyond normal encounters and cannot be explained, at least by science. To be honest, as a biologist and needing proof and data to fully accept things, Dennis did not recognize or accept these events at first. He thought he was imagining them. When they did happen, he discounted them with scientific reasoning. He eventually got to the point where these experiences could not be explained and had to start opening his mind and looking at other possibilities. Through the years, we have had several incredible and powerful experiences. Some of these experiences have been minor, others have been . . . more significant.

Denise and great horned owl during release.

Dennis was in the middle of his general biology lecture one bright winter day, teaching genetics to his enthusiastic class, when his phone rang. He had one hard and fast rule in his class: *no* cell phone use was allowed. He told students this rule the first day of class but also told them that he was going to break that rule himself occasionally, but for a very cool reason. If his phone rang in class and was answered instead of muted, then it was a wildlife call. Dennis pointed out to them that he was on call 24-7 and not only obliged to deal with the incident, but the class might have a cool opportunity to have something delivered while there. So Dennis answered his phone with the whole class waiting in anticipation because the last time he answered his phone in class, a baby javelina was brought in that they got to see.

He quickly took the information about the call, jotting down a few notes, and hung up. Turning to the class, Dennis told them, "Sorry guys, I have good news and bad news. The good news is that I have to leave immediately, and the rest of class is cancelled. The class erupted into a joyous roar because Dennis *never* cancelled class.

Finally, someone asked, "What's the bad news?"

He replied, "The bad news is that I am going to go get a very large golden eagle and you guys probably are never going to see it." The class groaned. Dennis asked his graduate assistant to lock up the lecture room for him and shot out the side exit and jumped into his truck.

The call was from a man who works at the local copper mine. He was on his way to work, admittedly late and speeding a bit, when he came up over a hill and surprised an eagle in the middle of the road eating a roadkill rabbit. The man slammed on the brakes and tried to swerve, but an oncoming car prevented him from missing the bird without causing a head-on collision. He said he hit the eagle solidly but had started braking and had slowed some. He described the eagle trying to fly up to avoid this and hitting the bird square in the chest with the front of his small pickup. Distraught over what he had just done and torn between the need to get to work on time and the need to save this animal, his decision was to call us as he continued driving to work.

This is the call Dennis received in class. "I just called Game and Fish and they told me to call you. I hit a humungous eagle with my truck on my way to work. I gotta go, but he walked just over the barbed wire fence on the side of the road. It is just past the City of Rocks turnoff on the road to Sherman. I put a towel on the fence to show you where he is. He should be right there," said a very excited gentleman talking a mile a minute. Dennis got a few other details from him and drove out there as soon as he could.

He arrived at the turnoff to the City of Rocks, a state park southeast of Silver City, and found the towel a mile or so down the road draped over the fence just like was described. Dennis was enthusiastic that this was going to be successful, and we could save another eagle. Eagle encounters are always special experiences, much less highly exciting. He climbed over the fence where the towel was and looked around. No eagle in sight. He looked and looked in the area close to the road and searched on the other side of the road, then both sides, searching diligently and making sure the eagle wasn't hiding behind a bush out of sight. No luck at all.

Dennis walked back to the towel. He looked out and tried to think like an eagle. After a quick search, he found some tracks of a walking eagle heading directly away from the fence, so followed them until they disappeared. He found no eagle. He walked all the way back to the towel and started a search pattern radiating out from that point, walking back and forth in an arc, farther and farther from the towel, and still no eagle. Remembering his hunting experiences where injured animals tend to work themselves downhill, Dennis decided to work his way in a pattern down a gentle slope away from the fence. He had already searched for an hour, and he searched for another half of one until he finally thought about giving up.

What happened next was one of the weirdest and coolest things Dennis had ever experienced. It was after some other events had started occurring, where he could feel animals, but it was confirmation to him that a Supreme Being is out there and, in this case, helping us with the wildlife we care for.

Extremely frustrated, Dennis stopped and put his hands on his hips, just standing there staring out toward the north from where he was. Ideas were flipping through his mind about what to do next, all the while the fear for this poor eagle building. The bird would surely die if not found. As he stood there, he noticed a large group of ravens flying in the distance. There were about twenty-five of them and they were headed across his field of view, about a half a mile away. Noticing that they were flying reasonably high and that they had "a bird's-eye view," Dennis called out and asked them something, but for some reason in his mind he looked at it as kind of a prayer. They weren't even close enough to hear him. He had never done anything like this before, but it just . . . happened. He was about to give up, so it was a last hope effort.

"Hey up there. Can you guys see the injured eagle? He needs help and I can't find him. Please help me," Dennis exclaimed out loud. He honestly felt pretty silly and was glad he was alone out there.

The flock of ravens were flying in single file to the east, all about the same elevation. The instant Dennis was through saying this, the lead bird dropped down to about half the altitude the rest were at, and his flock followed right behind. Then, as he watched, one bird out of the middle of the flock, cawing like crazy, dropped out of the group and

Mimbres

swooped down close to the ground. Then he quickly flew back up and joined the rest of the group. A second later, the whole flock, steered by their fearless leader in front, adjusted back to their original altitude and continued flying east. As the one bird swooped down, Dennis spotted a dark bush where he turned back up. He got a bearing lined up on this bush and headed straight at it in a jog, praying that these ravens were helping him. This all happened so fast, and so quickly and smoothly, that it just seemed like a dream. But sure enough, between two mesquite bushes, totally hidden from view unless you were right up on it, Dennis found the majestic golden eagle, standing there helpless and hanging his head. He would have never found him without the raven's help. The bird was huge with close to a seven-foot wingspan.

Dennis couldn't believe what had just happened but was so focused on saving the eagle that he didn't have time to think about it. He grabbed Mimbres, as we eventually named him (found in Mimbres Valley and near the Mimbres River), wrapping his arms around him from behind. He held the bird's legs so the feet and talons were away from him, keeping his wings in his bear hug so he could not open them. He walked quickly almost two miles back to the truck.

Dennis was a bit shaken by all this, and the scenario of the events that led to finding this bird had kind of left him in shock. When he heard a cry and saw another eagle up above him as he was walking, it didn't register, but it eventually would. The bird followed them the entire way back to the truck, circling and quietly vocalizing. As he was walking to the truck, Dennis noticed that the entire front of the bird was bloody. The bird's chest (the term in birds is the "breast") was bloody, with soaked feathers matting the front of his body. He knew the eagle was in trouble and saw clearly his needed course of action. He had to get this bird into surgery and quickly. There were not any veterinarians at the time in our area that had the ability to anesthetize a bird for surgery. We had not yet started working with the El Paso Zoo, so he started the process of transporting him up north to Española to the vet who is experienced with surgeries on raptors.

He called Denise at work and explained that an eagle had been hit by a car, and we needed to get him on the plane that left in half an hour from our local airport. Dennis asked her to find a sturdy box big enough for an eagle and grab some packing tape and meet him with it at the airport, which was about halfway between the two of us. Driving up at about the same time, we quickly applied some first aid to Mimbres, then placed him in the box and sealed it up tight for shipment.

Walking up to the ticket counter at our small regional Grant County Airport with the box, the girl at the counter gave us a worried look. "You need to get that out today?" she asked. "That may be a problem. We are full of passengers, luggage, and freight."

This was very unusual for this tiny airport where business is so slow that sometimes the plane to Albuquerque returns with no passengers. We explained to her that we need to get this eagle to surgery, or it will die. As we were talking, a businessman, clearly identified by his suit and briefcase, was listening in. He walked up to the counter, kind of shy and tentative, and said the most inconceivable thing: "I overheard the problem. Would it help any if I took the evening flight? Can that box be buckled into a passenger seat?"

We were floored. The guy was volunteering his seat so this eagle that needed emergency surgery could get his only chance at survival up in Española. There was applause in the small waiting room as other passengers who heard the whole thing realized what

Mimbres being released.

he had done. So Mimbres was put on the plane with some other passenger sitting right next to him, and he was off!

The bird was received by the vet and hustled off to surgery. We had not been back from the airport for more than an hour when the call came in. It looked like he was going to survive, but it was a tough one. His crop was torn all the way open. The crop is the first chamber that stores food in birds so they can quickly eat and then push it further into the system to digest completely. When a bird like a raptor eats, the crop gets full, and a large lump can be seen at the top of its breast from the food stored there. When Mimbres was hit by the truck it split open this crop, breaking through the skin and the wall of the crop, laying it wide open. There was a four-inch laceration where it split. Stopping the blood loss was the first task, and then the crop was sutured closed, followed by the skin of the chest. The prognosis we received was good—Mimbres should survive.

Six weeks later, we transported him to the area where he was found for release. We found a knoll near the City of Rocks that provided a good launching platform and got the bird out of the carrier, preparing for the release.

We were taking some last-minute photos and saying a prayer for him when we heard a loud eagle cry coming from directly above us. Remember the eagle crying at us when carrying Mimbres to the truck? Now it all was dawning on us. Looking up, we saw her way up there, almost a pinpoint. It must have been his mate, and the same bird that cried at Dennis and followed him when picking Mimbres up. We released him, and he flew off, gaining altitude, and the waiting mate dove out of the heights and plunged toward him. They joined together in midair, then flew off together. You could almost imagine them holding hands.

There is another spiritually related experience involving wildlife care that we hesitate a bit to bring up. Not only is it very personal, but the experience Dennis had may be beyond some people's level of belief or acceptance. That is fine. He knows it is true because it happened directly to him. For those of you who read this, and it helps you and is an inspiration, then we are grateful. For those of you who read this, and you think it isn't true, then just look at it as a nice novel you are reading and enjoy it anyway. We do not mean to offend, please do not be.

Here is Dennis's story:

I do not know exactly when it all started and have no idea how it began, this feeling inside me as I worked with wildlife. What I was feeling was something that started me to question my own spirituality. My belief in God had waivered throughout the years as is common when growing up Catholic in the fifties and sixties and being forced to go to church every Sunday, to be confirmed, to be an altar boy, and the whole thing. All the while the world was protesting all around me promoting free speech and free living. Most of us growing up during this time have at least wavered in our beliefs by now, if not outright tossed them out.

Once I was educated in biology and understood the mechanisms of evolution, I questioned my beliefs. Once I learned the details of the origins of life as science explains it, I questioned my spirituality and what I had been taught in church. Anyone who truly learns and understands the science and sees the facts knows it is the truth. It doesn't discount a Supreme Being though. Now at last in my science education, I was seeing a clear explanation of how the origins of life and the subsequent changes that could have occurred, with steps, evidence, and proof it was possible, and I could see it distinctly.

My parents and the church taught me a story of creation and where humans came from that was completely different from science and to me had no evidence or proof, something my brain needed. I was born with a calculating mind, a left-brain dominant mind that enables me to deal with math, science, and problem-solving easier than some, and has influenced my career choice. My mind needs data, evidence, and facts in order to accept things as the truth. I was having a hard time with the almost magical explanation from religion and that you *must* accept it unconditionally as my church was teaching me. So yes, eventually, I became a borderline atheist where I saw clear evidence that life could have formed and changed into what it is today by clear steps that can be explained through science.

But I still wondered if there wasn't a Supreme Being controlling it all. By the way, as a biology educator I felt it was my duty to teach the scientific explanations of the origins of life and the process of evolution where life changed after forming, but I also discussed religious explanations with my classes. I also showed how parts of the scientific explanations have some holes and those holes could be filled by including a Supreme Being in the process. What sparked that first cell to start metabolizing, for example, and moving from the realm of nonliving and inanimate to living and functioning?

So fast forward now to 2001, and I started having some weird feelings as I cared for injured wildlife, in particular when I examined a new patient. I couldn't explain it, just that I had a strange feeling. I *felt* them more. They seemed to feel me and respond to me more. I doubted it at first, but it soon became obvious. Since contact with wildlife is always kept to a minimum, I noticed this was the only time I touched them with bare hands, which was when I was examining them. They would calm down more frequently and make our assessments much easier.

I was examining a red-tailed hawk one day, holding him upside down on his back. I felt him very strong and watched him calm down with my touch. I eventually could let go of his dangerous talons and look at a wing with both hands, and he did not budge. I was single at the time and so was having some of these experiences with wildlife when I was by myself, where no one else witnessed it. These astonishing events eventually woke me up, as you will see, and it forced me to address my own feelings of spirituality. It wasn't a gentle awakening. It was like getting hit up the side of the head with a two-by-four. But in order for my mind to accept this, it probably had to be the two-by-four method. As a scientist, I needed hard evidence, and I got it.

Here is a partial entry from my journal, dated September 9, 2001, interestingly two days before the 9/11 terrorist attacks:

Just had the most awesome and amazing experience, stronger than any I ever had. I had to put down a deer fawn that was hit by a car. She came in yesterday and I should have put it down that evening but waited until this morning. She obviously needed to be put down now, her back was broken, but there were signs she struggled and suffered a bit during the night. After putting her down, I felt bad and good as usual, but a bit worse knowing that I should have euthanized her earlier. I started to deal with the body, which was still warm and only seconds ago was alive. I reached down and grabbed her leg to pick her up, but instead for some reason, I stopped, and I just gently held it. I said what I guess was a prayer, but I just asked for some help from the universe out there in recognizing when animals need to be put down so this didn't happen again.

In a fraction of a second, my hand felt like it was leaving my control and it tightened around the leg . . . very tight . . . and I started shaking. I felt something go up my hand and arm and into my chest. It was kind of a slow wave of warmth infused with tiny static charges. I immediately could feel her pain . . . I guess it was her pain. She was scared and I could feel her fright more than anything. I thought, "Don't be afraid, you are okay now," and immediately I could feel something leave her. Was it her fright? Was it her pain? Was she even still alive? I then felt something go from my chest, down my arm and hand, and into her, and a great wave of relief spread over me.

To be honest, this experience scared the crap out of me! I was shaking, kind of crying, confused, and shocked. This kind of thing doesn't happen to *me*! Was I dreaming? Had I been drugged? All sorts of crazy questions flashed through my brain in an instant. "What the hell just happened?" I thought. "Was that real?" Once I calmed down, I realized that I was not dreaming and tried to rationalize what happened. But my brain could not comprehend it. No explanation I could think of could even approach explaining what happened. It took the rest of the day for me to calm down, and I never did rationalize it. I remained confused for a few weeks . . . then it happened again.

Screech owl.

From my journal, October 14, 2001:

Two birds in today, a screech owl and a great horned owl. I had forgotten the events with the deer or at least did not connect that with the examinations I was about to perform. I looked at the screech owl first, and as soon as I laid him on the table and put my hand on him, I felt him. Once again, I had this feeling go up my arm and into my chest. I could feel his pain this time and felt some of it pulling out of him. I received an image in my brain, kind of like a flash that you see for just an instant. The image was of bright lights and an impact with something. Being hit by a car instantly came to mind. I wasn't sure if this was all coincidence or if it was real. I wrapped his wing and moved on to the great horned owl.

I did not feel anything when first handling him and was relieved. I cleaned his wound, treated it with ointment, and was getting ready to move her to a cage when she became very agitated and frightened. I took off my glove and put my bare hand on her breast and felt it again, the warm tingly feeling moving up my arm and into my chest. She instantly calmed down. I felt her pain too. But I also received another flash image that was so quick and vivid that I was frightened at first. I saw a clear picture, from the owl's view as she is flying and chasing a rabbit. Then she had a collision with barbed wire, and pain. So it has happened again.

I received another owl and two hawks during the next couple of months. Each time these events repeated, but they did not include revealing images of how they were injured. The feeling traveling up my arm and into my chest, feeling their pain, repeated with each case. So I decided I wasn't dreaming. I also decided there was not an explanation within my brain's capacity of understanding to explain these events. My only choice was that a Supreme Being was at work here. Not only was that the only choice, but it is what I felt in my heart. I started to realize that there really was clearly something out there bigger than all of us. I wondered what was in store for me next.

From my journal, January 4, 2002:

I received my first ever bald eagle today. It has lead poisoning. I didn't feel anything at first but put my hand on him after his examination and once again I felt him strong. That same sensation went up my hand from him and into my chest. I could feel his pain and deep fright. His heart rate was very fast. The pain I felt from him now turned around and went from my chest, out my arms, and out the tips of my fingers. Then, it was like the eagle made me reach back and touch him again, and I repeated the process. His heart rate quickly slowed, and he became calm. His pain was reduced. There was a brief flash picture that went through my consciousness quickly, but it was hard to see what it was. All I could make out was darkness, blackness, like oil or tar. Was this the lead poisoning in him? This all has left me very confused, but less frightened. If it helps the animals, should I worry?

Luna with lead poisoning.

These were the most powerful experiences that I had. Over the next year, these events occurred about half the time, usually when there was a question of how an animal's injury occurred. Sometimes it doesn't matter what happened, but sometimes poisoning has occurred and there are no outward signs as in the bald eagle. Or there may be internal injuries we would not know about if we didn't know it had been in a collision with a vehicle. When the injuries were obvious and no help was needed, then the experience didn't repeat itself as often. It also happened in those cases where the animal was extremely frightened and would not calm down. The process calmed them and allowed examination and treatment to occur with less stress.

The experiences had left me with a profound question: Why? Why me? You had to have experienced this yourself, but from the very first time it happened, I felt the reason was to wake me up to the fact that something was out there. Maybe this also was because there was a tool that I was not utilizing that was available, but I had to believe in order to use it. Since that year, the experiences have become less frequent, but they have never stopped completely. Recently, I seem to be feeling the animals a bit more but will just let it happen if and when it is supposed to. I think on this one, I am in someone else's hands and will let Him help us, however it comes, I certainly was a changed person and am certainly no longer an atheist.

CHAPTER THIRTEEN

Returning Them To Where They Belong

The ultimate goal of wildlife rehabilitation, and our paramount objective, is to return these animals back into the wild. They have been, in many cases, rudely jerked from their homes and hurt seriously either by an unsuspecting person, or purposely by a person we at Gila Wildlife Rescue don't consider a member of the human race. The violation against the animal is now finally at a point where they can continue their lives. The original harm is undone by release, and the animal is back to their deserved freedom. Now they can feed their spirit, can be renewed, and take back their place in the web of life.

Our granddaughter, oldest daughter, and her husband releasing Harris's hawks.

The negativity produced by the people causing these injuries to wildlife is balanced by the people who go out of their way to save them. Not just Gila Wildlife Rescue, but the numerous people, whose numbers are growing, that share this desire to leave less of a destructive footprint on this earth during their time here. They pick up wildlife and bring them to rehabilitators. These people are simply being a productive and integral part of their own web of life that has connections to multitudes of other living things around them, including wildlife.

Releases are the final steps of our efforts. Here is what makes all the blood, sweat, and tears worthwhile. The feeling we get when we release is way beyond what words could ever describe. We have had other people release animals and they have also experienced incredible feelings after doing this. They can release their burdens and heal their souls. But when *we* release, as the rehabilitators, who have picked the animal up injured, starving, or orphaned, whose death was assured and we worked with it, worried about it, cried at times, and grieved at times, to get them to the point of their final and deserved freedom . . . now *that* is an amazing feeling.

Denise giving red-tailed hawk a bit of advice and then releasing.

In the story of the golden eagle Thor, we related how we were able to see him again, to positively know that this is *the* bird we rehabbed successfully and could see with our own eyes how well he was doing. We have released thousands of animals, and we hope that we have made the right decision that they really were ready to be released. We never know if they are successful or how long they live after our care. To finally have confirmation with this eagle, after all these years, makes us hope that all our releases were as successful. Thor's reunion with his rescuers made our hearts grow three sizes that day.

Our typical release of a bird involves getting the animal out of the carrier and transferring it to the person releasing it.

We then say a prayer to send it on its way, asking for protection and good health and life, and we always give thanks for the opportunity to help the animal.

Then a last photo is taken, and the animal is ready to go.

Denise and Dennis returning Mimbres to the wild.

Denise and Dennis praying for Mimbres's success in the wild.

Mimbres ready
to release.

Although the transport carrier doors can be opened and wildlife can just walk out, we have seen an animal stay in the carrier and not want to come out. With some birds, we like to launch them into the air a bit in order to clear them of bushes and trees and get them some altitude to start off with. This is easy with something like a kestrel, but even though just around twelve pounds, with an eagle it is a bit more difficult.

Denise releasing
large eagle

When the actual release happens, there is a thrill that you get as the act unfolds and a warm glow that stays for a while afterward and maybe forever, if you let it. Releasing an animal that has been injured back into the wild can be a powerfully moving spiritual experience that we have seen many times and witnessed ourselves. It is possibly the connection the person holding the animal has with the wild animal, keeping it from flying at first, and then granting it the grace to return to its rightful freedom.

Release day is always an exciting one. The animal may not think so at first because we must enter the cage and quickly catch them without stressing them too much, then transport them in a vehicle, which further stresses them. But when we stop at the release site and get their carrier out, they sense the "different" and maybe familiar air of the wild and the impending freedom. Then they decide it is an exciting day too. They get aroused, they struggle to reach freedom inside their carrier, and they seem to know what is about to happen. You can imagine how these animals feel: the feeling of freedom and being given a second chance at life.

Red-tailed hawk release.

The animals are probably confused, too, over something that has been bugging them for a while. Up to this point in their lives, humans have only been a source of pain and suffering for them, a source of danger and death. Humans are an animal that they are justifiably afraid of, but, for a time, some humans have been caring for them and now, after humans basically jailed them for a while, they are letting them go? It has to be bewildering, but in reality, they probably don't care. Freedom is all they care about. As they should.

One of the most amazing releases we ever experienced was one that we incorporated into an educational talk about Gila Wildlife Rescue. We were asked to give the talk thirty miles north of us at the Gila Cliff Dwellings National Monument in the heart of the Gila Wilderness. The road to this beautiful site penetrates through the middle of a million-acre tract of wild land and ends fairly close to the center of the entire wilderness. The road itself and the monument are the only land not designated as wilderness, so one is completely surrounded by it at the site. It is a somewhat magical place as a

Our youngest daughter releasing a ferruginous hawk.

result. The event was coupled with a celebration of the wilderness and was well advertised, bringing about seventy-five people to listen and see.

We not only had an eagle to show during the talk, but she was ready to be released and what a better site to do it. Once the talk was over and questions answered, we all moved to the parking lot. The Visitor's Center is situated on a bench that places it a bit higher than the surrounding Gila River Valley, making it a perfect launching platform for this big girl. We got the eagle ready and said a few last words and a prayer, then off she flew.

Dennis and Denise giving presentation at Gila Cliff Dwellings (photo courtesy of Mary Alice Murphy)

She flew straight out, gaining altitude, and made a slow, wide bank to the northwest, soaring up the Gila Middle Fork and heading upstream to a renewed life. They told us there was not a dry eye in the place . . . including ours. It was a magical moment.

A friend of ours passed away from cancer a few years ago. When mutual friends suggested that her husband release an animal to aid with his grief, we thought it was a great idea. We happened to have a great horned owl at the time that was ready to go. We met at the release site and the widower was emotional when he saw that it was an owl.

He explained to us that he had no idea what he would be releasing and to see that it was an owl was perfect because his wife had loved owls and had a very special connection with them. We said a few words before the release, encouraging him to use this opportunity to release some grief. The owl was transferred to him, and we prepared for the release. The owl was situated in his grasp where her body was turned away from him, but for some reason the owl's head was turned around staring intently at who was now holding him. As he was getting ready to toss the bird gently but forcefully into the air, the owl would not break its gaze with him.

Her enormous eyes, each the size of half dollars, bright yellow with pupils wide, were locked to his. He moved her a bit like he was about to launch her, but she did not want to look forward. Worried about releasing her when she was not looking where she was going, he just held her for a while. With their eyes still locked together, we all could feel the movement of communication between the two of them. The owl finally broke eye contact. Then he sent it off to continue its life, while the owl helped him continue his.

Dennis releasing golden eagle at Gila Cliff Dwellings (photo courtesy of Mary Alice Murphy)

Great horned
owl release for
his wife.

Releasing barn
owls to bless
their home.

A unique use of an animal release is when our friends who had been working hard for quite a few years to complete a house released barn owls as a blessing to their newly finished home. We had a little ceremony and sent the animals off with blessings.

When releasing Swainson's hawks, a species that migrates in groups each year to South America and back, we often release birds we are caring for all together. The strategy is that they may stay together and migrate together, the older birds showing the younger birds the way. When release time is near the migration period in the fall, we usually release them in a group.

Friends, Denise, and middle daughter releasing Swainson's hawks.

When mammals are released, it is a completely different process. The transport cage is either opened and the animal shoots out like a bullet, or they have to be caught with a catch stick and pulled out of the cage and then released. Most of the time, this is a very quick process that is over in a flash, but the emotional and spiritual benefits of releasing linger for the rest of your life.

Here are a few other videos of hawk releases:

WNMURelease

ElPasoElectricRelease

SwainsonsReleaseBella

SwainsonsReleaseDenise

SwainsonsRelease

Gray fox captured and released.

Here are a few gray fox release videos:

GrayFoxRelease

GrayFoxRelease2

Mule deer release.

At other times, in particular with young animals, they tentatively smell and look, testing for dangers, then slowly walk out of the cage.

We have eight grandchildren and two great-grandchildren. Many of them have been exposed to quite a few animals in their young lives being around us. We hope that this exposure will remove unfounded fears and stimulate some interest and that will be valuable lessons for the future. We couldn't help putting a few photos as proud grandparents of releases with our grandchildren.

Gray fox release.

Grandson and great horned owl.

Top right: Granddaughter with roadrunner.

Granddaughter with Harris's hawk.

Oldest grandson with red-tailed hawk.

Here is an assortment of release videos that you may enjoy.

BarnOwlClose

BurrowingOwlReleaseInManMadeBurrow

BurrowingOwl

GHORelease

GHOReleaseClose

DennisTryingToCatchHawk

GoldenEagleFromCage

KestrelRelease

LoonRelease

LoonRelease2

CHAPTER FOURTEEN

Raptor Diversity

Long-eared owl.

This chapter is dedicated to exhibiting the diversity of wildlife in our unique area and to show just a small sample of the variety of animals Gila Wildlife Rescue has cared for. We have evolved through the years to now specialize in birds of prey, or raptors, and most mammals, and these two groups are a great example of the multitude of species found in this wonderful area. This chapter is not meant to survey every species found in Southwestern New Mexico, but to pick a few significant groups and highlight their diversity. Every species mentioned here has been cared for by Gila Wildlife Rescue and photos are all of birds and mammals that we have rehabilitated.

The diversity and large numbers of wild animals in our area is profound, and the reasons for this are usually a surprise to newcomers. We travel to other areas of the country and are often disappointed that we see very few animals. Few areas in our country have this amazing wildlife population and we should appreciate this fact more.

In a sixty-mile radius around Silver City we have a blend of desert, grassland, and forest, but the details are more important. We are located directly between the Sonoran Desert of Arizona and northwest Mexico, and the Chihuahuan Desert of New Mexico and northeast Mexico.[64] The forest biomes located here vary from the pinon/juniper at lower elevations, moving up in elevation to the pine/oak forests, the Douglas fir/aspen forests, and eventually at highest elevations the spruce fir forests and alpine tundra.[65] No other area in the United States has so many different habitats and biomes located in such a small area.

The amazing results of this are the presence of a huge mixture of the different characteristic animals and plants of each of these biomes placed together in one relatively small locale.

Juvenile red-tailed hawk on left, mature bird on right.

Buteo Hawks (Soaring Hawks)

Red-tailed hawks are one of the most common animals we care for. The largest hawk in most areas is a buteo, or soaring hawk, with long, broad wings to soar in thermals and hunt from above. The characteristic that influenced this bird's name can be a bit confusing. Just as bald eagles do not have a white head and tail or a yellow beak and yellow eyes until after the second year of their life, red-tailed hawks look different as juveniles as well. Young bald eagles are brown over most of their body and look similar to a golden eagle. Juvenile red-tails have a brown tail the first one or two years and then grow the characteristic red tail that makes identification easier.

Identification can be quite challenging because this hawk has the most variability of any hawk in the world as well as being the most common and widespread.[66] There can be very dark forms you would swear is a black hawk or small eagle. There are light forms that are almost totally white; some have a dark band across their chest; and others have a dark head and throat. Identification can be very challenging, but one sure method to identify this species of hawk is a characteristic that is visible from underneath, usually while the bird is flying. It is a dark band from the head to the elbow of the bird (about one-third of the length) on the leading edge of the wing. All red-tailed hawks have this dark stripe on the leading edge of their underwing and no other North American hawk does.[67]

Red-tailed hawk showing dark leading edge between head and elbow.

After handling more than a thousand of these birds, you get to know them. You get to know their personalities, their weaknesses, and their spirit. All mature adult red-tails have a warrior-type spirit where they are always vigilant and sharp and exude strength and courage. The juveniles, however, seem to act like baby hawks for a few years. They are more fearful and curious than adults. We must always be wary of these birds' feet as we care for them. Like other raptors, these talons are their weapon, not their beaks. They are a delight to work with and rival great horned owls in the amount of injury they can sustain and survive. These again are tough survivors.

Being the most common raptor in North America, this single species has a profound effect in the balance of prey populations and so has almost a ruling influence on any ecosystem they live in. Having one of the largest ranges of any raptor, they can live in almost any habitat. They can be found everywhere from southern deserts to northern forests and tundra.[68]

The very first animal that Gila Wildlife Rescue officially received was a red-tailed hawk. This was a hatchling, about the size of a baseball, and covered with fluffy white down feathers. It was brought to us after the border patrol took it away from some illegals that thought it was an eagle chick. They reportedly were coming across the border in their eyes to sell it to some dumb American. We had a hard time identifying it, having difficulty telling it from a Swainson's hawk chick or a couple of other species at first. It was this bird that taught us how fast bird feathers grow as discussed in the section on owls. He went from this ball-of-fuzz hatchling to a fully feathered fledging ready to learn to fly in a period of just over two weeks. It was a great experience and started this whole craziness.

Red-tailed hawk nestling on left, same bird two weeks later on right.

Let us clear up a confusing set of terms we have been using. The term "hatchling" is the term for a very young newborn, just out of the egg. A "nestling" is a bird that is still in the nest but has not tried to fly or leave it yet. A "fledgling" is a bird that is trying to or has left the nest and is starting to fly or "fledge."[69]

One spring, we were having a fundraiser at a local wine bar in Silver City, and an injured red-railed hawk was delivered to us at the event. It was a surreal opportunity for our supporters to see what we were doing and to observe our initial examination. The story on this raptor was that one of Dennis's former students (again) found the bird almost drowned in a metal stock tank, near Granite Gap near the New Mexico/Arizona border. When the bird arrived, wet and bedraggled looking, we determined she had no other injury. This was an easy one. She was fattened and exercised and released a few weeks later.

We returned her to Granite Gap for release, and once the bird was free, it flew off and then turned and flew back over us, like they often do. Then we heard another bird screaming their very characteristic cry. From a tall cliffside to the north came two other red-tails diving right at her. We were fearful at first that they were attacking the bird we just released, but our fears were unfounded. By the way they greeted each other, we realized we had just reunited a family group, and we watched in fascination as one bird clasped talons with the released bird and the third bird was flying above her and gently touching her back with its talons, leaving us breathless and with tears in our eyes.

Red-tailed hawks regularly breed in this area and as with great horned owls, in the spring after a big windstorm we get young ones that have been blown out of their nests. In most cases, it is not possible to get them back into the nest and they may fall right back out again anyway, so we take them in and raise them.

In rehabilitating many young raptors, it is imperative they are experienced at killing food before released into the wild. Raising red-tails then, as well as other raptors, involves kill training and we get many questions about how we do this. Our favorite answer when asked this is to jokingly say, "Well, we put a mouse in the cage, then run up to it and kill it with our feet and teeth to demonstrate to the youngsters how to do it and after a couple of dozen times they get it!" Everyone gets a good laugh, but it shows that the term "training" is not utilizing demonstration techniques but simply providing live food in an environment that makes it easy for them to catch. Flight cages are designed in a way that live food can't escape easily, so there is no place to run. After repeated opportunities where they can make multiple tries at catching a mouse or rat, they get experienced at it. Prior to this, we feed them the same type of mice or rats that we eventually feed live, so the prey is familiar to them. We start with small prey and work up to larger animals. After a bird has made six or eight kills of the largest food appropriate to them, they are ready for release. For example, for a red-tailed hawk it would be a large rat and for an eagle it would be a large rabbit. For a falcon it would be a large pigeon.

It is awesome to watch this hunting ability develop. Sometimes they pounce on food right away and know exactly what to do; other times, particularly with owls, they take a while to slowly develop the instincts needed to do the killing. At times, they will just play with it and chase it around for a while, but not catch it and kill it. On tough cases, we have been known to make it very easy for them by tying a thread to the leg of a mouse and the other end tied to a nail. The nail is then pushed into the ground and the mouse is "staked out" to make catching it very easy. It does sound a bit cruel, yet without the mother bringing mice that are half alive to "play" with, and to teach them other techniques by demonstrations, they may never learn.

Swainson's hawk showing underside of wing with light colors in front and dark wing feathers at the trailing edge.

For some birds, this process can be quick, a matter of days, or it can take months before they are ready. If they are not kill trained before release, it is not only cruel but guarantees their demise. Not kill training would be like taking a two-year-old child out in the wilderness and expecting him to survive.

Swainson's hawks are very similar to red-tails, although slightly smaller and lacking the red tail and the dark leading edge on the underwing.[70] They are gorgeous hawks with beautiful detail to their feathers, especially with juvenile birds. In the spring and summer, they can be as common as red-tails and are often confused with them. The quickest way to differentiate is from underneath. The wing is light colored on the leading edge of the wing and their feathers look dark on the trailing edge, which is the opposite of red-tailed hawks.

Swainson's hawk

In the winter in our area, 99 percent of the large hawks are red-tails, not Swainson's, because this species migrates to South America each fall. Usually traveling in large groups, most of them fly to the Argentina region where they gorge on grasshoppers.[71] We were driving to Arizona one day, traveling through a flat stretch before reaching Lordsburg, New Mexico, and we saw a group of these amazing birds gathering for migration. They were everywhere—on the ground, perched on fence posts, and on top of yucca stalks. It was obvious they were waiting for the signal to start their long trek. Can you imagine seeing a group of over a hundred large hawks migrating all together? This is very unusual for most raptors who generally migrate alone.

When we rehab this species of bird, the goal is to release them by the middle of October because if held longer they must stay until spring when their species migrates north. Due to Gila Wildlife Rescue being the farthest south of all rehabbers in the state, we have many rescue centers transfer their Swainson's to GWR to spend the winter with us because they return here so much earlier than other parts of the state and, as a result, can be released earlier. We have had as many as a dozen with us all winter, and we wait until we see other Swainson's in the spring before we release them.

Juvenile black hawk

We have only cared for two black hawks in the forty-plus years we have been doing this. This is an uncommon and unique hawk that is completely dark like a golden eagle, but much smaller, with a white band at the base of their tail. Similar in size to a red-tailed hawk, they are specialized feeders, eating primarily frogs and toads and occasionally crayfish, small fish, and lizards.[72] They readily take mice in captivity, but we also fed fish when we could. They are found along waterways in the Southwest as these riparian areas provide great sources of the aquatic creatures they feed on. One knows they are close to black hawks and their nests because their persistent vocalizations are a very loud, piercing cry that is hard to miss![73]

The first black hawk we cared for had a broken wing that healed and he was eventually released, but before he was, we also noticed something strange in his eye. We called in a local ophthalmologist for consultation. He educated us on trauma-caused cataracts[74] and showed us this bird had an eye injury that had healed. For some reason, it caused a milky buildup inside the eye and was starting to make the vision dimmer and blurry in that eye. We discussed treatments and since there were none, he was released with the hope that as the cataract reduced his vision, he would slowly compensate and survive fine. Large birds like this have been known to survive with one eye. Besides, frogs and toads are easy to catch, at least easier than fish or mice! Recent developments in surgical methods have possibly changed this with some success trying surgery.[75]

The second black hawk we cared for was a juvenile and had amazing plumage with incredible detailed barring and spotting. He was found on the ground just south of Silver City along the Big Ditch that runs through town and carries off excess runoff. This pretty stream provides enough riparian habitat and food sources, so we have had a few of these awesome raptors spend at least part of the year very close to town providing some nice opportunities for birders. His examination showed no clear injury but had possibly ingested something toxic based on his behavior. After a few weeks with us feeding heavily to flush his system, he recovered and was released. This was one of those great teaching moments where we arranged for a class from a local school, who were working in the area on a project, to be there for the release. Students voted for one girl to do the honors, and it was a wonderful experience for her and her classmates.

Black hawk with cataract.

Juvenile black hawk

Harris's
hawks

Harris's hawks are the most attractive of all the hawks. Having an entirely brown body like the black hawk, they have large red shoulder patches similar in color to the "red" tail of a red-tailed hawk.

We have cared for over four dozen of these rare birds. They are very similar in demeanor to a red-tailed hawk but a bit more timid. Harris's hawks are unique in the raptor group because of their hunting methods. Most other hawks lead solitary lives and hunt singly. These incredible hawks live in groups and hunt in packs like wolves![76] It has been documented that one bird will start chasing a jackrabbit down a ravine, forcing him into a narrower section, where a dozen or so other Harris's hawks are waiting. The one hawk could never take down and kill a jackrabbit, being smaller than a red-tailed hawk, but when all of them attack, they are quite efficient. They all share the kill. We have not observed this behavior in nature ourselves or with animals we have cared for, but knowing this shows us the importance of getting them back into the wild to join a group to better their chances for survival. One of our friends who assists in the program often and is a wood carver, wanted to give us a gift for our rehabilitation work, so he asked Dennis one day what his favorite hawk was. His immediate reply was a Harris's hawk, and six months later he presented us with a carving of one of them that was incredibly beautiful.

Here are some videos of buteo hawks:

RedTailMature

RedTailRelease

RedTailRelease2

Swainsons

HarrisHawkCry

BlackHawkRelease

Friend's carving of a Harris's hawk.

Ferruginous hawk

Ferruginous hawks are quite rare in this area, but Gila Wildlife Rescue has cared for four of them. Quite unusual because of their white undersides with brown-and-reddish-streaked wings, legs, and back. Close to the size of a red-tailed hawk, these birds are very shy and do not eat well in captivity compared to other hawks. Located occasionally along the Gila River Valley, they are rarely seen and rarely are injured.

Ferruginous hawks

Northern harrier

Accipiter Hawks (Forest Hawks or True Hawks)

An unusual hawk we have rehabbed often that looks and acts much different than other hawks is the northern harrier. Formerly named a marsh hawk and sometimes referred to as the "owl hawk," they at times can have an owlish appearance when they flare the feathers on their head. This medium-sized hawk has a dish-shaped face that functions like an owl to direct sound to the harrier's ears. They depend on hearing while hunting, flying low and carefully listening for mice and birds. Their distinct white rump patch and their low-flying habits help in this hawk's identification, along with the fact that they often fly with V-shaped wings like a vulture. They are also the only other raptor found in this area, besides kestrels, that show sexual dimorphism (difference in male and female) with the male being gray colored and the female brown.[77] These are quite common birds that are seen frequently hunting low to the ground in grasslands and savannas.

Cooper's hawk

Sharp-shinned and Cooper's hawks are somewhat plain-looking hawks that are small and speedy, darting around trees and scattering flocks of birds. They are very light and agile but, as a result, are commonly wounded and brought to us with wing injuries. They heal well but don't do well in long-term captivity of over a month or so. They just don't eat well and stay very hyperactive and afraid. They are a high-strung bird affected by disturbances more than other birds we care for.

These skillful fliers are sometimes unwanted guests at bird feeders, scattering the birds for hours. Both raptors are accipiters.[78] Unlike the buteos mentioned with larger hawks previously, they have short, rounded wings and a longer tail. These two birds are easily confused with the Cooper's hawk, being a bit larger with a head that looks

Sharp-shinned hawk

large, and the sharp-shinned being smaller with a head that looks smaller, almost like there was no neck. As they fly, you can see the sharp-shinned hawk has an erratic flight and the Cooper's has more steady wingbeats. Both birds can have red or orange eyes.

Another unusual bird we have cared for also belongs to this accipiter group, the Mississippi kite. Rarely seen in the Silver City area, it is found occasionally in marshy riparian areas along the Rio Grande River near El Paso, Texas. With a very unusual gray color in adults, they exhibit a unique behavior similar to falcons.

Gila Wildlife Rescue has cared for only one northern goshawk. A rare bird and a bird that rarely gets injured, one finally came in from the El Paso area transferred to us by the zoo. It was very similar to a large Cooper's hawk in looks and demeanor. This was an immature bird, so her plumage was similar to a Cooper's hawk. This bird will eventually change completely and have a very gray body with bright orange eyes. Unfortunately, we do not have a decent photo to show.

Immature northern goshawk.

Immature Mississippi kite.

Peregrine falcon—fastest animal on earth.

Falcons

 Falcons are definitely one of those special animals that give us a thrill when they come to us. They rival eagles in the excitement we get, and their releases are often spectacular with their aerial acrobatics. Like many of the animals we care for, their spirit, power, and beauty make it an honor to be able to help them.

Very different in looks and behavior compared to hawks, falcons are the lords of the air . . . well no, that should be reserved for eagles. How about fighter jet pilot of the air? These guys are fast! The peregrine falcon is the fastest animal on earth, having been clocked at speeds of 240 miles an hour in a dive, and reports of much higher speeds that were not confirmed due to the difficulties of being able to measure this accurately.[79] They even have adaptations in their skull and brain to accommodate for the g-forces they must withstand.[80] Falcons all have long, narrow wings for better speed and maneuverability. They are as agile as they are fast and, in fact, specialize in eating other birds, something that most predators can't catch. They have adapted to drop out of the sky, sometimes from great heights, and plummet down at high speeds and hit a bird with the force of a freight train in comparison and kill it instantly[81]. The noise generated when they are in a dive is amazing to hear, and you may think there is a jet coming at you! The birds they kill are heavier than they are so they cannot fly off with their prey but must eat it where it falls. These truly are fighter jets, with powerful ammunition, too, but just no payload.

We have cared for four species of falcons at Gila Wildlife Rescue. The coolest by far is the peregrine falcon. We have also cared for prairie falcons and have had one Aplomado falcon that was part of a reintroduction program in our area, but the falcon we care for the most are American kestrels.

Eye of peregrine falcon showing Gila River in reflection.

The Aplomado falcon we cared for was a gorgeous bird, but a frustrating case. He had a tracking device strapped to his back and was part of a reintroduction program for these rare birds in New Mexico. He came to us during a period when we had received quite a few barbed wire injuries, so it was no surprise. But what was surprising was that when we completed surgery to remove the wire, the wire had caught in the strap that was holding the tracking device. There was one barb deep in the chest and when it was removed, we knew he was in trouble. He died soon after. This made us angry at first, and, in fact, we contacted the research group. They explained that although they very rarely lose a bird to barbed wire like this, the necessity of finding out why so many of their releases have died made the use of the tracking device necessary.

Aplomado falcon caught in barbed wire.

Male American kestrel

The American kestrel is North America's smallest and most common falcon.[82] It is again primarily a bird eater, like most other falcons. Watching them dive into a flock of sparrows and pick one off is impressive to see. They have exquisitely detailed plumage and are some of the most beautiful of raptors in the world, especially the male with his bolder features. This is one of only a couple of raptors in North America that display sexual dimorphism, the other being the harrier. The only way to differentiate sexes in most other raptors is to compare sizes because the plumage of males and females look alike. In general, males are one-third smaller than females.[83]

These tiny, speedy guys are a miniature version of their role model, the peregrine, and predate on a group of smaller birds than the peregrine, so they don't compete. They are very vocal birds that seem to like to scream when upset. They have a very hyperactive disposition and are nervous and flighty all the time. Their metabolism is so high that they must be fed a number of times during the day, including adults. Starvation can occur in just a few days.

Kestrels are a riot to raise. They have the most ear-piercing cry we have ever experienced in our lives. We often get these in groups of four and five because this species has large clutches, and parents seem to be able to keep all of them fed. With multiple groups of these coming in all at once, we sometimes have over twenty at a time. The first animal Dennis ever had to put down as an un-releasable animal was a kestrel. It served a good purpose to teach us the valuable lessons on euthanasia that we required for many years in the future.

Male American kestrel

In our annual report for the first year of rehabilitation, we listed a kestrel that we were keeping that was unable to fly. Dennis was quickly contacted by the U.S. Fish and Wildlife Service and was told that we could not keep him more than a few months, then it had to be either released or euthanized or placed in a zoo. Being a very common species, no zoo could be found willing to adopt him, so he had to be euthanized. This was very difficult. We have now developed methods that make it easier and can be accomplished quickly, but each time we have had to euthanize an animal it kind of ruins our day, and we are a bit sad and grouchy for a while. Dennis seems to feel it in his heart. This is balanced with the knowledge that they cannot be kept in captivity and need to be flying free in the wild. Knowing that this is best for the bird to stop its suffering helps to calm our hearts a bit. We end up euthanizing fifteen to twenty birds each year.

The last falcon we have in our area and another that has been cared for by Gila Wildlife Rescue is the merlin. This falcon, once rare in our area, has been sighted more frequently, and we have cared for a dozen or so. Looking and acting more like a Cooper's hawk, this feisty speedster is definitely a falcon with long, narrow, pointed wings and a tomial tooth, which is a notched point on the side of all falcons' beaks.[84] We have cared primarily for immature birds and have at times had to look closely to determine what species we were looking at.

Video Link: KestrelRelease

Merlin showing tomial tooth of falcons.

Osprey

Osprey—The Fishing Hawk

The osprey is one of the most unique birds of prey in the world. It is the only raptor whose diet consists exclusively of fish.[85] Other raptors like bald eagles will also eat other prey and carrion. Ospreys have a four-and-a-half-foot wingspan that is longer than most raptors of a similar body size. This allows them to dive quickly and crash into the water, sometimes going as deep as two feet to grab a fish. Their amazing adaptations to catch fish include specialized talons that have gripping scales and longer claws that give them the ability to keep their slippery prey from escaping from their grasp.[86] Their eyesight has also adapted to water hunting. Like most birds of prey, they have excellent vision. What makes this bird unique is they cannot only see fish from great heights, but their eyes can also adjust for the refraction of light in the water.[87] This adaptation allows them to strike their prey very accurately.

Osprey—keen eyesight that adjusts for water refraction.

Ospreys have been shown to be of paramount importance to the varied aquatic and marine ecosystems they live in. As a result, many areas of the country have had concerted efforts to encourage them to nest and take up residence in areas where they once were common and had all but disappeared.[88] From Montana to Florida, nesting poles have been erected along waterways to draw them in. Amazing birds to watch hunting, they are often confusing to many people as to what exactly they are looking at. These birds are fairly common in aquatic habitats in our area.

WARNING!

PHOTOGRAPHS OF OWLS
ON NEXT PAGES

(Explanation to Come)

Mysterious Owls

Dennis had been bringing owls into the classroom for years, but one day learned the hard way that he had to be careful. While teaching a summer school biology class at WNMU, he performed his typical first day of class ritual of walking in with an animal of some sort to generate interest. As he walked into the classroom with a large adult great horned owl, the closest student to the door, a Native American girl, immediately had a fearful look on her face. She listened and watched for less than ten seconds and then bolted out of the room, grabbing her books as she left. Recognizing immediately that he had blundered into an American Indian cultural problem with owls, Dennis finished his introduction using the owl and then walked out the door to check on the student. She was just outside the door and was distraught. The major cause of her distress was walking out of class and being rude to Dennis. She thought that he was going to have a problem with her because of it. He got her to calm down and understood that he was the one who should be sorry and that he recognized this as something she reacted to because of her culture, and not rudeness.

She explained to Dennis that she was in a particular Navajo clan that has strong beliefs about owls, but not all clans do.[89] She said that in her clan, if you are surprised by an owl—startled by them as she was—then it could be a foretelling of a bad event happening in the near future. He understood that if he had only told her he had an owl before she was startled by it, there would not have been a problem. She apologized, he apologized, and they went back into class.

The next day, she was waiting for him as he arrived at his office. She tried to assure him that it was not his fault, but she found out last night that her best friend was killed in a car accident the day before, and she had to go home for the funeral ceremonies. Of course, he felt awful. It was difficult to teach the rest of the day, it weighed so heavily on his mind. Ever since then he has been careful to announce to the class before he walked in that he was bringing in an owl to show them. His Native American student assured him that this would be all he needed to do to handle this. We are even careful now during fundraisers not to display owl photos where someone could be surprised by them and place those photos in a box that people can look through if they are interested. The warning about owl photos in the front of this section is for this purpose.

Humans regard owls with fascination and awe. They are mysterious and sacred to some, scary and cursed to others, but we see a side that most people do not, and we have a deep respect for them. They are survivors in a tough world to live in. They go about their lives in the cloak of darkness, silently and secretly hunting, unknowingly providing an essential service to the ecosystem. For owls are one of those top predators mentioned earlier that are so essential in controlling rodent populations. We see the fighter in them as well as the shy, timid side of them. Unlike other animals we have cared for, owl hatchlings don't seem to exhibit behaviors of a baby but display the demeanor of an adult. Aggressiveness is expressed early on, and they almost never have problems with imprinting.

Owls have been significant in cultures all over the world. The significance varies widely from owls being considered wise (the wise old owl) to them being an evil animal that is often linked with witchcraft and death. Few other creatures have such contradictory beliefs attached to them. In some Native American folklore, owls portray wisdom and helpfulness and have powers of prophecy. Yet, in other tribes the meaning is clearly associated with death. Members of the Dakota tribes see the burrowing owl as a protective spirit. Other North American natives believed that after death, the brave and virtuous became great horned owls. The wicked, however, were doomed to become barn owls. To an Apache, dreaming of an owl signified approaching death. To the Cherokee, if an owl's shadow falls over you, you will die in battle that day.[90]

Great horned owls are one of the most common owls in North America, and one of the most successful predators. They occupy the same habitats as red-tailed hawks, often nesting and hunting in the same area but without competing. This is due to the owl's well-known nocturnal habits. The red-tailed hawk is the solar or daytime equivalent of the lunar or nocturnal great horned owl.[91]

Great horned owl fledgling taking very first flight.

A large adult female great horned owl can stand almost two feet tall, can have a five-foot wingspan, and is the most widely distributed owl of the Americas.[92] They have proportionally one of the largest eyes of any vertebrate animal with incredible night vision capabilities.[93]

Eye of great horned owl.

Owls' eyes cannot move like humans' eyes can, so they must move their entire head. To hunt quietly, moving only their head, they can rotate it a full 270 degrees.[94] This leads to the false reputation that owls can turn their head round and round. With spinal cords and vertebrae in the neck there is a limit, but it is amazingly flexible. If you saw an owl that had just turned his head 270 degrees to look at you, he could turn it 270 degrees back to the normal position and continue 270 degrees more the other way, spinning it 540 degrees. No wonder the reputation!

Their incredible talons can exert over three hundred pounds of force, rivaling the force of an eagle's talons.[95] Their feathers, like most owls', have soft edges to them and when examined closely have what looks like frayed edges. This contributes to an owl's best hunting tool, silent flight.[96] Even in the flight cages, owls are totally silent as they fly, unlike other raptors we care for. By the way, the noisiest by far is the flight of a peregrine falcon when flapping to get speed up!

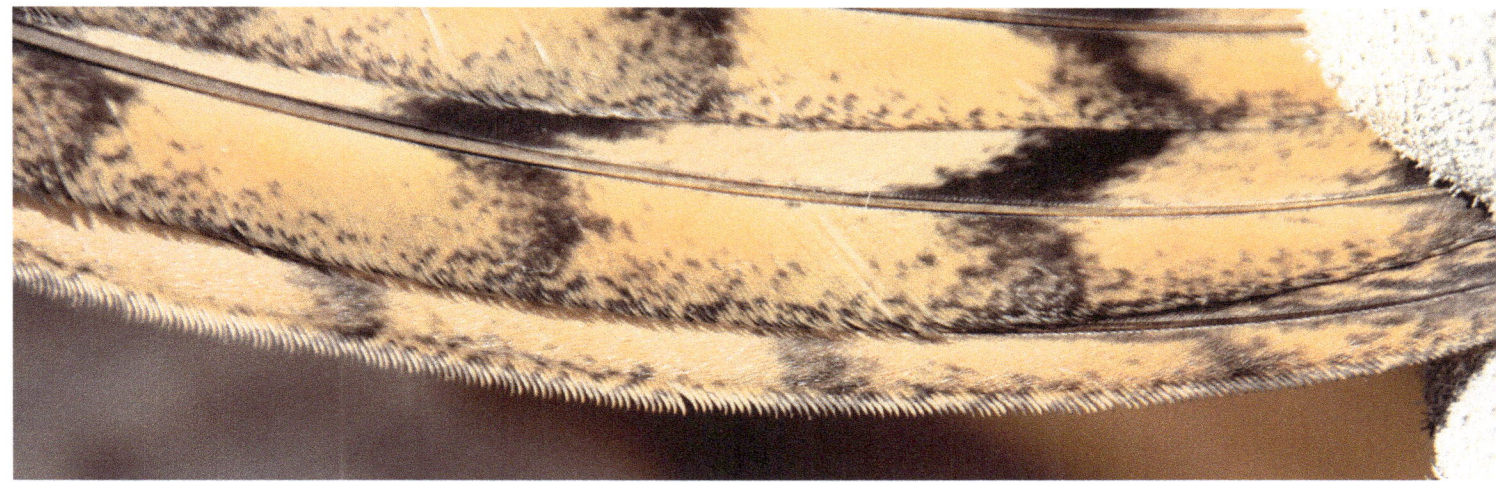

"Frayed" edge of feathers of barn owl.

We have cared for well over a thousand owls. They are resilient animals that are very successful in their habitats. We have cared for uncommon owls like flammulated and pygmy owls, but many barn owls and even more great horned owls, which are one of the most common animals we care for. There is an amazing diversity of owls in our area (like everything else) because we have also cared for burrowing owls, screech owls, long-eared owls, short-eared owls, saw-whet owls, and spotted owls. Despite the fact they are owls, each species displays a personality that is very distinct from the others. But they all display a sleepy, "leave me alone" attitude when they are disturbed while sleeping during the day.

Barn owl

Burrowing owl

Western
screech owl

Northern
pygmy owl

Long-eared
owl

Short-eared
owl fledgling

Saw-whet
owl

Flammulated
owl

Here are some of our favorite owl videos:

GHORelease2   BurrowingOwlRelease   FlammulatedPygmyOwl

Great horned
owl

The most common injuries we see with great horned owls are caused by either collisions with automobiles or entanglements in barbed wire. We have had long sessions in surgery getting them untangled from wire and suturing the damage that has been done. Treatments with injections to attempt to bring owls out of concussions have been administered by the scores. This may be one of the disadvantages of being a nocturnal hunter of the air. They have the disadvantage of commonly finding roadkill animals and, as a result, are down on the road feeding and they have to dodge cars racing by. Some of these wounds are horrendous and involve euthanasia once the level of damage has been assessed. To show how tough and resilient these birds are, we have had many birds come in, still alive, with multiple injuries, including some who have had a broken wing, damaged eye, concussion, and a broken leg. They are amazingly tough birds to be able to survive all that. Of course, we have to euthanize birds in this shape, but if they were never found and brought to us, they could survive for many weeks before finally passing and suffering the entire time.

One day we received a call from the local copper mine that one of their workers hit an owl on his way to work, and it was still stuck in the grill of the guy's pickup truck. Once arriving at the truck, all that Dennis could see in the grill was a big owl's face looking at him like he had no care in the world. Upon closer inspection, he had hit the grill on impact, knocking a hole in it, something a hard-thrown baseball may have had a hard time doing because of the grill's honeycomb structure. The owl had wedged itself between the radiator fan and the back of the grill with his head sticking out of the hole he had made. After carefully extracting him through the open hood, Dennis was amazed that he had no major injury. He was sore and bruised, but basically the bird walked away from the whole episode without a scratch. How he didn't get chewed up in the radiator fan we don't know, and to survive such an impact? This was one tough and lucky bird but a great example of how resilient they are!

Great horned owl trapped behind grill after being hit on highway.

Great horned
owl shipment
from El Paso
Zoo.

Great horned
owl shipment
from El Paso
Zoo.

A similar episode occurred with a woman who hit an owl on the highway and when she got home, he was still stuck behind the grill and had to be removed. She called us and we drove out to their house south of town and carefully removed the bird. It was humorous to walk into their garage and see this big owl looking out at us, almost like saying let me out of here! Once again, no major injuries!

Great horned owl hatchlings come to us every spring. Often, we get multiple animals at the same time from different nests. We have had as many as twenty-eight, all raised together. The logistics of this gets a bit challenging but with three large flight cages, we can place the youngest owls together in one flight, the medium-aged that are nearly starting to fly in another, and the oldest owls that are starting to fly strong in the largest third cage. As the older group gets released, the shift occurs with moving the birds eventually into the last largest flight cage that will be better to exercise their wing muscles and prepare them for release. In one day, we can go through the experience of capturing owls for release, capturing the medium-aged birds to the large flight, then moving the younger owls into the medium-sized flight. We end up handling nearly thirty owls within an hour!

Great horned
owl fledglings.

It is a riot to watch how they interact with each other, with their fluffy little bodies trying to act like big adult owls. Like other large raptors we have raised, their growth rate is phenomenal. They go from a tiny egg, half the size of a chicken egg, and within days become so large they could not fit into an ostrich egg. They grow from this tiny size to adult size in just three months or so. This rapid growth from egg to adult size is rivaled by few others in the animal world.[97] Equate this with humans. These owls live about twenty-five years, so in one-quarter of a year they mature, this being 1/100 of their life span. As humans, we are physically mature around the age of twenty, live to an average age of say eighty, and this ends up being one-quarter of our life span. Rapid body growth is coupled with rapid feather growth once they have reached a certain stage. We have seen owls and hawk nestlings progress from being completely covered with down feathers to being fully feathered enough to fly in just a few weeks.

Great horned owl hatchling two weeks old.

Great horned owl nestling four weeks old.

Great horned owl fledgling, eight weeks old and flying.

Great horned owl twelve weeks old and ready to release.

Great horned owl fledgling trying to make himself look bigger.

Owls have a "unique" spirit. Where other raptors have this intense, fierce spirit full of fight, owls have a quiet, almost haughty demeanor. It is like everyone is beneath them, and they have an intensity about them that you can almost feel. With great horned owls, their spirit is substantial and powerful. With small owls like screech owls, it is a small, spritelike power they exude.

Great horned owl adult.

One of our rarest owls displaying the most unique owl spirit and behavior is the Mexican spotted owl,[98] only two of which have we cared for. The first arrived late one summer after some widespread forest fires in the area the previous year. He was found in someone's backyard in a community many miles from any suitable habitat. This was a young bird, and our guess is that he was not able to find enough food after the effects of the fire started kicking in, which had dropped the mouse population. He was emaciated and starving as well as scared and stressed.

Mexican spotted owl

Spotted owls have a unique personality that seems to jump from being completely drugged and out of it to acting like they are scared to death. They are much less afraid of humans than other owls and can readily be drawn in and observed or even captured by using recorded owl calls and baiting them in with mice, as researchers have learned.[99]

This spotted owl was fully feathered but still had small down feathers visible from his previous plumage as a hatchling, so he was just around five months old. He was

Spotted owl after release.

easy to rehab, we just needed to fatten him up and give him some flying therapy in one of our flight cages. When he was ready for release, we located a suitable habitat for him and a longtime friend of ours and supporter of Gila Wildlife Rescue released him. Like many releases, pain and worries can symbolically be released as the bird flies free, and hope for better futures can be carried on their wings. It can be a wonderfully healing experience and with the recent death of her father, she let this bird help her do just that.

Spotted owl release.

Spotted owl caught in barbed wire.

The only other spotted owl we have cared for was rescued just recently as we were making editing changes to this book. It was found by tourists visiting the Gila Cliff Dwellings National Monument and reported to the people at the entrance to the monument. They had found it a mile or so down the valley caught in a barbed wire fence and had cut the fence rather than trying to untangle it, exactly like we would have advised and done ourselves. A retired game warden helped to remove the wire and the bird was quickly transported to us. Unfortunately, the bird did not live through the night but was obviously hanging in the fence for at least a week. It was too bad the bird was not found earlier and could have a chance to be saved.

This is an endangered species in our area, and we reported it to the U.S. Fish and Wildlife Service like we are required to do. When they received the news, they asked us to ship the carcass to their spotted owl researcher in Flagstaff, Arizona, for analysis in their ongoing study of the species. At least it provided some needed information for science.

Barn owls are different than all other owls. Not only do they look different with their heart-shaped faces and smaller dark eyes, but they act very different and have a unique spirit.

We admire them and see a different side of them than most people do, but if ever there was an owl that could give you a scary, spooky feeling, this is it. Perched in a tree, this skinny owl is almost invisible. Its coloration that shows when perched blends in perfectly. When flying at night, the solid white undersides of the wings are strikingly visible, especially when reflected off the headlights of a car. We have had many people swear to us they have seen a completely white owl. When questioned, they report the whole body is completely white, making it a snowy owl found only in the arctic. We sometimes tease them and ask if they saw the polar bear and caribou, too, because they are just as unlikely!

We have cared for nestlings all the way through adults and have had many eggs that had to be rescued from nests that we incubate and hatch and raise to maturity.

Barn owl

Left: Barn owl eggs in process of hatching.

Right: Barn owl hatchlings.

Barn owls' behavior is bizarre. They can definitely give you the "spooks." Lowering their heads close to the ground, they swing them back and forth slowly, like a metronome, sometimes also shaking their heads from side to side. Then they start hissing! At first it sounds like a snake hissing, but at times it quickly changes into something that sounds evil. It is a guttural scream coming out with great force, and it can be extremely loud. The combination of the bird's head swinging and the loud scream certainly makes a person or another wild animal wary of this creature, so this helps to protect it. You would swear that an evil being is coming out of it!

Plumage on back of barn owl.

Dennis remembers the call from the local copper mine that there was a big snake they wanted him to catch. When he got there, he heard this hissing noise, which they had thought was a snake, and he reached into a crevice where the noise was coming from and pulled out two baby barn owls, screaming away. Thinking he was pretty macho when he reached for a "snake," they were embarrassed when it was two harmless barn owl hatchlings.

Barn owl babies are some of the ugliest babies of all raptors, maybe of any bird. When the growing nestlings start their screaming behavior, and with their small, almost repulsive bodies barely covered with down feathers—making them look even uglier—they are very scary indeed. They eventually become something quite beautiful and regal.

On the other hand, more than any other owl, barn owls show a soft side that is touching—nuzzling each other and soft, coy looks. The plumage on their back is so exquisitely detailed that you are in awe when you look closely. This beauty in their feathers can never be appreciated by seeing them in nature even with binoculars. Only by being very close to the bird or holding it in your hands can you appreciate this awesome detail. We never forget how fortunate we are . . . and are always thankful.

Barn owl videos are amazing!

BarnOwlHatchlings

BarnOwlHatchlingsBeingFed

BarnOwl2

BarnOwlFledgeScream

BarnOwlAdultScream

Detail of face plumage of barn owl.

269

In the Company of Eagles

Early on in rehabilitating wildlife, eagles became our favorites, the animal that gave us a thrill of excitement every time we encountered them. We dealt with them very closely as we cared for them, but we were seeing them in nature quite often as well. When we spot an eagle, we consider it a blessing. It is always a good day when we get to see one.

These magnificent birds, so powerful, and so full of spirit, are truly the lords of the air. When you see them flying or perched close on a branch, they can look quite large, but only if there is something to reference its size with. Often, they look fairly small, and you don't appreciate their dimensions. On the other hand, when you have one in your arms, wow . . . you really get the impression of their bulk and their power! We say, "Have one in your arms," because it is such a large and strong bird that you cannot handle them by holding them by the legs like we do other raptors. The only way to handle them is to grab their legs from above them (sliding your hands down the sides of the bird from its back) and pulling the whole bird to you and into your chest. So the bird is in your arms with its wings pinned under your arms and you can hold its legs and body to keep it from getting away. To show how large they are, Dennis was holding a large female golden eagle one day that had just been brought to him during one of his classes at the university. The students were remarking, "Look how big she is. The tail is almost touching his feet and he has to pull his face back from being nipped!"

Golden eagle

They are huge, and like all raptors, females are larger than males, sometimes as much as a third larger.[100] Our experience with eagles has been almost totally with goldens, caring for over one hundred golden eagles, and having cared for only three bald eagles up to this point. Golden eagles have one of the largest wingspans of all eagles but are not as heavy or as long as the shorter-winged "larger" eagles of the jungles like harpy eagles or Philippine eagles. Even the bald eagle, although heavier and longer by just a bit, has a shorter average wingspan than a golden. We have had large females with wingspans well over seven feet, and the average span is the fourth-longest wingspan of any of the sixty-plus species of eagles around the world.[101] They are enormous, formidable animals that we always treat with respect and awe.

Holding a struggling golden eagle.

Golden eagle

Eagles are revered worldwide by many cultures. Unlike owls, which can have negative connotations in some cultures, eagles are universally treated as a sacred animal. To Native American cultures, the eagle is known to be the highest flier among all others and, therefore, has a different perspective of the earth. They link this to the perspective of the Creator who watches his creations from up above. Hence, the eagle became a symbol for the all-encompassing divine spirit.[102]

Not many people can say they have looked an eagle in the eye, but if you ever get the chance, you will see this superb creature look back at you with a stare, a look, that speaks volumes. Gaze into an eagle's eyes and you will see power, defiance, a brilliantly radiating fierce spirit, and you will come away with an experience that will stun you and deeply move you. They exude their character and spirit like the sun radiates heat, and you cannot help but feel it.

It is difficult to age a golden eagle once they reach maturity. Juveniles normally have distinct white spots on their wings, and the white stripe at the base of the tail is not as pronounced. But adults, once reaching the age of five or so, can be roughly aged by observing their eyes. Younger birds have darker eyes and as they age, the eyes get lighter colored and often have gold flecks.

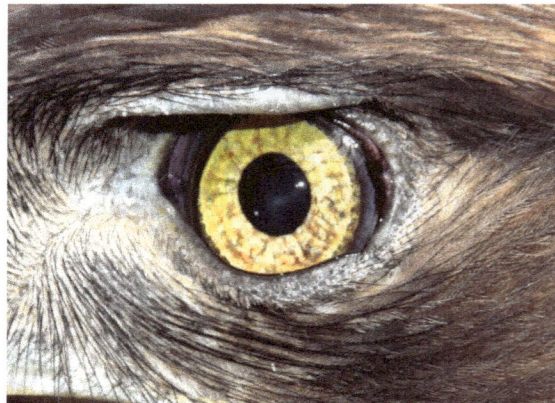

Golden eagle under one year - notice yellow mouth.

Two- to ten-year-old eagle.

Mature eagle ten-plus years old.

This does not give any exact age but can tell us if the bird is in the five- to ten-year-old group, which is a mature but young bird, or if it is a ten- to twenty-year-old bird that is nearing the end of its life. More definitive answers on the age of an eagle can be achieved by analyzing DNA and other measurements like the length of the skull.[103] We get mature animals in from time to time that are not injured in any way nor have any physical problem at all, but their bodies are failing. They are dying of old age just like all animals do.

An eagle came to us one time that was exactly like this. We could find no injury, or infection, or toxicity, and realized he was dying of old age. His eyes were light golden with not only zigzag streaks through the iris, but with lots of tiny, bright flakes that looked like flakes of gold in a miner's pan.

We knew he was quite old, near the end of his twenty- to twenty-five-year life span.[104] He was examined and held in intensive care in the clinic and had been there for a few days. We both looked at each other once we realized the situation, and Denise said, "Dennis,

Old golden eagle.

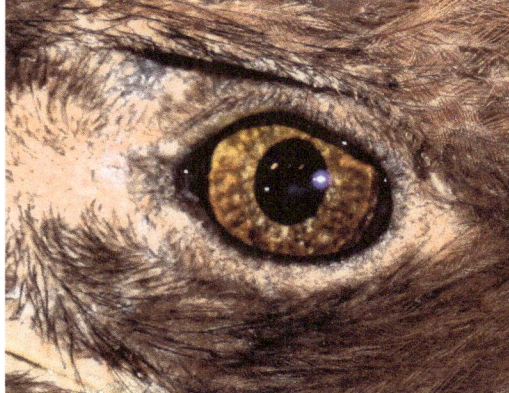

Eye showing old age.

let's take him out of here where it is dark and oppressive and let's put him outside into the sun where he can stay warm and see out and get some fresh air in his last hours."

We placed him in one of our pens and in the sun where he could stay warm. We watched and checked on him throughout the day. He started to hang his head down,

Elderly golden eagle basking in the sun.

with the crest of feathers on the back of his head flared, and late in the afternoon with a setting sun shining on him, he lay down and took one last shuddering breath. We were glad we could make his transition a bit more serene.

The spirit that eagles exude is amazingly powerful and profound to experience. To feel that spirit firsthand is something that, well, you just have to experience personally to understand. All we can say is that every time we come away from dealing with an

eagle, especially when Dennis has to capture the massive bird and hold it for treatment or transport, Dennis is a bit shaken by the ordeal. This is not a bad thing necessarily. There is excitement and danger, adrenaline flowing, but there is a thrill, an elation that he gets that no other experience in life can duplicate. Maybe he has a connection with these birds that they may sense. Maybe they can sense his excitement, and his respect, but whatever the reason, this makes it easier to treat them and without as much fear.

Dennis is not a large guy, being five foot six and 135 pounds. Some people wonder how a man of his size can capture an animal as large and as aggressive as an eagle without getting hurt. They look like they are about his size at times and look like they would weigh about the same. What he just described helps a great deal. He also goes about it with a specific attitude that works well to keep him safe. When he catches eagles in nature, they can be somewhat dangerous but are always injured or sick and not able to fight back much. It is when they are in the flight cage and have been brought back to good health and he must catch a healthy spirited bird that things can get hairy.

Catching an eagle in flight cage.

We do this as infrequently as possible. We may need to catch the eagle for transport, or to examine a healing wound or break, or to administer medications. Dennis will walk into the cage with the assertiveness of say . . . an eagle! He goes right in with a purpose and calmly but firmly captures the bird with no delay or tentativeness—or fear. He lets them know right away that he is the boss now and they *will* be captured, like it or not. Of course they do not like it, but just the approach he uses helps to quickly subdue and capture them, and they submit to his gentle but insistent request. It is impressive to watch. The next time this needs to be done, they are a bit easier to catch because they are now used to his boldness and firmness. Maybe it is brazenness, or as some people may think about us handling all these dangerous creatures, craziness. But it works!

Video Link: GoldenEagleCapture

Golden eagle showing feathers they are named for.

We have cared for a variety of conditions with eagles, some quite complicated, as with the bald eagle we recently cared for with lead poisoning, and others a bit easier. We have experienced gunshot wounds, barbed wire fence gashes, concussions, lead poisoning, West Nile virus, avian influenza, and emaciated juveniles and orphans just to name a few. In some cases, we may have them for only a few days, or we may have them for many months or close to a year, as with our West Nile virus cases. We have seen horrendous damage to some eagles with combinations of broken bones, lacerations, and head injuries that force us to euthanize. In general, we have a very high success rate with them, higher than most other animals we care for. One reason is that they are so large and tough. They

Immature bald eagle with severe wing break— note the brown head, eyes, and beak of a juvenile bird.

have much larger and stronger bones than most other birds, so when they do break a bone, it has to be a comparatively massive collision or trauma to have caused the injury. They are also delicate creatures in some ways that are—as mentioned earlier—prone to head injuries and lead poisoning and are very susceptible to West Nile virus and more recently avian influenza.[105] Although they may seem large, they are still a bird and one that needs to fly precisely to catch food. As a result, they do not weigh much, only between six and fifteen pounds.[106] Due to this, they are affected by winds and storms more than most birds, with their long wingspans acting like a large kite. This invariably leads to serious injury. Poor Thor. . .

We mentioned that we have only cared for three bald eagles. As described in a previous chapter, a large adult female with nearly an eight-foot wingspan came to us with a very severe case of lead poisoning and did not survive. The bird did teach us valuable lessons about how to care for lead poisoning in the future, but this bird's lead levels were too high to save her.

Bald eagle recovered from lead poisoning.

The second bird was a young juvenile, probably less than a year old, who was found in the Gila Wilderness with a severe wing break that was at least six weeks old. His break was so severe and old that he had to be euthanized. It was a sad one to deal with because he was so beautiful but suffering and needed our help.

The third bald eagle was also mentioned in an earlier chapter. This was a more recent experience for us and involved the Mescalero Apache tribe's help.

This bald eagle was filmed fishing recently on one of our local lakes:

BaldEagleFishingBillEvans

Bald eagle Mescalero.

Common raven

The Intelligent Raven

Before leaving this chapter on raptor diversity, we must mention one other bird we care for that is *not* a bird of prey. One of the most common animals brought to us, and one of the most intelligent,[107] ravens are always an adventure to care for. We have tended to everything from adults with broken bones and poisonings, to young raised from eggs or fledglings almost ready to fly.

They are funny, curious, bright, and a bit crazy. Recent studies have shown that this may be the most intelligent of all birds and the level it has reached is much higher than once thought, rivaling human babies' intelligence levels.[108] This research has also shown that their intelligence is present in the entire family that ravens belong to, the Corvid family.[109] This means that crows, jays, and even nuthatches have similar brainpower.

Raven eggs in incubator.

Ravens are one of the most misidentified birds we care for, most often called a crow in our area. Ravens are larger and more robust than crow, and it is easy for them to be distinguished in our area because we very rarely find crows in southern New Mexico as this bird's range maps show.[110] This means that almost all large, black, crow-looking birds are actually ravens in southern areas of New Mexico and Arizona. Still again, this misnomer is tough to change in some people's minds. We have two species, the common raven and the Chihuahuan raven, the latter being a bit stouter but smaller, and with a shorter and stouter beak than the common raven.[111] Another easy way to tell them apart is to see the color of the base of the neck feathers. This is visible only if the wind is blowing their feathers up or if the bird is in hand. When holding the bird, a soft blow on the neck will ruffle these neck feathers and if it is gray, then it is a common raven; if white, then it is the Chihuahuan raven. In fact, this bird formerly was called the white-necked raven in older field guides.[112]

Chihuahuan raven showing bright white nape feather bases.

Raven hatchlings are among the best examples of the ugly duckling syndrome. They start out life being almost repulsive. They are amazingly ugly, but very slowly develop into an incredibly beautiful bird that has plumage with a soft iridescence, making them exceptionally handsome.

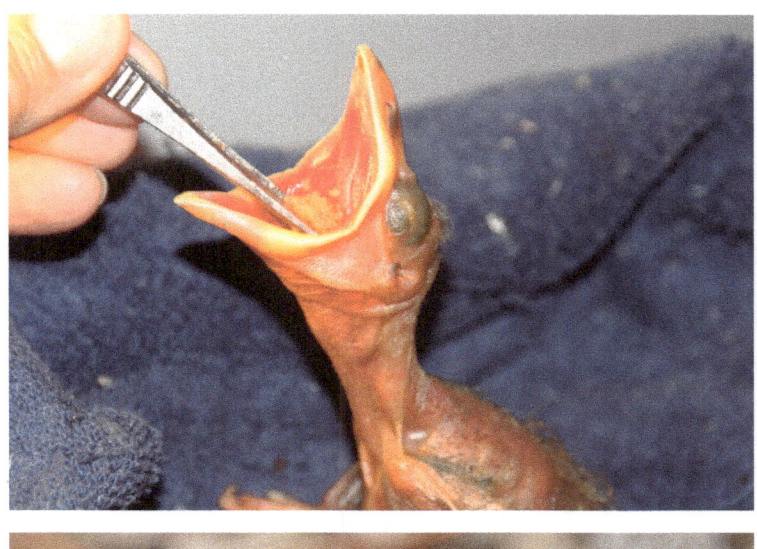

Along with their intelligence comes a unique character that is a bit different in each bird. We have raised five or six of them together and have seen this develop. They are flock animals, and being gregarious tends to place individuals at various levels of hierarchy within a group. The differences in personalities that develop usually have to do with what level they are within the flock.

Raven hatchlings, nestling, and fledgling ready to release.

By the way, we use the term "flock" here and might be tempted to use the term "mob," which describes the behavior of a big group of them at times. We refuse to use the correct term for a group of ravens, which is an "unkindness" of ravens.[113] It is even worse for crows, for they are referred to as a "murder" of crows! We are confused about why these highly successful animals have been labeled with such negative connotations. Some theorize that because they are scavengers, they were ever present on battlefields and so were associated with death and the macabre. As many other humans have discovered, due to their intelligence, they interact with humans more than most other birds. Denise is excellent at duplicating the clicking noises they communicate with and can call them in at times as they are flying by.

Chihuahuan raven

Cultures around the world show raven symbolisms in both positive and negative meanings, and there are hundreds of tales with ravens that have been passed down through generations. Scandinavian cultures, as well as the Inuit Alaskan culture and Native

American cultures, have ravens in many of their legends and beliefs. Ravens interact with humans more than other animals possibly because of their intelligence, and these interactions have strongly influenced humans and their cultures.[114]

Ravens are an amazing mixture of behaviors and characteristics that show themselves in different circumstances. Coyotes are labeled as "tricksters" by southwestern North American tribes, and we see the same trickster behavior often in ravens. When we have a group of them together, they play with each other in this manner, always teasing each other and tussling. We learned the hard way that we can't leave frozen mice out to thaw quickly in the sun because ravens that happen to fly by will steal them. We also observe highly calculated behavior, where you can watch them learn something swiftly. We have observed their vicious predatory side, predating on hatchlings of other birds frequently, and have seen their soft, caring side. They can easily be imprinted and attached to you as you hand-feed them, even before their eyes open. They are one of this earth's most successful creatures and owe their success to their intelligence, superior flying abilities, and in part to humans and human activities.[115]

CHAPTER FIFTEEN

Carnivore Diversity

Raccoon testing freedom after release.

Raccoons and Relatives

Little mischievous bandits are what we call these furry guys, who are omnivores consuming both meat and plants. They are surprisingly strong and aggressive when the predator comes out in them. A friend of ours had an experience with this firsthand one night when he tried to keep a raccoon from killing his prized turkey. He described the crazed look in the raccoon's eyes and the animal pouncing on the back of his turkey, using his "hands" to pluck out enough feathers to get a bite into its neck. He was not only fearful for the turkey, but for himself, especially when he turned his flashlight to the wall behind it and saw a dozen or so pairs of eyes glowing green.

Raccoon "hand."

They are astounding animals, strong survivors in nature, and one of the most successful animals in the wide variety of habitats that they live in. Those paws that look very "handlike" don't have an opposable thumb that allows them to grasp but still are very flexible and dexterous that allow them to grip and, as in this case, pluck![116]

They leave behind a very recognizable star-shaped track that can be found along all waterways in America and is clear evidence of their presence and activity.

Most of our experience in directly caring for raccoons has been with orphaned babies. We have dealt with scores of adult raccoons in the part of our job where we must relocate away from where they are causing problems. In these cases, we capture them in live traps and relocate them immediately. Orphans in the past came to us an average of two a year, so that made sixty to seventy of them we have raised and released. They normally came to us in batches, so we raised three to six of them at a time.

Raccoon print in mud.

Raccoon orphan.

Raccoon baby.

Raccoon babies are fairly easy to raise. They feed well and can be quickly weaned to convert them to solid food and prevent scours. They seem to stay afraid of you, as long as you don't pet them or talk to them and is necessary to prevent any imprinting problems. They stick together in the cage, rarely venturing away from the others, so when one goes exploring in the cage, the others follow right behind. They always curl up together in a big ball to sleep. They are very cute and cuddly looking but can bite like any predator and readily do if you are not careful.

Raccoon babies from White Sands Missile Range.

Why do we call them mischievous bandits? They get into anything and everything, as much out of curiosity as the constant search for something to eat. As they are getting into things, they knock stuff down, break things, tear everything up, and wreak havoc. People returning to their homes after raccoons have broken into them swear at first that their house has been ransacked and searched by someone. They are escape artists, and one time on the morning some of our raccoons were going to be released, we went into the pen and all four of the ones we raised were gone! They had escaped through a small hole a branch had poked in the roof. As we looked up through that hole, we could see all four of them looking right back at us, still in the tree next to the cage! They were quickly recaptured and released to a more suitable area.

They are very dirty, always pooping in their water dish, making us have to put two in the cage so they can use one for their "toilet." They are always picking and tugging at parts of the cage with their hands trying to get out. We often see little arms reaching out trying to grasp leaves on nearby trees and see those little star-shaped hands spread wide. When we enter the cage to clean, they scurry into their den, usually a pet carrier, where they sleep. They are nocturnal, but at times are diurnal, being active in the day. The raccoons we have raised seem to become somewhat diurnal while we have them, and we get to observe their behavior a bit more. They are a riot to watch! Always playing and picking on each other, they seem to be just like the group of kids in *The Little Rascals* or even *The Three Stooges*.

One year we had three raccoons that had been raised together and we released them at the Gila River Bird Area, a wonderfully healthy and beautiful spot. We had transported them to the release site in a pet carrier. It happened to be the same carrier that they were raised in and that they had been using as a den. As usual, when we went into the cage to catch them for release, they scurried into their "den." We just had to close the door and carry the cage to the truck. Once we got to the release site, we took the carrier out and opened it. They would not come out! They wanted to stay in their den that was their security blanket. We eventually had to grab the carrier and shake it to get them out and on their way to freedom.

Raccoon having to be "coaxed" into freedom.

Here is a video of an adult raccoon being released:

RaccoonRelease

Released raccoons—looking back at us saying thank you (or cursing us!)

Two other raccoon relatives reside in our amazingly biologically diverse area, belonging to the same family. Both are unique in their own way but are still obviously a raccoon relative. These are the rarely seen ringtails and coatimundis. These very unusual mammals are increasing in population in our area and have spread farther north in the past decade. We have discussed them in detail in chapter 7, "Unusual Animals."

Both mammals are clearly raccoons with masks on their faces and rings on their tails. Basically, a ringtail is the Chihuahuan desert's version of a raccoon, and the coatimundi is the Sonoran Desert's raccoon. With our immense mixture of life zones and biomes, we get all three species residing and breeding here.[117]

Ringtail - a Chihuahuan Desert raccoon

Here are more videos of ringtails and coatimundi:

RingtailRelease RingtailRelease2 CoatiRelease

Orphaned bobcat.

Secretive Cats

If raptors are the birds that exhibit the most spirit, then our choice for the mammal that exhibits this level of spirit must be the cats. We only have a few species in North America compared to the rest of the world, and if you look at Canada and the US, excluding the states of New Mexico, Arizona, and Texas (which have a couple of more occasionally), then we only have three. This includes mountain lions, bobcats, and the lynx. Although lynx do not technically live in New Mexico, they are being reintroduced into Colorado just north of us.[118] They occasionally cross into New Mexico at the border but are not found anywhere else in the state.[119]

The biological influence of the Sonoran and Chihuahuan Deserts has added three very rare and unique cats to the list in the three states that make up 90 percent of the border between the US and Mexico. Along this border, from Brownsville, Texas, to Yuma, Arizona, there has been an occasional straying over the border of these elusive cats into Texas, New Mexico, and Arizona. Although, we are not sure if this will continue with the construction of security walls along the border.

Those beautiful and secretive cats are the ocelot, the jaguarundi, and yes, the jaguar.[120,121,122] To our knowledge, none of these cats have formed populations in the US, but they are making forays, or even raids—which may be more accurate—north into more remote areas. Some of these cats may be expanding their ranges north as global warming affects their habitats. We have evidence of this in birds, so it is probable in cats also, but the change is slow and not significant enough yet to include anywhere north of the Mexican border as part of their official ranges.

We have never had any experience with an ocelot, but it would be a thrill. We really hope we don't ever see one because that means that one has been hurt or orphaned. Game cameras have caught them coming into water at night, primarily close to the border with Mexico.

Jaguarundis have been seen as far north as Silver City according to our own experiences. We have increasingly received calls over the past ten years about this cat being spied in Arenas Valley and in Pinos Altos, New Mexico. A friend of ours kept having something eat peaches from his tree. He had fenced it off, but still had problems. He started seeing strange tracks, then the animal became bolder, and he saw him feeding in the tree during the daytime. He observed the jaguarundi make an easy leap, he said, as if it could jump much higher, and sailed over the five-foot fence out of his yard. He was able to take a few photos to document this and reported it to the state mammologist at the New Mexico Department of Game and Fish as a new sighting.

They are a very strange-looking and acting cat with a small head, long neck, and long, sleek body with short legs. They are sometimes called the weasel cat or otter cat. This very dark brown, unspotted cat weighs seven to seventeen pounds and is three to four and a half feet long with the tail; they are not much larger than a big house cat.[123] With a length like that though, it sounds like a larger cat, but the tail can be longer than the body making the body fairly small. Everyone who has reported this animal has had a hard time figuring out that it was even a cat and had no idea until they talked to us. We have never had the opportunity to care for a jaguarundi at Gila Wildlife Rescue.

We also have never cared for a jaguar and only recently have been equipped to care for a large cat like this. Dennis did have one experience that involved jaguars that he will never forget that occurred twenty-five years ago. He got a call one afternoon from a friend and former student who had become a successful biology teacher himself. Dennis knew him well and had been hunting and fishing with him often. When he called with a fairly outrageous claim, Dennis believed him because he was just that type of guy. He would rather be conservative than stretch the truth.

"Mr. Miller,"—he would never use "Dennis"—"you are going to think I am crazy, but I just almost hit a very big cat along Highway 90. I have seen quite a few mountain lions around here, but this was huge! And he had a very deep chest!"

"How big was it?" Dennis asked.

"His body stretched the width of the front of my small truck, not counting the tail," he answered.

Kind of confused, not yet considering the possibilities, Dennis said, "This sounds like a big mountain lion to me. I am glad you didn't hit him."

He replied, "Yeah, I had to hit the brakes to keep from making him a new hood ornament, *but* Mr. Miller. He was solid *black*!"

It took a second to register what he was saying, then realized he was talking about sighting a black panther!

Dennis's mind screamed, "Holy crap! My first jaguar encounter and it is in black panther form." Dennis told him to stay right there because he described how the cat had jumped in front of him on Highway 90 on the hill by the turnoff to the Tyrone Mine, just a few miles south of Silver City. He knew exactly where that cat ran, and we thought we may be able to make a cast of a track. Dennis ran to the university to get some casting material and drove out there as fast as he could.

The first thing the young man did was to downplay it once more saying it probably was just a dark lion. He showed Dennis where he had to dodge the animal. We found a trail and followed it across the center median and across the other lane of traffic to the east. This was right where the base of a large mountain started and there was a twenty-foot-high road cut that the cat bounded up after he crossed. He described the animal making that leap in one bound like it was nothing and continuing up the hill. It was heavily forested past this, so he lost sight of him and called Dennis.

We walked back along that trail looking for a print that could be cast. Getting a good cast is more luck than anything. Most of the time the surface an animal is walking on is not soft enough, or it is not the best type of substrate to make a print. When reaching the edge of the road again, we found a good track, although it was located in gravel. It looked huge. But realizing there was more needed to document this as a genuine jaguar sighting, Dennis tried to not let it influence him. It could easily have been a large mountain lion, possibly melanistic. We mixed the casting material and poured it over the track. While it was setting, we climbed the hill a short distance to see if we could pick up the animal's trail, but from there on out the ground was a hard and crumbly granite that never leaves tracks. We got back and lifted the cast. It turned out great, despite the gravel.

That night, Dennis researched as much as he could find about black panther forms of jaguars in New Mexico. As he suspected, they are unheard of in the US, but there are rare reports of black panthers in the rugged and remote mountains of central Mexico.[124] They move up from Central America where they are more commonly found. He also studied the possibility of this being a melanistic mountain lion, one that develops an excess of the pigment melanin and looks very dark. The opposite of this is albinism where there is no pigment present. A black panther is a melanistic form of a jaguar or a leopard. The melanistic forms occur occasionally in tropical jungles because of its advantage in a dark rainforest habitat.[125]

He found that melanism is not found in mountain lions at all, but the color is still a bit brown, and sometimes with the belly and neck being lighter. The young man that sighted the cat described him as having solid shiny black fur, no lighter belly or any other color. He also said his chest was much deeper than the mountain lions he has seen. After reviewing this, Dennis discounted the mountain lion based on color alone. They just don't get dark black. There was adequate light for the young man to see colors clearly.

The next morning, Dennis contacted the Game and Fish office in Santa Fe and talked to the state mammologist. He reported what he had been told, and the mammalogist was intrigued, but skeptical. He had a problem with the eyewitness account and needed a photo or something to prove it. Once he found out we had a cast of a track, he was more optimistic but warned us that the track could show it was a jaguar, but not a black form. We shipped the cast to him that morning. Our discussions continued and we were trying to figure out other possibilities. The only thing we could come up with was that maybe this was an unsuccessful staged exotic hunt, and the intended prey got away. This is legal in some states like Texas, and maybe into Mexico, believe it or not, but certainly not in New Mexico. Could he have strayed that far?

Six weeks later, we finally got the cast back with the evaluation. It was sent to five experts for analysis.[126] Two said definitely a jaguar, two said definitely a mountain lion, and the fifth said that it could be either one. It was disappointing but that was the end of it. This did not count as an official jaguar sighting. And the part about it being black? Forgotten? Dennis's former student was positive about what he saw. Ranchers and home-owners in areas south of where this happened reported sighting a large black cat after this for about two years. We're just sayin'…

Mountain lion as he leaps to freedom.

Just a handful of mountain lions have been cared for by Gila Wildlife Rescue, but each of them was very exciting. Known by many names—cougar, puma, panther, catamount, wildcat—they can reach sizes close to three hundred pounds and normally range between 103 and 190 pounds.[127] The record, killed just across the border in Arizona, weighed 275 pounds with its intestines removed, so probably weighed over three hundred.[128]

Large mammals like this, including adult deer and elk that we could care for, are extremely difficult to rehabilitate. Capture is challenging. The use of tranquilizers, nets, and traps all have a high degree of mortality. Capture myopathy, discussed in this book in the chapter about deer, is worse in adult wildlife than young and can cause death in a few hours or a few days. Transport is a headache because often these animals freak out once moving and hurt themselves in the trailer or cage. Housing can be a problem. These adult animals are so wild that they may jump out, dig or tear a way out, or hurt themselves trying to get out.

Much of our experience with all of these large animals is with their young. We have only cared for lions that are cubs or yearlings, but we did have the opportunity to deal with one adult. These are physically powerful animals that we are very aware can be a danger to us. Extra care and protection are used around these stalwart mammals.

Some detailed stories about mountain lions we have cared for are in two other chapters in this book, both "Dangerous Encounters" and "Frustrations and Heartaches."

Bobcats

We have successfully raised nearly fifty bobcats, some from being just days old to other emaciated youngsters that were close to release age. They are remarkably cute with small spots, soft fluffy fur, and big curious eyes. They are even more adorable than mountain lion kittens. They are so tiny and delicate compared to lion cubs. One of the cutest litters of bobcat kittens we raised was a group of three we named Winkin, Blinkin, and Nod. They were rescued from the Playas copper smelter south of us as it was being demolished with no sign of the mother

around. Being so adorable, we succumbed to the temptation to name an animal we care for, which we don't normally do. The fact that they were named didn't affect our ability to let go when it was time to set them free. It is so rewarding to see them run free after being raised in captivity that any attachment is immaterial.

Orphaned bobcat raised by GWR and ready for release.

295

Winkin, Blinkin, and Nod.

These mammals do better if raised with another of their kind, as we have described with raccoons, and, fortunately, almost all our kittens came in with the entire litter from a dead or missing mother. The largest group we raised together was four, and they were a handful. Once again, what is paramount in the restoration of these animals back into the wild is to keep them wild with no imprinting or habituation to humans. Again, no talking or petting was allowed. We were much more careful to toss food (mice and rats once weaned) into their pen without them seeing us. Places were provided in the pen for them to defecate and cover it up, so contact with them for cleaning was kept to a minimum because we didn't have to clean as often and could quickly come in and change their "litter box."

Live food was placed in the cage at an early age starting with pinky mice and rabbits and eventually to adult mice, rats, and rabbits. What always impresses us is that every cat we cared for from kitten stage on would instantaneously attack any live food placed in the pen.

BobcatKittensPlaying

The attack is swift, and the kills are quick. They then leisurely eat it, like they are savoring a good meal. One of our local rabbit breeders donated live rabbits for the kill training, and we know they are ready to release when they can kill with ease. We cared for two bobcat kittens one time that would kill rabbits quite a bit larger than them. They dispatched them so quickly that if you blinked or looked away for a second, you would miss it. It was quite impressive to see the wildness come out in them and to observe

Young bobcat killing prey

how this instinctive behavior is such an innate one. There is no mother around to teach them how to kill and they do quite well. Mother may teach them where to look for food and how to search for it, a skill we cannot teach like she could. We try to compensate for this by hiding food in places in the pen and get them to search to stimulate behavior that they are born with or is innate.

With repetitive and varied methods, they become very skilled at hunting. Eventually, experience in nature can teach them these lessons. Our job is to provide enough experiences for them so that they have enough skills to survive until this learning can be reinforced once back in the wild. By the time bobcats are released, they are quite adept at being a predator and we think they succeed quite well.

The steps we use to raise wildlife are designed to keep them wild and are very effective. We proved it one time with a bobcat youngster about four months old that was brought to us by being left in a box on the front doorstep of our house. With the pet carrier was a note that said, "Got him from a den to make into a pet. After he killed all my chickens and cats and tore up all the curtains in my house, I am giving him to you. These don't make good pets!"

Although he cried for three days, we tried our best to block it out and waited him out. He finally stopped, and with our methods of feeding and reduced interactions with him, he slowly became more and more wild. It took three or four months, but he did wild up and developed the fierce and powerful spirit that these animals need to survive. This was once again one of those cases that confuse us as to people's motives. What selfishness . . . they stole him from his mother right out of the den!

Once reaching full adult size, bobcats can be very aggressive and dangerous, although sometimes it is just a bluff. Our friends got firsthand experience at this one time when they were helping us on a weekend we were out of town. We had quite a few animals that needed to be fed daily, and they volunteered to come in and feed. We had two bobcat kittens in our large mammal pen that had been set up with branches and ropes for them to exercise on. The pen had doors with latches on the outside that catch as the door is closed. In order to get back out we always have a string that runs through a hole and into the cage so you can pull on the cord and it unlatches the door.

When our friend walked into the cage to feed the bobcats, she asked her husband, "What is this string here for?" and proceeded to pull it out of the hole. Of course, the door closed, and they were locked in. Not realizing it at first, they completed their feeding duties and when they turned to go, they realized what they had done. "THAT'S what that string is for," she said nervously laughing.

Young bobcat.

His reply was classic: "Yeah, but now we are locked in with two killer bobcats and we're f***ed!" They calmed down and he tried to reach the latch with his long arms, opening the door as much as he could to reach out. He couldn't reach it and they started to worry because they had run in quickly to do this but had left their car running out front with their dogs in it. Finally, his wife reached with her smaller fingers through to open the latch and they were free, having been locked in for close to an hour. The "killer" bobcats just watched and snarled at them the entire time.

"Killer" bobcats.

As cute as these bobcats may seem, even as young cubs, they still can be very aggressive and will bite and scratch at any opportunity. They look so much smaller than a mountain lion, and you get the impression they are just a bit larger than a house cat and therefore not dangerous. Think again. These guys are the cat with "little man syndrome" and are always going around acting tough and mean. We do see their soft side and have observed incredible gentleness with each other, but even after being raised by hand, they are still tough kitties. Here is one that we raised and were trying to catch for release. Does he look imprinted and not wild anymore?

BobcatCapture

BobcatRelease

Very angry bobcat raised by hand but still very wild.

Gray fox

Elegant Foxes

Only one species of fox lives in our immediate area, despite the variations in colors that occur. There is a tiny species called a kit fox that lives in deserts south and west of us, but we have never seen one or cared for one. We often get calls about a "red fox," but we do not have that species here and gray foxes have some red in them. Gray foxes are the only canid in North America that can climb, which is rare in any member of the dog family, and they can easily and readily scale trees, fences, walls, and can even climb onto the roof of a house.[129,130]

Gray foxes are handsome as adults and adorably cute as pups. Twice we have been confused as to what species the animal was that was brought to us, and both times it ended up being a newborn fox. One day while at the university, a fox puppy was brought to us with eyes still closed, less than a week old, and between all of the biology professors examining it, we couldn't be sure at first as to what we actually had.

Gray fox pups.

Gray fox pups with eyes barely opening.

They are about the size of a short, fat cigar, fitting in one's palm, with very short fur and toes not well-developed. Once eyes open and they start running around, they are covered with dense, fluffy, almost kinky fur and with tiny, bright eyes full of spunk. At this point, we start weaning them. Unlike when raising deer, foxes and bobcats cannot be fed on a rack in a pen because at first their eyes are closed. They must be bottle fed by hand. We are very careful, though, not to treat them in any other way except like they are—a wild animal.

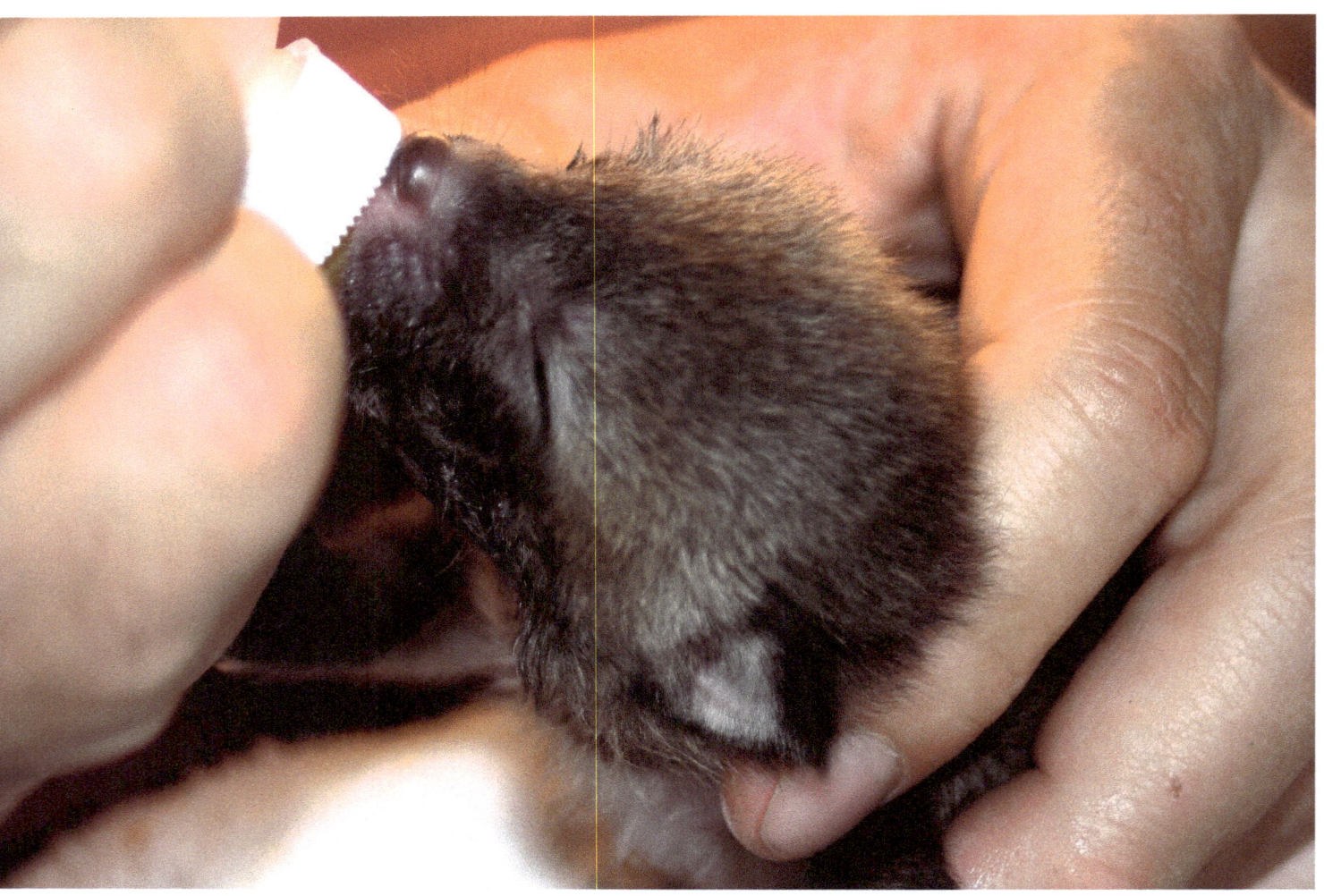

Gray fox pups hand-fed until they can lap from a bowl.

The imprinting that starts to occur as they transition from a bottle to lapping up milk from a bowl and eventual weaning is easily undone by keeping them isolated from us as they mature from this point on. Crying for milk is short-lived as they feel solid food fill their bellies.

If foxes are raised singly, it is more difficult to get them through this stage, but if they are raised with others, they comfort each other and act like any other pack animal and stick together like glue.

Gray fox
youngster.

Gray fox

As you can see by our photos, foxes are quite handsome. They are hyperactive animals as they near adulthood, and you can watch their intelligence develop as they grow. Once adults, they are very clever and start trying to break out of cages and digging out. They are telling us they are ready to be free . . . and we listen to them.

A few years back we had a large outbreak of rabies in foxes in Southwestern New Mexico that even started spreading into the bobcat populations.[131] Dead foxes were being found and rabid foxes were interacting with humans. This problem was compounded by an urban fox population that may have become too high, similar to what we see in deer and skunks. We had several adults brought directly to us that we had to put down as well as some that we had to go out and capture and euthanize. Some of these foxes were foaming at the mouth, walking in circles, staggering, falling down, and suffering greatly.

After months of this problem with it growing each day, we were driving toward our house, going up a hill on the highway that had large medians. As we drove by, Denise spotted a fox in the median that was showing signs of rabies, staggering and foaming at the mouth. We turned around and prepared to deal with it. The only thing to do was to euthanize it. Capturing a fox in a median would be almost impossible, they are too quick. If it gets away, all directions lead to houses and people and the possibility of the disease spreading. Telling Denise to cover her ears tight, Dennis pulled up to the median and using both hands, fired his .357 Magnum pistol and dispatched it, solving the problem. It was quick and the most prudent thing to do but damaged his hearing in the process. He could not cover his ears and due to the percussion being made worse by being inside a closed vehicle, his ears rang for days and now have a bit of hearing loss. Like Denise says, there is never a dull moment!

Just after this, we received four fox puppies about four weeks old. They were found in an abandoned car that was being hauled away. The man put the car on a trailer and drove to Las Cruces, a two-hour drive southeast of here. When he stopped to get gas, he found them. Not having anything to put them in, he cut the top off a quart milk carton and placed them in it. When he got back to town and brought the babies to us, he handed Dennis the milk carton, not saying anything at first. We saw one baby on top, the others were underneath. As we turned the carton on its side on the counter, out came one, then two, then three tiny fox pups. Thinking that was all, we glanced into the carton again and there was one more, even smaller, cowering in the back. He was the runt and was always more afraid than the others while raising them.

These guys were successfully raised together and released together. Just as we do with most wildlife, in particular mammals like foxes, bobcats, and raccoons, we release them in as remote an area as possible. If there is any imprinting or habituation of being around humans, we know from experience in our own cages that given enough time, left alone with no human contact, their natural instincts come out and they lose that familiarity and become afraid. Being released in remote areas is what will protect them. We have released animals in the "bootheel" of New Mexico, in remote mountain ranges in the southwest part of the state, in wilderness areas, and in remote areas that require serious four-wheel drive vehicles to get to.

We released these foxes in a beautiful grassy meadow near the Continental Divide in the Aldo Leopold Wilderness. As always, we sent them off with a prayer, and our thanks for the opportunity to help them, and said to them, "Live long and prosper," the only time we ever spoke directly to them for the last nine months.

Gray fox pups found in abandoned car—eyes still closed.

Gray fox released—one of four orphans released together.

FoxTrapRelease

Gray fox

CHAPTER SIXTEEN

Final Thoughts

As we complete this book, a saga of our lives dedicated to wildlife, we would like to leave you with some thoughts. Throughout this book, stories have unfolded that at times are heartwarming and stimulating, but others are sad and somewhat depressing examples of how thoughtless and ignorant some people can be in dealing with wildlife. We may have given the wrong impression. A great majority of people we deal with are caring and concerned about doing what is right with wildlife and are eager to learn and to help.

Current changing attitudes on how humans deal with wildlife are wonderfully encouraging. Certainly, in the past there has been ignorance and even downright maliciousness

Peregrine falcon

by a few individuals toward wildlife, but in the late 1970s, when Gila Wildlife Rescue was founded, things were a bit different. Humans were just starting to realize that we are not the rulers of the earth and have control of all the creatures in it like we once thought. We were just beginning to see more and more evidence of how human actions have caused ecological damage and damage that eventually affects ourselves as humans in profound ways. No longer could we say that humans had the right to let wildlife serve them. We could start to see that our actions of the past may have done more harm than good. Today, this attitude is the norm rather than just some radical "damned environmentalist's" idea like it was in the sixties and seventies. Most residents in the area at that time viewed these ideals as being only thoughts from crazy hippies. After all, we had annual visits to our forest from the Rainbow Gathering nudists each summer!

Great horned owl

Humans worldwide have slowly been exposed to more and more examples of how we are an integral part of a bigger picture, one where we are not the rulers over the other life we live with on earth but are almost equal partners with other species in a complex web of interactions where each of us plays an integral role. The "almost" part of this is that humans have a superior brain that allows them to see the bigger picture and to see what the future could bring, unlike the rest of the animal kingdom that has no ability for that kind of thought. This gives us a unique responsibility to be the stewards of the health of this earth because we are the only organisms with a consciousness of the fact that we could destroy the earth and all life in it. This knowledge has helped us make great strides in the health of the earth and in getting closer to ensuring our own survival. With our knowledge of global warming, the effects of pollution, the effects of nuclear bombs and nuclear radiation, the effects of overpopulation, and a slew of health-related discoveries, we have made some major advances in the survival of this earth. We still have a great deal of work to do but the work completed so far has helped at least, and we are increasing our awareness and acceptance of responsibility for the future of the entire planet.

Directly in this specific area of Southwestern New Mexico, changes in attitudes have resulted in a majority of people realizing how important it is to keep not only ourselves healthy but realizing our responsibility to keep the area around us healthy, too, or it will affect us and possibly our own health and well-being. We see more habitat restoration work as well as we observe more ranches and farms becoming responsible and reducing the amount of damaging chemicals they use and improving ranching and farming practices. We find a growing support for wildlife rehabilitation and, in general, a growing sense of pride in how unique and biologically healthy an area we all share here.

There are still some who are resistant to change and do not realize the responsibility we humans have. At least we are working at it and improving slowly. The very controversial issue of putting a dam on the Gila River has shown how support for the protection of the environment has increased in our area. There are a large number of people who are against the dam and have organized and are fighting to protect this river, one of the last free flowing or undammed rivers in the nation. The fight may not result in stopping the dam, the government agency may do what it wants without the approval of the public living in the area, but the issue has brought people together to fight for an environmental cause, and this growing support will continue for years to come and hopefully do a great deal of good.

One of the best examples of the scope of the problem is that each year, there are more deer killed by automobiles in our country than the total number of deer harvested by hunters nationwide. If you look at the growing problem in Pennsylvania and other surrounding states, you can start to see how big a problem this really is.

Similar to what has happened recently in this specific area, nationwide it is becoming more and more common that bow hunters are authorized to hunt within the city limits and areas bordering urban areas to reduce urban herd sizes. Across the country, hunting is poised for a comeback because it is a useful tool in managing the overpopulation of wildlife. This may not sit well with everyone, particularly in a period of time when people are becoming more protective of wildlife and want to keep their populations healthy. These somewhat severe methods have become necessary to counterbalance the highly successful efforts of the past in the recovery of some species of wildlife.

Too many wild animals can be almost as bad for the animals as too few. This is why across the country people find themselves forced with a conundrum. The same environmental sensitivity that brought species back from near extinction now makes it painful for some to do what experts say must be done; a large number of them need to be killed. The nation as a whole has been very successful in our recovery efforts of some populations, so now there is a need to have things corrected before they cause damage to themselves simply by being overpopulated. What a change! We went from almost totally wiping out deer, bears, turkey, pronghorn, and elk to now dealing with serious overpopulation problems in certain areas.[132]

The damage was done in the last part of the nineteenth century and the first half of the twentieth century with unregulated hunting (and allowing commercial hunting) and habitat destruction. With changing attitudes about wildlife and an effort to not only stop habitat destruction but to regain the lost habitat, we have had an overabundance of success in some areas. By 1907, 34 percent of forest in the United States had been destroyed, much of it in the east. But since then, we have maintained the forest at over 70 percent of what it originally was. Much of this has also been replaced by agriculture and is still environmentally useful.[133]

The result of this recovery is that wildlife has benefited and now they have reached unhealthy levels that in some areas have brought wildlife populations to levels higher than when Columbus first set foot here.[134] This problem is compounded by a large amount of replanting occurring around our homes, in our parks and golf courses, and in metropolitan areas, attracting wildlife into cities and our yards instead of in the wild where they should be. Problems are multiplied even further by people feeding wildlife, thinking they are helping them. This brings increased numbers of wildlife directly into our communities and causes a multitude of problems. Once again, it was our own doing. Now we have to look at some radical methods to regain the balance that we desperately need.

The future actually looks bright. This certainly is a big turnaround from the destructive past. What an amazing thing to go from wildlife almost exterminated to now dealing with how to handle too many of them! Again, the changing attitudes of the public is what has brought this about, and now we need the attitude to change once more and get people to realize that they may need to deal with the wildlife around them a bit differently. Accepting hunting as a control method, realizing that feeding wildlife is harmful, working at not destroying habitat and instead working to "improve" it are some of the changes we need to still work on. The pride we can take in our success and the balanced and healthy ecosystems we will live in can be the impetus to continue.

Pronghorn

As far as Gila Wildlife Rescue, the future looks bright as well. We have so much outpouring of support it is truly heartwarming. The community recognizes the need for our services, and they are very grateful for our commitment. They appreciate and respond to our warnings and notices about wildlife problems and issues that come up. In fact, after telling many of these stories to friends and to the public during talks and presentations to groups, they are the ones who have encouraged us to write this book and spread the message. We look forward to the years to come in caring for the wildlife of our area. We will eventually start looking at how to continue our work once we are not around. That may be our biggest challenge yet. . . .

1   John C. Craighead and Frank C. Craighead Jr., *Hawks, Owls and Wildlife* (Dover, 1969), 311-315.

2   R. D. Sage, "Wild Mice," in *The Mouse in Biomedical Research*, eds. H. L. Foster, J. D. Small, and J. G. Fox (Academic Press, 1981), 40–90.

3   Rebecca L. Grambo, *Eagles* (Voyageur Press, 1999), 11.

4   Capainolo, Peter., Butler, Carol A. How Fast Can A Falcon Dive? Fascinating Answers to Questions about Birds of Prey. (United States: Rutgers University Press, 2010), 159-159.

5   David H. Johnson, "Wing Loading in 15 Species of North American Owls," in *Biology and Conservation of Owls of the Northern Hemisphere*, eds. James R. Duncan, David H. Johnson, and Thomas H. Nicholls (U.S. Department of Agriculture, 1997), 553-559.

6   Nicole Nemeth, Daniel Gould, Richard Bowen, and Nicholas Komar, "Natural and Experimental West Nile Virus Infections of Five Raptor Species," *Journal of Wildlife Diseases* 42, no. 1 (2006): 1–13.

7   Iñigo Zuberogoitia, Jabi Zabala-Albizua, and José Enrique Martínez, "Moult in Birds of Prey: A Review of Current Knowledge and Future Challenges for Research," *Ardeola* 65, no. 2 (1 July 2018): 183–207, https://doi.org/10.13157/arla.65.2.2018.rp1.

8   Finn Salomonsen, "The Moult Migration," *Wildfowl* 19 (January 1968): 5–24, https://wildfowl.wwt.org.uk/index.php/wildfowl/article/view/331/331.

9   J. Christian Franson and Robin E. Russell, "Lead and eagles: demographic and pathological characteristics of poisoning, and exposure levels associated with other causes of mortality," *Ecotoxicology* 23 (2014): 1722–1731, https://doi.org/10.1007/s10646-014-1337-0.

10   Nigel W. H. Barton and David C. Houston, "A comparison of digestive efficiency in birds of prey," *Ibis* 135, no. 4 (1993): 363–371.

11   Vincent A. Slabe, James T. Anderson, Brian A. Millsap, Jeffrey L. Cooper, Alan R. Harmata, Marco Restani et al., "Demographic implications of lead poisoning for eagles across North America," *Science* 375, no. 6582 (2022): 779–782, doi:10.1126/science.abj3068.

12   Francisco Lopez-Jimenez, M.D., "Can Chelation Therapy Treat Heart Disease?" Mayo Clinic, June 13, 2023, https://www.mayoclinic.org/diseases-conditions/heart-disease/expert-answers/chelation-therapy/faq-20157449

13   Jesse A. Fallon, Patrick Redig, Tricia A. Miller, Michael Lanzone, and Todd Katzner, "Guidelines for Evaluation and Treatment of Lead Poisoning of Wild Raptors," *Wildlife Society Bulletin* 41, no. 2 (2017): 205–211.

14   Jenny P. Pope, Debra L. Miller, Matthew C. Riley, Eman Anis, and Rebecca P. Wilkes, "Characterization of a novel *Canine distemper virus* causing disease in wildlife," *Journal of Veterinary Diagnostic Investigation* 28, no. 5 (2016): 506–513, doi:10.1177/1040638716656025.

15 K. M. Charlton, W. A. Webster, G. A. Casey, C. E. Rupprecht, "Skunk Rabies," *Reviews of Infectious Diseases* 10, no. 4 (November–December 1988): S626–S628, https://doi.org/10.1093/clinids/10.Supplement_4.S626.

16 Herb Wilson, "The Sense of Smell in Birds," Maine Birds, December 11, 2023, https://web.colby.edu/mainebirds/2023/12/11/the-sense-of-smell-in-birds/.

17 Simon Potier, "Olfaction in Raptors," *Zoological Journal of the Linnean Society* 189, no. 3 (July 2020): 713–721, https://doi.org/10.1093/zoolinnean/zlz121.

18 Andy Dobson, "Raccoon Rabies in Space and Time," *Proceedings of the National Academy of Sciences* 97, no. 26 (December 19, 2000): 14041–14043, doi: 10.1073/pnas.97.26.14041.

19 Goodell J, Joseph V, Atkinson C, Atkinson J. 2018. Conditioning and Release Strategies for the Golden Eagle: Techniques to Increase Survivorship and Mitigate Take.

20 Gary Brown, The Great Bear Almanac (Lyons & Burford, 1993), 16-22.

21 Emily G. Pieracci, Christine M. Pearson, Ryan M. Wallace, Jesse D. Blanton, Erin R. Whitehouse, Xiaoyue Ma et al., "*Vital Signs:* Trends in Human Rabies Deaths and Exposures—United States, 1938–2018," U. S. Centers for Disease Control and Prevention, *Morbidity and Mortality Weekly Report* 68, no. 23 (June 2019): 524–528, http://dx.doi.org/10.15585/mmwr.mm6823e1.

22 Arnaud Tarantola, "Four Thousand Years of Concepts Relating to Rabies in Animals and Humans, Its Prevention and Its Cure," *Tropical Medicine and Infectious Disease* 2, no. 2 (2017): 5, 27-32. https://doi.org/10.3390/tropicalmed2020005.

23 Rebecca F. Wisch, "Table of State Rabies Vaccination Laws for Companion Animals," Michigan State University College of Law, Animal Legal and Historical Center, 2002, https://www.animallaw.info/topic/table-rabies-vaccination-laws

24 "Rabies: Information for Diagnostic Laboratories," U.S. Centers for Disease Control and Prevention, 2024, https://www.cdc.gov/rabies/php/laboratories/diagnostic.html.

25 John Marzluff and Tony Angell, *Gifts of the Crow: How Perception, Emotion, and Thought Allow Smart Birds to Behave Like Humans* (Atria Books, 2013), 1-10.

26 James Ferguson-Lees and David Christie, *Raptors of the World: A Field Guide* (Houghton Mifflin Harcourt, 2001), [88].

27   Janet Sullivan, "Taxidea taxus," in Fire Effects Information System, U.S. Department of Agriculture, Forest Service, Rocky Mountain Research Station, Fire Sciences Laboratory,1996, www.fs.usda.gov/database/feis/animals/mammal/tata/all.html.

28 Michael Wink, "Phylogeny of Old and New World Vultures (Aves: Accipitridae and Cathartidae) Inferred from Nucleotide Sequences of the Mitochondrial Cytochrome b Gene," *Zeitschrift für Naturforschung C* 50, no. 11–12 (1995): 868–882, https://doi.org/10.1515/znc-1995-11-1220.

29 Manuel Hernández Fernández and Elizabeth S. Vbra, "A complete estimate of the phylogenetic relationships in Ruminantia: a date species-level supertree of extant ruminants," *Biological Reviews* 80, no. 2 (2005): 269–302.

30 George A. Bubenik and Anthony B. Bubenik, eds., *Horns, Pronghorns, and Antlers: Evolution, Morphology, Physiology, and Social Significance* (Springer, 1990), 3-12.

31 Bart W. O'Gara and James D. Yoakum, *Pronghorn: Ecology and Management* (University Press of Colorado, Wildlife Management Institute, 2004), 24-27.

32 Samuel I. Zeveloff, *Raccoons: A Natural History* (Smithsonian Books, 2002), 33–37.

33 David Valenzuela, "Natural history of the white-nosed coati, *Nasua narica*, in a tropical dry forest of western Mexico," Revista Mexicana de Mastozoología, Nueva Época 3, no. 1 (1998): 26–44.

34 Ben T. Hirsch, Margaret A. Stanton, and Jesus E. Maldonado, "Kinship Shapes Affiliative Social Networks but Not Aggression in Ring-Tailed Coatis," *Plos ONE* 7, no. 5 (2012): e37301, https://doi.org/10.1371/journal.pone.0037301.

35 William S. Longland, "Reversed Sexual Size Dimorphism: Its Effect on Prey Selection by the Great Horned Owl, *Bubo Virginianus*," *Oikos* 54, no. 3 (1989): 395–98, https://doi.org/10.2307/3565301.

36 A. S. Perry, I. Yamamoto, I. Ishaaya, and R. Perry, "Rodenticides," in *Insecticides in Agriculture and Environment*, Applied Agriculture (Springer Verlag, 1998), 181–186, https://doi.org/10.1007/978-3-662-03656-3_27.

37 Donald B. Snyder, "Strychnine as a Potential Control for Redwinged Blackbirds," *The Journal of Wildlife Management* 25, no. 1 (1961): 96–99, https://doi.org/10.2307/3797003.

38 Alina Petre, "What Is Activated Charcoal? Benefits and Uses," Healthline, February 23, 2023, https://www.healthline.com/nutrition/activated-charcoal.

39 2023–2024 New Mexico Furbearer Rules and Information, New Mexico Department of Game and Fish, April 18, 2023, 11. https://wildlife.dgf.nm.gov/download/2023-2024-new-mexico-furbearer-rules-and-info/.

40 N.M. Code R. § 7.4.2.12

41 "Rabies in the United States: Protecting Public Health," U.S. Centers for Disease Control and Prevention, June 21, 2024, https://www.cdc.gov/rabies/php/protecting-public-health/index.html.

42 "Chemist Has the Power to Tame Skunk's Spray," *Chicago Tribune*, November 25, 1994, updated August 9, 2021, https://www.chicagotribune.com/1994/11/25/chemist-has-the-power-to-tame-skunks-spray/.

43 Migratory Bird Treaty Act of 1918, 16 U.S. Code § 703, "Taking, killing, or possessing migratory birds unlawful."

44 New Mexico Administrative Code, Title 19: Natural Resources and Wildlife; Chapter 35: Captive Wildlife Uses; Part 7: Importation of Live Non-Domestic Animals, Birds, and Fish; Section 19.35.7.19: Release from Captivity for Imported Animals.

45 New Mexico Department of Game and Fish State Statutes, Chapter 17: Game and Fish and Outdoor Recreation; Chapter 30: Criminal Offenses; Chapter 66 NMSA: Motor Vehicles; and Rules in 19.30.1–19.36.3 NMAC. 1978.

46 Migratory Bird Treaty Act of 1918, 16 U.S.C. 703–712.

47 The Bald and Golden Eagle Protection Act of 1940, U.S. Fish & Wildlife Service, 16 U.S.C. 668–668d.

48   Endangered Species Act of 1973, U.S. Fish & Wildlife Service., 16 U.S.C. 1531–1544.

49   "List of Bird Species To Which the Migratory Bird Treaty Act Does Not Apply," *Federal Register* 85, no. 74 (April 16, 2020).

50   E. S. Williams and E. T. Thorne, "Exertional Myopathy (Capture Myopathy)" in *Noninfectious Diseases of Wildlife, Second Edition,* eds. Anne Fairbrother, Louis N. Locke, and Gerald L. Hoff (Iowa State University Press, 1996), 181–193.

51   Juan Krauer and Samantha Wisely, "Diarrhea in Farmed White-tailed Deer Fawns," University of Florida IFAS Extension, 2020.

52   M. Dinesh, Jigari C. Thakor, Hiteshwar Singh Yadav, R. Manikandan, S. Anbazhagan, E. Kalaiselvan et al., "Capture Myopathy: An Important Non-infectious Disease of Wild Animals," *International Journal of Current Microbiology and Applied Sciences* 9, no. 4 (April 2020): 952–962.

53   Saul McLeod, "Konrad Lorenz: Theory of Imprinting in Psychology," Simply Psychology: Famous Experiments, updated June 16, 2023, https://www.simplypsychology.org/konrad-lorenz.html.

54   "Deer Fawn Facts," Maryland Department of Natural Resources, https://dnr.maryland.gov/wildlife/Pages/plants_wildlife/Deer_Fawn_FAQ.aspx.

55   Vikki Simons-Krupp, "Understanding Deer," Native Animal Rescue Publications, 2024, https://www.nativeanimalrescue.org/understanding-deer/.

56   Erwin L. Boeker, Virgil E. Scott, Hudson G. Reynolds, and Byron A. Donaldson, "Seasonal Food Habits of Mule Deer in Southwestern New Mexico," *The Journal of Wildlife Management* 36, no. 1 (1972): 56–63, https://doi.org/10.2307/3799188.

57   Laura A. Romin and John A. Bissonette, "Deer: Vehicle Collisions: Status of State Monitoring Activities and Mitigation Efforts," *Wildlife Society Bulletin* 24, no. 2 (1996): 276–83, http://www.jstor.org/stable/3783118.

58   New Mexico Code R. 19.30.2.8 (D), "Techniques/Intervention."

59   "Facts + Statistics: Deer Vehicle Collisions," Insurance Information Institute, 2022–2023, https://www.iii.org/fact-statistic/facts-statistics-deer-vehicle-collisions.

60   "Search Continues for Lion that Killed Pinos Altos Man," New Mexico Department of Game and Fish News Release, June 23, 2008, https://www.wildlife.state.nm.us/legacy/publications/press_releases/documents/2008/062308pinosaltoslion.html.

61   John A. Byers, "Peaceable Peccaries," in *The Natural History Reader in Animal Behavior,* ed. Howard Topoff (Columbia University Press, 1987), 177–185.

62   Bret A. Moore and Fabiano Montiani-Ferreira, "Ophthalmology of Accipitrimorphae, Strigidae, and Falconidae: Hawks, Eagles, Vultures, Owls, Falcons, and Relatives," in *Wild and Exotic Animal Ophthalmology,* eds. Fabiano Montiani-Ferreira, Bret A. Moore, and Gil Ben-Shlomo (Springer, 2002), https://doi.org/10.1007/978-3-030-71302-7_20.

63   Steven I. Rabin, "Growth Plate Fractures (Physeal Fractures)," Medscape, December 8, 2023, https://emedicine.medscape.com/article/1260663-overview?form=fpf.

64 Gorden L. Bender, ed., *Reference Handbook on the Deserts of North America* (Bloomsbury Academic, 1982), 37-51.

65 Vernon Bailey, "Life Zones and Crop Zones of New Mexico," *North American Fauna Volumes 35–36*, U.S. Government Printing Office, 1913.

66 William S. Clark and Brian K. Wheeler, *Hawks of North America* Second Edition, Peterson Field Guide Series (Houghton Mifflin Harcourt, 2001), 213.

67 Charles R. Preston, *Wild Bird Guides: Red-tailed Hawk* (Stackpole Books, 2000), 11.

68 Noel Snyder and Helen Snyder, *Raptors of North America Natural History and Conservation* (Voyageur Press, 2006), 158.

69 Mike Unwin, *The Life Cycle of Birds* (Heinemann/Raintree, 2003), [37-38].

70 Clark, *A Field Guide to Hawks of North America*, 198-202.

71 National Audubon Society, *National Audubon*, John Farrand Jr., *The Audubon Society Master Guide to Birding Volume 1: Loons to Sandpipers* (Alfred Knopf, 1983), 240.

72 *Society Birds of North America* (Knopf Doubleday, 2021), 639.

73 *The Birds of North America: Common Black Hawk.* (n.p., 1994), 1-3.

74 Natthanet Sritrakoon, Kaset Sutasha, Chaiyan Kasorndorkbua, Winyu Karntip, Noppasin Jindawattana, and Aree Thayananuphat, "Bilateral cataracts extraction by lens aspiration and foldable intraocular lens implantation in a black kite (*Milvus migrans*)," *Open Veterinary Journal* 11, no. 3 (Jul–Sep 2021): 441–446.

75 David H. Ellis, James C. Bednarz, Dwight G. Smith, Stephen P. Flemming, "Social Foraging Classes in Raptorial Birds: Highly developed cooperative hunting may be important for many raptors," *BioScience* 43, no. 1 (January 1993): 14–20, https://doi.org/10.2307/1312102.

76 Kenn Kaufman, *Lives of North American Birds* (Houghton Mifflin, 1996), 122.

77 John Farrand Jr., *The Audubon Society Master Guide to Birding Volume 1: Loons to Sandpipers* (Alfred Knopf, 1983), 216.

78 Capainolo, Peter., Butler, Carol A., "How Fast Can a Falcon Dive? Fascinating Answers to Questions about Birds of Prey". (United States: Rutgers University Press, 2010): 45-55.

79 D. A. Orton, "The Speed of a Peregrine's Dive," *The Field* (1975), 588–590.

80 McMillan, M., Falcon Attack: "How Peregrine Falcons Maneuver At Nearly 225 MPH", Forbes, August 5, 2022. https://www.forbes.com/sites/fionamcmillan/2018/04/13/falcon-attack-how-peregrine-falcons-maneuver-at-nearly-225-mph/

81 Kate Davis, *Falcons of North America* (Mountain Press Publishing Company, 2008), 150.

82 John Farrand Jr., *The Audubon Society Master Guide to Birding Volume 1: Loons to Sandpipers* (Alfred Knopf, 1983), 30.

83 Ferguson-Lees, James., Christie, David A., *Raptors of the World*. United Kingdom: (Houghton Mifflin, 2001), 66.

84 Tim Mackrill, *The Osprey* (Bloomsbury Publishing, 2024), 37-42.

85 Mackrill, *The Osprey*, 29.

86 Richard O. Bierregaard, Alan F. Poole, and Brian E. Washburn, "Ospreys (*Pandion haliaetus*) in the 21st Century: Populations, Migration, Management, and Research Priorities," *Journal of Raptor Research* 48, no. 4 (December 2014): 301–308, https://doi.org/10.3356/0892-1016-48.4.301.

87 Bierregaard, "Ospreys (*Pandion haliaetus*) in the 21st Century," 302.

88 Carina Bissett, "A Parliament of Owls: Native American Myths of the Southwest," Carina Bissett (blog), March 24, 2017, https://carinabissett.com/2017/03/24/a-parliment-of-owls-myths-of-the-southwest/.

89 Hamilton A. Tyler, *Pueblo Birds and Myths* (UNKNO, 1991), 156-172.

90 Michael N. Kochert, "Are red-tailed hawks and great horned owls diurnal-nocturnal dietary counterparts?" *The Wilson Bulletin* 107, no 4 (1995): 615–628, https://pubs.usgs.gov/publication/1015915.

91 John Farrand Jr., *The Audubon Society Master Guide to Birding Volume 2: Gulls to Dippers* (Alfred Knopf, 1983), 162.

92 Christian Artuso, C. Stuart Houston, Dwight G. Smith, and Christopher Rohner, "Great Horned Owl: *Bubo virginianus*," Cornell Lab *Birds of the World*, October 24, 2022, https://birdsoftheworld.org/bow/species/grhowl/cur/introduction.

93 James R. Duncan, *Owls of the World: Their Lives, Behavior and Survival* (Firefly Books, 2003), 40-47.

94 Carol Lee, "Powerful feet and talons help birds of prey make their living," *Lubbock Avalanche Journal*, March 26, 2006.

95 Leslie Evans Odgen, "The Silent Flight of Owls, Explained," Audubon, July 28, 2017, https://www.audubon.org/news/the-silent-flight-owls-explained.

96 Arthur Cleveland Bent, *Life Histories of North American Birds of Prey* (Dover Publications, 1961), 10-15.

97 Jean-Luc E. Cartron, *Raptors of New Mexico* (University of New Mexico Press, 2010), 597-619.

98 Eric D. Forsman, "Methods and Materials, for Locating and Studying Spotted Owls," U.S. Department of Agriculture, Forest Service General Technical Report PNW-162, December 1983.

99 Mary Louise Grossman and John Hamlet, *Birds of Prey of the World* (Bonanza Books, 1964), 27-28.

100 Ferguson-Lees, *Raptors of the World*, 25-34.

101 "Importance of Eagles to Native Americans: Golden Eagles as a National Symbol," American Eagle Foundation, https://eagles.org/what-we-do/educate/learn-about-eagles/golden-eagle-as-a-national-symbol/.

102 Al Harmata, "Morphometric Sex Determination of North American Golden Eagles," *Journal of Raptor Research* 47, no. 2 (June 2013): 108–116, https://doi.org/10.3356/JRR-12-28.1.

103 Leslie Brown and Dean Amadon, *Eagles, Hawks and Falcons of the World* (McGraw Hill, 1968), 133-145.

104 Brian A. Millsap, Guthrie S. Zimmerman, William L. Kendall, Joseph G. Barnes, Melissa A. Braham, Bryan E. Bedrosian et al., "Age-specific survival rates, causes of death, and allowable take of golden eagles in the western United States," *Ecological Applications* 32, no. 3 (2022): e2544, https://doi.org/10.1002/eap.2544.

105 Cartron, *Raptors of New Mexico*, 371.

106 Candace Savage, *Bird Brains: The Intelligence of Crows, Ravens, Magpies, and Jays* (Sierra Club Books, 1997), 3-36.

107 Savage, *Bird Brains*, 56-58.

108 Roger Tory Peterson, *Peterson Field Guide to Birds of North America* (Houghton Mifflin Harcourt, 2008), 252.

109 David Allen Sibley, *The Sibley Guide to Birds* (Knopf, 2014), 309.

110 Udvardy, *National Audubon Society Field Guide to North American Birds, Western Region*, 526, 685-686.

111 Udvardy, *National Audubon Society Field Guide to North American Birds, Western Region*, 526.

112 James Lipton, *An Exaltation of Larks* (Viking, 1991), 48.

113 Franz Boas, "Mythology and Folk-Tales of the North American Indians," *The Journal of American Folklore* 27, no. 106 (October–December 1914): 374–410, doi:10.2307/534740.

114 Joan Garcia-Porta, Daniel Sol, Matt Pennell, Ferran Sayol, Antigoni Kaliontzopoulou, and Carlos A. Botero, "Niche expansion and adaptive divergence in the global radiation of crows and ravens," *Nature Communications* 13, no. 2086 (2022): https://doi.org/10.1038/s41467-022-29707-5.

115 Tim Traver, "Raccoons: It's All in The Hands," *The Outside Story* in Northern Woodlands, March 31, 2014, https://northernwoodlands.org/outside_story/article/raccoons-hands.

116 Jean-Luc E. Cartron and Jennifer K. Frey, eds., *Wild Carnivores of New Mexico* (University of New Mexico Press, 2024), 895-913, 947-969, 919-942.

117 Colorado Parks & Wildlife Lynx Reintroduction. Colorado Parks & Wildlife. June 2014 https://cpw.state.co.us/species/lynx

118 Elizabeth Miller, "Linked to Lynx: Could New Mexico's Mountains Land on the Map for Canada Lynx Habitat?" *Santa Fe Reporter*, October 11, 2016, https://sfreporter.com/archives/linked-lynx/.

119 Anthony J. Giordano, "Ecology and status of the jaguarundi *Puma yagouaroundi*: a synthesis of existing knowledge," *Mammal Review* 46, no. 1 (2016): 30–43, https://doi.org/10.1111/mam.12051.

120 Carlos A. López González, David E. Brown, and Juan P. Gallo-Reynoso, "The ocelot *Leopardus pardalis* in north-western Mexico: ecology, distribution and conservation status," *Oryx, The International Journal of Conservation* 37, no. 3 (2003): 358–364.

121 Alan R. Rabinowitz, "The Present Status of Jaguars (*Panthera onca*) in the Southwestern United States," *The Southwestern Naturalist* 44, no. 1 (1999): 96–100, http://www.jstor.org/stable/30055410.

122 Fiona Reid, *Peterson Field Guide to Mammals of North America: Fourth Edition* (HarperCollins, 2006), 435.

123 Emil B. McCain and Jack L. Childs, "Evidence of Resident Jaguars (*Panthera onca*) in the Southwestern United States and the Implications for Conservation," *Journal of Mammalogy* 89, no. 1 (19 February 2008): 1–10, https://doi.org/10.1644/07-MAMM-F-268.1.

124 Michael S. Mooring, Amy A. Eppert, and Ryan T. Botts, "Natural Selection of Melanism in Costa Rican Jaguar and Oncilla: A Test of Gloger's Rule and the Temporal Segregation Hypothesis," *Tropical Conservation Science* 13 (March 11, 2020): 1–15, doi:10.1177/1940082920910364.

125 Carlos De Angelo, Agustin Paviolo, and Mario Di Bitetti, "Traditional Versus Multivariate Methods for Identifying Jaguar, Puma, and Large Canid Tracks," *Journal of Wildlife Management* 74, no. 5 (July 2010): 1141–1153.

126 Donald F. Hoffmeister, *Mammals of Arizona* (University of Arizona Press, 1986), 521.

127 Maurice Hornocker and Sharon Negri, eds., *Cougar: Ecology and Conservation* (University of Chicago Press, 2009), 149.

128 Erik K. Fritzell and Kurt J. Haroldson, "Urocyon cinereoargenteus," *Mammalian Species* 189 (November 1982): 1–8, doi:10.2307/350395.

129 "Gray Fox," New York State Department of Environmental Conservation, DFW, Bureau of Wildlife, Albany, NY, accessed October 18, 2024, https://dec.ny.gov/nature/animals-fish-plants/gray-fox.

130 Logan Hawkes, "Rabies Outbreak Spreads in New Mexico," Farm Progress, May 10, 2012, https://www.farmprogress.com/livestock/rabies-outbreak-spreads-in-new-mexico.

131 David G. Hewitt, ed., *Biology and Management of White-tailed Deer* (CRC Press, 2011), 355-375.

132 "U.S. Forest Facts and Historical Trends," U.S. Department of Agriculture, Forest Service, Government Printing Office FS-696-M September 2001.

133 "Deer Population Facts," Cornell Deer Project, http://wildlifecontrol.info/cornell-deer-study/deer-populations/

Old Flight   Mammal Pen   New Flight   Octagon   Mews   Clinic   Eagle flight cage

Our Facilities

A local news reporter came to our house one day to interview us for an article in his publication. Once he found the house, he interviewed us and saw our cages and left. We read the article a few days later. It started out by saying, "When you drive up to Dennis and Denise Miller's house it is very unassuming, and you wonder if you have the wrong place for a wildlife rescue facility. Then they take you into the backyard and you enter another world!" We do live in an unassuming home, a place on the outskirts of Silver City, which has been altered quite a bit from the original, but the backyard has been completely transformed from its bare beginnings. Now every square inch of room is used for cages, and it *is* quite another world.

We have three large flight cages, a cage designed to house mammals, a clinic, a bank of three mews, a metal octagonal cage, a metal transport trailer, and a metal mammal pen.

Flight Cages

The most important housing for large predatory birds are our flight cages, or aviaries, as they are sometimes called. We use the term "flight cage" because this is where we put birds and mammals that are ready to fly and move around. They may have been in the clinic in intensive care, or one of our smaller intermediate cages. The animal's injury may have left it weakened, but especially in birds, their flight muscles atrophy without daily use. To release a bird that has not been in a flight cage and has not exercised those muscles would guarantee that it will not survive. Some of these recovering birds may be able to fly, but not fly well enough to catch food. It takes perfectly honed flying skills with all muscles in perfect condition to survive in the tough world they live in. We must put them in flights to make sure they are ready when released.

The U.S. Fish and Wildlife Service is very strict on the federal wildlife rehabilitation permitting for birds. One of the most important things they look at is the sizes of flights the permittee or the new applicant has. We are required to take photos and draw maps of our facilities with accurate measurements of cage sizes. If a person wants to be a raptor rehabilitator, they must have a flight cage at least one hundred feet long or their permit will not include the care of eagles. It would be illegal for them to care for eagles even for a short time. There are minimum cage size requirements for hawks, owls, and even long flight cages required for smaller raptors that are swift fliers like falcons.

Large Flight/Eagle Cage

Our largest flight cage is just over one hundred feet long, twenty feet wide, and eighteen feet tall and is specifically designed for eagles and other large raptors. With a shelter on one end and large log perches located on both ends, it is a big, tough cage for these massive creatures. Like all of our flight cages, the bottom of the sides are made of solid plywood to keep live food (mice and rats) from escaping before they are eaten. The sides are made of 2" x 2" wooden furring strips attached vertically and two inches apart. Construction with wood—never using wire—is a requirement for these cages to prevent feather and beak damage, and they're attached with screws and not nails that could work out and become a danger. We cover the roof and some of the sides with a Nyco knit nylon cloth, which is incredibly strong netting that is sometimes used for poultry pens. We refer to this product as poultry netting.

Largest flight cage—100' x 20' x 18' tall—required for eagles.

Dennis catching golden eagle "El Paso" for release.

Smallest and oldest flight cage.

Smallest Flight Cage

Our smallest flight is fifty feet long and forty feet wide. It is built in an L-shape to encourage birds to turn and bank and to get those muscles for quick flight back into shape. It is designed for smaller hawks and owls. It has a shelter on one end and a variety of perch sizes for different size birds. It has housed hundreds of hawks, owls, and eagles, along with many orphaned mammals. This cage has also housed and raised raccoons, bobcats, and coyotes. This is the next cage in line for being rebuilt, being twenty-four years old now.

Medium-Sized Flight Cage
Mammal Pen
Multiuse Cage

Our third flight cage is our newest. It is seventy feet long, sixteen feet wide, and fourteen feet tall, so a medium-sized flight cage. Pre-entry rooms have been added to reduce escapes when doors are opened. It has shelters on both ends, both high for birds and on the ground for mammals. It has also been specifically designed to function not only as a flight cage but as a mammal pen. This cage is also lined with poultry netting and has wire mesh buried along the outside base to keep animals from digging out.

Interior of small flight cage for hawks, owls, and orphaned mammals—two golden eagles inside.

Flight cage / mammal pen.

Inside of flight cage/mammal pen—two barn owls in top right.

With the poultry netting, this cage can house any bird from an eagle to a humming-bird. We also added features to accommodate mammals. We have raised baby deer in this pen along with javelina, bobcats, raccoons, pronghorn, and many other mammals.

Pre-entry room on west end to prevent escapes.

The other features we built into this new flight cage are a pre-entry room on the far end of the cage that runs the length of that end. This has observation doors, photography doors, and racks to feed babies that bottles fit in. These bottle racks, mentioned previously in the section on deer, have been extremely effective in keeping the deer we have raised from being imprinted and keeping them wild.

Bottle rack from inside cage.

Bottle racks and observation/ photography doors insidepre-entry room.

View out observation window at barn owls.

Clinic

Our clinic was a godsend when we first built it. We were examining animals on our kitchen island, housing intensive care animals in pet taxis in a back bedroom, and even putting injured ducks in our bathtub! Our freezer was also a problem with a mixture of our food and mice and rats for the wildlife!

With the clinic, it is possible to do all this in a more controlled and sterile environment rather than in our house. A local veterinarian donated a bank of steel cages that can be sterilized, the same type you see in a vet's office. We have a dedicated refrigerator, freezer, blender (yes, we have to blend mice!), large counters for surgeries and examinations, and all animal food, medications, and first aid supplies are stored in cabinets. This room can be heated or cooled, which is important for recovering animals. It is used primarily for examinations, surgeries, and intensive care, but more recently the clinic has become necessary to quarantine newly acquired animals to isolate for avian influenza and West Nile virus that we do not want to spread to our other charges. Once healthy enough, animals are transferred to flight cages, or mammal pens, or to one of the mews where they can get fresh air and more exercise.

Clinic with intensive care cages, examination and surgery tables, etc.

Mews

Mews are small cages primarily to house birds of prey. The name is a falconry term for cages that hold falcons and hawks. They are imperative to use when rehabbing these animals. They are small, only about four feet wide and five feet long, but ten feet tall. They are designed to house birds but to keep them from moving too much. In raptor rehab, they are effective in transitioning a bird from intensive care in the clinic to a flight cage. The bird may be healing and not needing to be cooped up in a small intensive-care cage that is two feet wide and two feet deep. If the bird has a broken wing, for example, once it is set, we don't want the bird to have restricted movement. The wing will be wrapped, and it will be kept in intensive care.

Once the wing has started to heal and the wrap is off, we may want him to stretch that wing and move it some, but not to put the full stresses of flight too soon in his recovery. The mews are perfect for allowing them a bit more movement, but it is not large enough for them to fly. They get sunshine and fresh air, which helps a great deal with their

Mews—a bank of three cages for intermediate care before transfer into flight cage.

View from inside mews.

recovery. From here, they are transferred to one of the flights. These are awesomecages made of metal, well designed, and strong enough for even large mammals. The next couple of cages we will describe are made of the same material. The mews are a bank of three cages, one larger than the other two, and all three are inside of a larger cage that is ten feet wide and twenty feet deep.

The cage-within-a-cage concept is to keep animals from escaping as doors are opened. If they get out of a mew, they are still in another cage. We have one set up with smaller perches for smaller raptors like kestrels or small owls, another with medium-sized perches for hawks like harriers or barn owls, and the third is a bit bigger and is set up with large perches for eagles, red-tailed hawks, and great horned owls. Poultry netting is once again used to line the inside of each of the mews to protect feathers and it works perfectly! It also makes it dark and shaded to help calm them.

Octagonal Multiuse Cage

One of our other cages is a multiuse octagonal steel cage, again lined with poultry netting. It is fifteen feet in diameter and is connected to the mews we just described. This allows us to walk into the main mews cage and access the three mews and this octagon to prevent escapes. It has been fitted with a wire bottom to prevent animals from digging out but is covered in deep sand. The netting allows us to use this cage for birds, but it is also designed for small mammals. Within days of completion, we received three baby raccoons that we raised in the new cage and it was the perfect facility for them. We built shelters, perches, and branches to climb on.

Octagon and mews.

Octagonal cage with perches and shelters.

Mammal Pen

Our last cage is exactly like the cages just described. Remember we previously showed how the mews are attached to the octagonal cages? Well, this one we put together as one large cage that has an octagonal cage on one end with shelters and such, and it connects to the ten-by-twenty-foot rectangular cage. This makes a cage that is thirty-five feet long, made of metal, and perfect to house mammals, particularly those that could break out of a cage made of wood. This is where we house carnivorous mammals such as bobcats, bears, mountain lions, and many others. The bottom is concrete to prevent them from digging out. If we have grazers like deer and javelina, we will put them in the new flight cage/mammal pen because it is larger for them to run and exercise. This mammal cage is designed more for carnivores. It is not lined with poultry netting this time so is not designed for the care of birds, just exclusively mammals.

Mammal pen during construction— now covered with wood fencing for privacy.

This mammal cage can be set up for cats and foxes and similar animals with shelters, climbing logs, and places to dig. At other times, everything can be removed to make it useful for grazing mammals when needed.

With the completion of these cages, along with the completion of our new flight/mammal pen, this gives us the ultimate setup. Hopefully, we will not have to build any more cages because we have everything we need as it stands right now. We also don't have any more room in the backyard anyway!

Shelters inside mammal pen

SPECIES LIST

This is a species list of the animals we have cared for at Gila Wildlife Rescue. These are in a general sequence of the most common to the least common animals we have encountered within each section. After twenty years of caring for all species of wildlife, then specializing for the next twenty-plus years on mammals, raptors, and other large birds, the list is extensive and gives the reader an idea of the diversity of wildlife in this area as well as the diversity we have cared for. Those with an asterisk (*) make up 80 percent of the animals we care for. Those with a plus sign (+) have had less than five individuals of that species we have cared for.

Raptors

Red-tailed hawk*	Great horned owl*
Swainson's hawk*	American kestrel*
Barn owl*	Northern harrier*
Cooper's hawk*	Sharp-shinned hawk*
Peregrine falcon *	Golden eagle*
Turkey vulture	Harris's hawk
Western screech owl	Common black hawk +
Zone-tailed hawk +	Long-eared owl +
Short-eared owl +	Prairie falcon +
Ferruginous hawk +	Flammulated owl +
Burrowing owl +	Rough-legged hawk +
Bald eagle +	Osprey +
Mississippi kite +	Northern goshawk +
Aplomado falcon +	Spotted owl +
Northern pygmy owl +	Saw-whet owl +

Waterfowl and Shorebirds

American coot*	Lesser scaup*
Mallard duck*	Pied-billed grebe*
Western grebe*	American wigeon*
Northern shoveler*	Ruddy duck*

Ring-necked duck*
Pintail duck
Cinnamon teal
Canvasback duck
Bufflehead duck
Sandhill crane
Common loon
Red-throated loon
Eared grebe
Brown pelican +
Double-crested cormorant +
Snowy egret +
American bittern +
White ibis +
Green heron +
Snow goose +
Black-necked stilt +
Wilson's phalarope +
Ring-billed gull +

Great blue heron*
Green-winged teal
Blue-winged teal
Redhead duck
Common merganser
Killdeer
Cattle egret
Horned grebe
White pelican
Soar +
Hooded merganser +
Little blue heron +
Black-crowned night heron +
White-faced ibis +
Canada goose +
Wood duck +
American avocet +
Western sandpiper +
California gull +

Game Birds and Assorted Other Birds

Mourning dove
White-winged dove
Common nighthawk
Montezuma quail
Belted kingfisher
Ruby-throated hummingbird
Rufous hummingbird
Yellow-bellied sapsucker

Gambel's quail
Greater roadrunner
Scaled quail
Wild turkey
Broad-billed hummingbird
Broad-tailed hummingbird
Northern flicker
Ladder-backed woodpecker

Songbirds

Common raven*
Cliff swallow
Western kingbird
American robin
Pinyon jay
Spotted towhee
Western meadowlark
Northern mockingbird
Pyrrhuloxia

Chihuahuan raven*
House finch
Cassin's kingbird
Western scrub jay
Curve-billed thrasher
Green-tailed towhee
Barn swallow
Northern cardinal
Phainopepla

Loggerhead shrike

Black-headed grosbeak

Western tanager

Bronzed cowbird

Mammals

Mule deer*

Bobcat*

Ringtail*

Javelina

Cottontail

Chipmunk

Pronghorn

Little brown bat

Pallid bat +

Mexican free-tailed bat

Zebra +

White-tailed deer

Raccoon*

Coatimundi

Rock squirrel

Jackrabbit

Black bear

Badger

Big brown bat

Townsend's big-eared bat

Mountain lion +

Jaguar +

Reptiles

Bull snake*

Prairie rattlesnake

Western box turtle*

Black-necked garter snake

Western diamondback
rattlesnake

Black-tailed rattlesnake

Red-eared slider

The writing of this book was made possible by the wonderful wildlife that we have been so blessed to care for. All credit should go to them.

As far as humans, we deeply thank Pete Nebbia; Jeff LeBlanc and his wife, Melanie Zipin; Jodi Crocker; Kacie Peterson; Buck Burns; Mark and Francisca Weber; and Eric Kennedy, may he rest in peace, for all of their volunteer work in covering for us when we snuck out of town, for help in construction, and for being wonderful friends.

We would also like to thank local author Phil Conners, who originally encouraged us to write this book. Our thanks also go to two additional authors, John Fayhee and the late Richard Mahler, who guided and advised us on getting this published. Thanks to Luan Mitchell who volunteered her editing services.

To the many donors throughout the years from small to large, from individuals to corporations, again, we and the animals are deeply grateful and could not have done this without you. In particular, Freeport-McMoRan Copper and Gold deserves a big hand in their regular funding of Gila Wildlife Rescue, and also for taking a proactive stand on animals being injured at their local facilities. We are also thankful for our second corporate sponsor, El Paso Electric Company.

Thanks also goes to the Arenas Valley Animal Clinic. Starting with Dr. Hopson, then Dr. Wenzel, and now Dr. Allred, these guys have helped us out for all of these forty-plus years. We also need to mention the expertise that we more recently have received from Dr. Vicki and her dedicated staff at the El Paso Zoo, who now provide an even higher level of expertise for the treatment of our injured animals, having specialized in raptor rehabilitation like us. Thank all of you—your volunteer work and donation of services and medications have and always will be crucial to what we do.

Thanks to Jim Kolb and Jake Politte for sponsoring fundraisers at the Twisted Vine and 1Zero6. They still are, hands down, the best parties ever to be thrown in Silver City. Thanks to all the bands that played and to Jason Hammond (RIP) and Joe Doyle for all the audio help.

Thank all of you who love wildlife and want to help them rather than harm. We hope you have enjoyed our stories and have learned from them. Be good stewards. Don't be ecologically immoral!

Dennis and Denise

The End!